	RED	YELLOW		
APPROACH	Energetic and direct	Optimistic and spontaneous		rrect
MANNER	Businesslike	Visible	Sensitive	Formal
WORK-STYLE	Hard-working Ambitious Professional Effective Exact	Committed Personal Flexible Stimulating Articulate	Personal Relaxed Friendly Informal Low-key	Structured Organized Specialized Methodic Succinct
WORK PACE	Fast and decisive	Fast and spontaneous	Slow and consistent	Slow and systematic
PRIORITIZES	The task and the result	Relationships and influence	Retaining good relationships	The task and work method
AFRAID OF	Losing control	Losing prestige	Confrontation	Making a fool of oneself
BEHAVES UNDER PRESSURE	Dictates conditions and asserts oneself	Attacks and is ironic	Backs down and agrees	Withdraws and avoids
WANTS	Results	Inspiration	Stability	Quality
WANTS YOU TO BE	Straightforward	Stimulating	Kind	Exact
WANTS TO BE	The one who decides	The one who is admired	The one who is liked	The one who is correct
IS IRRITATED BY	Inefficiency and indecision	Passivity and routines	Insensitivity and impatience	Surprises and whims
WANTS TO HAVE	Success and control	Status and flexibility	Calm & quiet and close relationships	Credibility and time to prepare
BEHAVES	Businesslike	Elegant	Friendly	Law-abiding
LIVES IN	The present	The future	The past (when everything was better)	One's own thoughts
RELIES UPON	Gut feeling	Recognition	One's self	Specialists
DON'T LIKE	Sitting still	Being alone	Unpredictability	Hurry

Surrounded
by Setbacks

. . . .

Surrounded by Setbacks

Turning Obstacles into Success
(When Everything Goes to Hell)

Thomas Erikson

ST. MARTIN'S
ESSENTIALS
NEW YORK

First published in the United States by St. Martin's Essentials,
an imprint of St. Martin's Publishing Group

SURROUNDED BY SETBACKS. Copyright © 2021 by Thomas Erikson. Translation copyright © 2021 by Rod Bradbury. All rights reserved. Printed in the United States of America. For information, address St. Martin's Publishing Group, 120 Broadway, New York, NY 10271.

www.stmartins.com

Library of Congress Cataloging-in-Publication Data

Names: Erikson, Thomas, 1965– author.
Title: Surrounded by setbacks : turning obstacles into success (when everything goes to hell) / Thomas Erikson.
Other titles: Omgiven av motgångar. English
Description: First U.S. edition. | New York, NY : St. Martin's Essentials, [2021] | "Originally published in Sweden by Forum in 2020"—Verso. | Includes bibliographical references and index.
Identifiers: LCCN 2021016088 | ISBN 9781250789518 (hardcover) | ISBN 9781250838933 (international, sold outside the U.S., subject to rights availability) | ISBN 9781250789525 (ebook)
Subjects: LCSH: Success. | Goal (Psychology)
Classification: LCC BF637.S8 E7413 2021 | DDC 158—dc23
LC record available at https://lccn.loc.gov/2021016088

Our books may be purchased in bulk for promotional, educational, or business use. Please contact your local bookseller or the Macmillan Corporate and Premium Sales Department at 1-800-221-7945, extension 5442, or by email at MacmillanSpecialMarkets@macmillan.com.

Originally published in Sweden by Forum in 2020.

First U.S. Edition: 2021

10 9 8 7 6 5 4 3 2 1

Contents

Part I. The Best Way to Deal with Setbacks, or Everything That Can Go to Hell, and What You Can Do About It

Part II. Creating Lifelong Success, or How to Win Every Time

Introduction

When It All Goes to Hell

WHEN IT ALL GOES WRONG

Sometimes it just happens. Things go bad. In a big way.

You're about to celebrate your daughter's graduation with a party in the backyard; the family has prepared for this for months, fifty guests have arrived, and suddenly the heavens open, the rain pours down, and the whole affair is ruined.

When you check the balance of the equity fund the bank recommended so highly and realize that your financial advisor really didn't know more than you. Now you're broke—again.

When you realize that the presentation you've been working on for several weeks, the one that is going to catapult you directly to the corner office, was on the other USB stick.

When the house you've dreamed about since you were a kid finally comes on the market, but the bank says no.

When you've just reestablished contact with an old friend, only to learn that he only has six months left to live.

When you're walking down the sidewalk one fine morning and happen to put your left shoe right into a pile of dog shit.

When your worst enemy in the company gets the top job you thought had your name on it.

When you just open your eyes in the morning and everything goes wrong.

Sometimes you feel as though you're surrounded by setbacks, obstacles, and adversities. Little ones and big ones. And each time, you're overwhelmed by a feeling of hopelessness.

You've picked up a book with a slightly depressing title. But this book isn't really about setbacks. It's about how you can deal with what you perceive as setbacks, and instead learn to achieve success. Life is what it is; it's more a question of what you make of it than of what happens around you.

Like a wise person once said: it isn't about what happens to you, but about how you deal with it.

This planet can be a tricky place to live. A wonderful place, too, but nevertheless a rather weird one. And we aren't always great at adjusting to the circumstances.

Some people manage to get through life fairly well without serious damage, but nobody manages to completely avoid difficulties and setbacks. Some people only have to deal with minor irritations. And then there are those who get such a rough deal from life that it makes you wonder why the powers above don't descend and give them a helping hand. They get hit so hard that you wouldn't want anyone to suffer that way.

Despite unimaginable difficulties, some of these people do keep going. How? What is their secret? Why don't they just lie down and give up?

Somewhere I heard an expression that stuck in my mind: "If you find yourself in a rowboat way out at sea—by all means say a prayer, but start rowing toward land at the same time."

That's a good approach to difficulties and setbacks in life. Sometimes you need to hope that it will get better, but you also need to act.

And here we have one of the most important keys to dealing with setbacks and building your path toward success: you have to do something.

THIS BOOK DOESN'T CLAIM TO BE TOTALLY COMPREHENSIVE

There's research that can confirm much of what I am going to share with you. I will refer to some of it, and at the end of the book you will find a list of books to read on many of the subjects that I'll discuss.

A lot of what we're going to look at is based on my own experiences. Experiences that I've spent years trying to understand myself. I've also observed the journeys of others I've encountered over thirty years of professional life.

The approach that I share in this book has saved me from serious problems on more than one occasion. It's given me the ability to pitch unpleasant experiences overboard, retain my focus, and keep rowing my boat.

So has everything gone perfectly? Certainly not. I make my own mistakes and end up in trouble, just like everybody else. Even in situations where I really should have known better, I've sometimes managed to mess things up all by myself. And sometimes the world doesn't go my way at all. A few situations come to mind:

- When I was ten years old, my family moved hundreds of miles away from everyone I knew.
- I misjudged the willingness of a potential client to do a deal, and that carelessness meant a missed contract for a *lot* of money.
- On one occasion, I wrote a grumpy letter of complaint to my employer (the biggest business bank in Scandinavia).

The letter went right up to the CEO, who phoned me and gave me what for.

- At first, nobody was interested in the original Swedish manuscript of *Surrounded by Idiots,* my first book. About twenty publishers said no. Some of them rather brutally. I had to publish it myself.
- After the publication of my first book, I was pursued by a malevolent stalker.
- I've gone through two divorces.

Of course, this list of failures, setbacks, and difficulties could be far longer. Nevertheless, I've succeeded with some things. And you can read about the methods that have helped me in this book. You'll learn how to:

- never forget where you're going in life;
- not worry about what other people think of you;
- know which people really wish you well, and who doesn't;
- learn from every setback, so that you won't run into a brick wall again;
- stay on track, even when the people around you are doubtful;
- turn a setback into a success;
- stop wasting your time on the wrong things;
- deal with your fears;
- achieve long-term success without giving up on the way.

KNOWLEDGE IS NOT POWER

That familiar old expression "Knowledge is power" is indeed deceptive. Knowledge is *not* power. The world is full of enormously well-educated people who (if we're being honest about it) aren't doing particularly well. People with all the right letters before and after their names. They know just about everything and can quote every possible theory, but they don't even have power over their immediate environment.

So what is knowledge? Well, knowledge is *potential* power. If you use it, that is.

It makes no difference what you know and what you are capable of doing. Not even if you have an IQ higher than anyone south of the North Pole. However well-read you might be, and whomever you may have listened to, whichever books written by the world's cleverest people you may have read—it makes no difference.

No. Difference. At. All.

What you are *capable of* is beside the point. What you *know* is irrelevant. The only thing that matters when it comes to dealing with obstacles and creating success is what you actually *do*.

In the United States, 44 percent of all doctors are overweight (*Newsweek*, October 2008). I haven't managed to find any equivalent statistics for the Swedish medical profession, but all the doctors I've met are definitely not in the best shape. How can that be? They know better than anyone what you should eat and that you should exercise regularly, and they've seen all the sad effects of being overweight and smoking. Nevertheless, many of them also have challenges with their health. It doesn't add up.

This kind of thinking may determine what you do with the content of this book. You can always nod and say, *Yeah, so what?* Or say, *I don't believe that.* Or you can test it yourself. You won't know whether it works for you until you've given it a try.

The problem is bigger than that. We tend to stick to our normal ways of thinking, even when new insights come our way. Ideas that we've lived with for a long time, perhaps many years, aren't easy to let go of. Sometimes we need to change perspective.

Recently, I heard that the definition of "intelligence" shouldn't be how high your IQ is, but rather your ability to neutrally observe something that doesn't fit in with your existing picture of the world and actually take it in. And even change your own opinion on the issue.

YOUR RESULTS ARE ALL THAT COUNTS

We don't really need loads of new ideas to achieve success and to deal with setbacks. Perhaps as you read this book you'll find yourself thinking, *Meh, I've heard this before!* When that thought crops up, because it will, I want you to ask yourself three questions:

1. Are you doing it today?
2. Have you mastered it?
3. Do your *results* show that you have mastered it?

If you say that you already live an active, healthy life, I'm going to believe your waist measurement, not your words. If you claim that you're in full control of your financial situation, I'm going to rely on your bank statement, not your words. If you say that it's easy for you to apologize to others, I'm going to look at how your relationships work, not listen to your words.

Does that sound tough? Maybe it is. But if you want to start an interesting journey toward a bright future, I can promise you some interesting insights.

But remember: knowing something is not the same thing as doing it.

THE RESULTS WILL TAKE THEIR TIME . . .

A warning might be appropriate here. In some of the chapters, you may start wondering whether the author is completely crazy and think that I'm a workaholic with no personal life or ability to enjoy life at all. You may be tempted to close the book and think that you are never, anyway, going to get anywhere if this is what success requires.

To you, I want to say the following: when I describe how I spend my time, I do so knowing that I have things to achieve and goals to reach. Later on, when I talk about how it's a waste of time to watch TV, it's based on the understanding that that time does nothing to actively contribute to your goals. As general entertainment, there is nothing wrong with TV.

The tips and the ideas I present are only relevant for those who want to get more out of life than they do today. They're for people who want to reach a certain goal within a particular time frame. During calmer periods of life, things will likely look different.

You might find my advice unreasonable but remember that I'm talking about achieving long-term success. The purpose is to give you the tools to move you forward and prevent you from staying stuck where you are, treading water. When I talk to you through the book, I do so assuming that you want to move ahead in life. So I'll tell it like it is and assume that you're looking for change.

But remember this: you won't get six-pack abs in thirty days. Probably not even in six months.

You won't be offered a cool management position just because you finished your final exams.

That dream boyfriend or girlfriend won't waltz around the corner just because you're a nice guy.

You won't become financially independent in five minutes. Perhaps not even in twelve months. It's going to take longer than that.

Or like the financial genius Warren Buffett has said, "No matter how great the talent or efforts, some things just take time. You can't produce a baby in one month by getting nine women pregnant."

On the other hand, time passes regardless. Why not do something good while we wait?

PART I

The Best Way to Deal with Setbacks, or Everything That Can Go to Hell, and What You Can Do About It

. . . .

1

It's Not Them. It's . . . You

Do you want to avoid setbacks as much as possible and instead experience as much success as you can? In one respect, you're just like everybody else: you want to lead a good life.

I think that all of us deserve a good life. You, me, and everyone else should be given the chance to have a good life from the moment we find ourselves here on Mother Earth. Life is so short, in some cases little more than a few decades. But regardless of whether you will live to age 50, 60, 75, or—why not—110, I think that you deserve to have a good life during the time you're here. Even though the planet is presenting us with more problems than we had perhaps foreseen, even though the world is not always a beautiful place, and regardless of the fact that our society sometimes feels totally sick—we have a duty to make the best of what we have.

To achieve these delightful possibilities, there's really only one thing you need to do. Forget long lists with endless action items; put aside all that good advice. You don't need to sit down in a corner and meditate, start analyzing your dreams, have a vision, or become a world champion at a single thing. No, there is only one thing you need to do for good fortune to come to you. If you do this single thing, then everything will sort itself out.

Are you ready?

The only thing you need to do is to take 100 percent responsibility for yourself.

Now.

The single most important factor for avoiding problems and creating a bright future for yourself is the ability to take responsibility. Nobody is ever going to achieve his or her dreams without accepting full responsibility.

When I say responsibility, I mean it in a positive sense. Not a burdensome responsibility for the failings of others, or responsibility for the development of society. Or responsibility for global conflict. Or taking on responsibility for whatever mess your boss made without ever getting a "thank you." No, I mean the responsibility you take for yourself and for your own life. And this is where many of us have a lot to learn.

You are no doubt a responsible person in many respects. I am sure you take care of your family, you're loyal at work, you don't subject yourself to unnecessary risks, you stick to the speed limit in school zones, and so on. Absolutely.

But sometimes it goes wrong anyway.

Let's say that somebody got a nice bonus last month. And her way of celebrating was to spend the whole evening out with the girls on the town.

The result: they had a really great evening, but she's just as broke as before. Short-term pleasure, instead of a sound life in a long-term sense. And that's a problem. All of us know this, but we still fail to do the right thing. For various reasons, we hide the truth from ourselves. And we don't always take responsibility for our situation.

We'll try again:

Somebody got a nice bonus last month. She invested the money in a sensible equity fund, which has now started to increase in value.

The result: she's increased her assets and will continue to do so. Suddenly we have a positive result because she was a great deal more responsible.

Let's look at the three types of responsibility you need to take.

The First Responsibility: *Everything That You Do*

Your responsibility is basically never-ending.

What does that mean?

It means that everything you *do* is your responsibility. Your actions, regardless of whether they are evil or good, are entirely your responsibility. Even if someone else asks you to do a particular thing, the decision to *do it,* and *how* you do it, is your responsibility. When your partner asks you to do something that you find repulsive, then it's your responsibility to say yes or no. If your boss asks you to do something that you don't think is really right—it can be something morally wrong or ethically questionable—it's your responsibility if you actually do it. It makes no difference that she demanded that you do it. Some people would have said no. When your children nag you about privileges and treats they think they have a right to, and you give in even though you know that it's entirely wrong, that was your responsibility. To blame your decision on possible consequences won't work. Other people would not have agreed.

If you're angry about your rotten sales figures at work, while simultaneously ridiculing the outside consultant who is trying to show you a better way of doing business, well, then you're responsible for having refused to listen to good advice.

When you drive through a red traffic light because you thought you would get through in time, you're responsible for all the potential catastrophes that may arise as a result of your decision. You can tell yourself you didn't "see" the light change because you were so worried about being late to pick up your child from school. But tell that to the police officer who stops you two hundred yards down the road. Or to the dad of the child you nearly ran over.

If you sit too long with your cell phone in your hand in front of the TV and are completely unaware of your teenager's nervous anxiety before the school dance tomorrow, that, too, is *your* responsibility. It doesn't make any difference that you felt that you simply had to watch this cute cat play piano. It was *your* choice to give priority to your cell phone rather than talk with your child about her worries.

If you wake up on a Saturday morning after the most raucous after-work gathering in modern history, with a hangover of epic proportions, that's your responsibility. The fact that you've gone to an after-work happy hour every Friday for God-knows-how-long doesn't matter; *you're* the person who decided to go. Trying to explain this away to yourself or your partner by saying, *Everybody else drank too much, too,* doesn't cut it. It was you who lifted the glass to your lips time after time. The hangover is completely and entirely your own responsibility. Telling your family *I can't drive you to the football game because I "don't feel too well today"* is completely transparent. Nobody falls for it.

A blockhead brought some donuts to the office; you ate two and your diet is all messed up. Come on! Who decided to eat those donuts? Whose body was affected? Your work colleagues'? No, it's your waistline that is now challenging your clothes budget.

You can't claim that she did this, so I was forced to do that. No, no. You made an active choice, that is what you did. Necessary or otherwise, you are the one who made the choice.

You can always control your own actions.

If you save money and invest wisely and become economically independent before reaching the age of forty, that is also your responsibility. And you can definitely take the credit for it. It works both ways.

Everything *you* do is *your* own responsibility.

You Either Create or Allow Everything That Happens to You

To avoid setbacks and achieve real success, you need to accept that you are the person who governs your own life. This attitude is far from new, and not everybody agrees with it, but let me show you some examples. When I say that you "create" what happens, I mean that to a great degree your own actions influence the result.

If you step into a bar in the wrong part of town on a dark night, walk up to four beefy dudes with shaved heads and tattoos all over their faces, who have been drinking beer since four o'clock in the afternoon, and say, "Goodness, I've never seen anything this ugly," then you'll know perfectly well why you ended up in the hospital.

But here is an example that's harder to take in: You stagger home every evening after working overtime again. In a comalike state, you force yourself to eat dinner while—in total silence—you think horrible thoughts about your boss. After that, you vegetate for hours in front of the TV and are bombarded with news about murders, acts of terrorism, corrupt politicians, and doomsday prophecies about our climate. You're so stressed and tense that it feels like it's impossible to do anything else. Like, for example, go for a walk together with your partner, or play with your kids for a while before their bedtime. Your partner wants to talk to you about important things, but you're too tired, so you bluntly say that you need to rest. After three years of this familial bliss, you come home late one evening to a silent, empty house. Your partner has left and taken the children, too. Perhaps there's a note in the kitchen: *You don't love me anymore.*

A simple truth: this, too, was a situation that you were involved in creating. It just took a bit longer to realize it.

The Second Responsibility: *Everything You Don't Do*

It's easy to forget that you are also responsible for everything you *do not* do.

Every time you know that you ought to go for a walk instead of pour a glass of wine, it's your responsibility. It doesn't matter whether you "forgot" or deliberately avoided it (in other words, just couldn't give a damn). Similarly, if you see somebody who needs some help at work, something that you could do in five minutes, but you choose to look the other way because it isn't actually your job, then that's your responsibility. Your decision to be a less-helpful colleague will always be your responsibility. You will discover the consequence of that choice the day you're the one who needs help.

Every time you press "snooze" on your alarm instead of getting out of bed and reading a book for half an hour, it's your responsibility. Every time you don't listen to your partner because you think that you already know what she or he is going to say, it's your responsibility. If you get a flirty text from a female colleague and you avoid telling her it isn't okay because you're married, then you've made a fool of yourself. Your ego has nothing to do with it. A failure to make things clear is your responsibility.

None of these are things that you can blame somebody else for. In your heart, you know that I'm right, even though all of us sometimes hide behind apologies and empty excuses. Defense mechanisms are indeed natural. They're there to protect us from possible dangers, but they aren't much use when they simply trick us into thinking that we have done the right thing, when really what we have done is wrong.

Sorry? You were late for the meeting because the printer was being used by somebody else? But who chose to wait until the absolute last second to print those damned documents? Who chose *not* to plan ahead?

What did you say? Your team didn't do what they should have, and now your boss thinks you messed things up? But who was it *didn't bother* to follow up with his team?

If you should study but don't study, and instead play computer games for six hours, then you only have yourself to blame. It was you who *couldn't care less* about studying, and now the exam is coming up regardless.

You didn't follow up on your threat of turning off the internet if the kids didn't start tidying up after themselves, and now your home looks like a war zone.

You never demanded that she come with you to the therapist, so now your relationship is worse than ever.

You refused to participate in the company's in-house training program because you assumed you already knew everything, and now the newly hired twenty-three-year-old has been named the Manager of the Year and is well on his way to becoming your next boss.

You attended a seminar and learned all about the DISC method and its four colors. But despite the fact that you now know that your Yellow behavior means that you're careless with details, you did nothing to correct it. Now you've messed up the contract with the company's biggest client, and your boss's boss wants to talk to you about your future at the firm.

You never got around to taking your dogs to training classes, and now all three are totally out of control.

You need to realize that in none of these situations are you a victim of anything but your own passivity. You said nothing, you demanded nothing, you waited too long, you never said yes or no, you never tried anything new. Instead, you just sat there.

It's not nice to hear it, I know.

2

Seeing the Warning Signs in Time

Very rarely does lightning strike out of a clear blue sky. Oftentimes, we need to train our ability to react to the warning signs that precede unpleasant events. You might feel there's something in the air: you see something strange, somebody makes a stray comment, your gut says something is off. But sometimes we choose to put the warnings aside and don't notice things like:

- your repeated headaches every Sunday night before work;
- your teenage son's endless absence from the dinner table;
- your belt that seems to have become too short again;
- the weird sound from somewhere under your car;
- that strange alcohol smell you notice on someone;
- the lipstick smear on a shirt collar;
- your boss's odd look when you make suggestions.

And so it goes on. But sometimes you do need to act when you feel that something isn't quite right. If you have that feeling, do something about it. If your partner comes home late every Tuesday after work, that's a pattern that needs to be handled, however unpleasant it may be. Confront the person, because that is how successful people act. They don't wait passively and hope that it will blow over. They raise the point of concern and ask for feedback. Of course, nobody loves negative feedback or hearing bad news, but once you get it, you can act. It's better to know about a problem than to go around in ignorance. When the shoe finally drops, it will be much worse than if you had raised the problem early.

You know that I'm right. You can feel it in your entire body, can't you?

WHY DON'T WE DO ANYTHING EVEN WHEN WE SEE THE YELLOW LIGHT?

Why don't we react to things that look a bit weird or sound strange? It's about risk. We don't want to risk what we have, so we accept some things that we shouldn't accept. There's a danger in confronting people around you. Going to your boss and telling it like it is sometimes requires courage. Dealing with unpleasant things with your partner can be unbelievably frightening.

We've seen the warning signs. But we often pretend that we haven't seen anything, since that's so much simpler. We keep quiet to avoid confrontation, conflict, and the risk of discovering an unpleasant truth.

For many years I went around with an uneasy feeling in my gut about certain people, both in my personal life and at work. But I learned to escape from the uncomfortable feeling of deceptive denial and to address even very difficult behaviors in others. And I've never reverted to pretending to be satisfied when in reality I'm not. You can do the same.

Stop living in passivity and start acting to achieve the life you could have. Don't stay on in a bad relationship. You'll only become bitter. Don't remain in a job you detest. Nobody is going to thank you for it. Ditch your bad eating habits. It's your body that is suffering, nobody else's.

There are no rights to claim. The world does not owe you anything. You, and you alone, can change your own situation. Nobody is going to do it for you.

Stop putting things off or turning a blind eye to reality.

Accept this simple fact: *you're responsible for everything you don't do.*

But it doesn't stop there.

The Third Responsibility: *Your Reaction to Everything That Happens*

What happens to you is often in large part your responsibility. At this point, many people get irritated and claim that *it wasn't my fault that the traffic was chaotic and I was thirty minutes late for my interview for a new job. How the hell can that be my responsibility? It isn't my fault!*

Uhmm, well, even if it wasn't you who ran over that deer near the crosswalk that stopped all the traffic for five miles in every direction, it was you who didn't allow for potential mess-ups on your way to the interview. It was you who didn't allow sufficient time to deal with unpleasant surprises. And it is you who reacted with anger at the traffic chaos.

This is important. Even if you didn't create the incident in question, you are responsible for how you reacted to it. The fact that you're now angry for having been delayed on your way is your responsibility. If you look around at the lines of cars, you'll see quite a lot of people sitting calmly in their cars and listening to music or just enjoying a moment's relaxation. Some people have chosen to appreciate the moment of silence during their day. It's just another way of approaching the situation.

It rains on everybody—rich, poor, short, tall, thin, fat, young, old. The question is: Who makes a fuss about it and acts like it's the end of the world, and who accepts the rain and starts to collect the water?

To avoid the feeling of continuous setbacks bombarding your life, you need to realize that you are (and nobody else is) responsible for how you react to what happens. There is always an alternative reaction.

Note that I'm talking about everyday things and not about how you react if, for example, somebody close to you tragically dies. But you're smart enough to distinguish between the small difficulties of life and the true tragedies.

The problem with not taking responsibility for one's reactions is that everything becomes impossible. Oddly enough, the same laws of nature apply to all of us. While you and I might grumble about how the state of the economy is terrible, somebody else is making a fortune under the same conditions. If your excuses about your boss, the company, and all the idiots around you were true, then nobody would ever succeed at anything.

Ingvar Kamprad would never have founded IKEA and established stores across the world. Spotify would have never gone beyond an idea on a piece of paper. The Rockefeller family would be destitute. Stephen King would never have written a single book. We would never have heard of Greta Thunberg. Barack Obama would never have been America's first Black president. None of the major religions would have been founded. Microsoft, Google, Volvo, Tesla, or Apple wouldn't have existed at all.

Even though we all have many of the same limiting factors around us, those factors only seem to restrict certain people. Some people don't understand that what they're doing is impossible. They just go out and do it anyway.

It's not about what happens around you; it's about what you choose to make of it. Unfortunately, many of us unconsciously restrict ourselves with our limiting thought processes and with self-destructive habits. We ignore useful feedback; we fail to continually develop ourselves; we carelessly waste a lot of time on lots of stupid things; we help to spread meaningless gossip. We eat far too much unhealthy food; we don't bother to go to the gym; we spend money we don't have on things we don't need to impress people we don't like. We don't bother to invest in our future; we avoid necessary conflicts; we neglect to speak important truths to people around us; we don't ask for help when we need it—and then we wonder why life doesn't go the way we wish it would!

Unfortunately, many—far too many—people live their lives exactly like that. And when they encounter setbacks, they always have an explanation (or rather, an excuse) for why everything went to pot. But the fact that you're sitting in the same boat as everyone else is cold comfort, is it not? Why not at least get a little boat of your very own?

You can manage your own reactions much better than you think.

You missed your flight. Tough. You swear and grumble. That's your choice, in that case. Of course, you can be angry, disappointed, shattered, destroyed.

You can also choose to go back to why you missed the plane in the first place. Perhaps you overslept? Left home a little too late? Had no margin of time. Why did that happen? Er, you pressed "snooze" three times because you were too tired. But why were you so tired? Because you stayed up too late the night before.

Now you can choose a completely different reaction: lucky for me I now know that if I'm going to get up early the next morning, then

I need go to bed before ten o'clock. An important insight. And above all: *your own choice.*

You can change your way of thinking, change your way of communicating with others, change the images inside your head. You can definitely change your own behavior, regardless of whether you are a Red, Yellow, Green, or Blue (more on the color profiles later!); you can adjust your behavior to the circumstances. These are things that only you have control over. Unfortunately, many of us are stuck in our habits, in our bad habits. We're stuck in our repetitive reactions to our partner, our children, our boss, our employees. And to the rest of the world, too, for that matter.

In some strange way, we rely on predictable reactions that seem to happen outside our control. We need to regain control of our own thoughts, our inner dialogue, our dreams, and our behavior. We can't continue as we always have, because then we'll get the same results we've always gotten. And believe me when I say that very few people want that.

THE THIRD PSYCHOLOGIST

Taking full responsibility is not a new idea. In fact, we find it in the work of the greatest psychologist of all time, a man many of us have never heard of.

Freud and Jung had a contemporary colleague who is not nearly as well known as they are. Partly because he didn't care about whether he was going to be remembered, and partly because his ideas were more important than the man himself. He established concepts like the "inferiority complex"; he invented conversation therapy (nowadays seen as self-evident); he analyzed how family constellations and family dynamics influence children; and he thought that not only the past but also the future ought to play a part in therapy. Today he's almost forgotten, but you will find his ideas in every modern form of therapy.

The man we are talking about is Alfred Adler. Freud taught that what you experience within yourself has been caused by factors outside you. If you had parents who treated you badly, then you'll always be a victim. The trauma in your childhood will leave its mark on who you are. You are, so to speak, condemned from the very start. Adler had a different take.

Adler didn't agree with that at all. He thought that it is you, yourself, that creates the feeling of trauma. He didn't deny that there are nasty parents, and he didn't ignore the fact that a person is obviously affected by being treated badly during childhood. But he was of the opinion that you can choose how you look at your history. Portraying yourself as a victim can benefit you. You get sympathy from those around you. People will become involved in your well-being. Which isn't bad for somebody who was born into the world with unloving parents. But do you really want to be a victim?

Within psychology, during the last ten years or so, many have started to question the value of digging too much into people's pasts. In many cases, it's like scratching at scabs that are in the process of healing. This is a major and relatively little-researched area, but progress is being made, and psychotherapy is now leaning more in Adler's direction than in Freud's.

It's not easy to liberate oneself from the past. All of us have some "baggage" that weighs us down. But once we've managed to liberate ourselves, we're free of it. The past shouldn't have so much importance in people's lives. It doesn't even exist, apart from inside our heads. What's done is done. The question is: What should happen now?

Clinging to the past won't change what has happened, but it may affect the future, and often in a negative way.

THOUGHTS VS. EMOTIONS

We are emotional beings who make decisions, even very big ones, based on feeling. But that is not the same thing as being governed by our emotions. You will certainly be able to recall situations in which, for example, you've lost your temper and the results weren't great. But what would have happened if you'd been able to control that anger?

Anger is not always negative, but on the occasions when it doesn't lead anywhere constructive, it would have been better to be able to control it. To loudly scold a waiter because he spilled coffee on you might feel good for a moment, but a better approach would probably be to deal with it as calmly as possible. I can promise you that the service will be better if you succeed in controlling yourself.

What comes first, thought or emotion?

If you think about it, you'll probably find that the thought comes first. In most cases, the thought triggers the emotion. The emotion, on the other hand, is commonly what triggers action. We've all heard that response from people who have done the weirdest things. Why did you do that? It *felt* good. But if you can manage your thoughts in a rational manner, you won't need to be a victim of your emotions every time.

There's a story about two brothers who grow up with a father who drinks and fights and can never keep a job. He supports himself with petty theft and goes to prison time after time over the course of his sons' childhood.

One of the sons grows up to become a drunken habitual criminal. When asked how his life turned out like that, he answers, *With a father like that, what else could I do?*

The other brother leaves home, studies, gets a top job at a bank, and marries the prettiest girl in the district. He brings up three wonderful children. When asked how his life turned out like that, he answers, *With a father like that, what else could I do?*

The same background. Different ways of dealing with it.

How does that happen? If we were always victims of our past, we would always react similarly to the same events. That's a completely impossible idea.

Sure, we're all unique individuals. But you can definitely choose how you think about a particular event and draw different conclusions. The reflection *My dad was a drunken bastard, and the last thing I want to do is be like him* will create a very specific feeling of revenge. And that in turn will lead to specific actions.

But the thought *My dad was a drunken bastard, and the apple never falls far from the tree* is going to create a feeling of resignation. And that will in turn lead to extremely destructive actions.

Becoming a victim—of your tough childhood, destructive parents, being bullied, being born with dyslexia, chronic morning fatigue on your mother's side, poor health, obesity within the family—is absolutely understandable. But when you come across a person who is trapped in the past, think about this: What does this person gain from retaining the feeling of hopelessness? Because there can be something beneficial from remaining in the role of victim. Sometimes you need to look closely to really see it. And understand it.

WHY A WALKER ISN'T ALWAYS FOR THE BEST

If I had bad grades at school—regardless of the reason—I can always insist that I'm not clever enough to learn new things.

If I was overweight as a child, I can always blame my weight on something wrong with my hormones, and there's no point even trying to stop eating pizza.

If I was bullied in school, I can always mention that at my workplace and get lots of sympathy and attention.

If I have the slightest headache, I can make a big thing of it and have people wait on me hand and foot.

I've seen an example of that among my acquaintances. An elderly lady uses a walker and hobbles about unsteadily every time family members are at home. Concerned about her frailty, they visit often and help as much as they can. When nobody is at home, she whips around the house without the slightest difficulty. (The neighbor sees her through the windows).

This lady is not evil or mean or grumpy or demanding. She has simply settled into a sort of victim mentality. She might not even be aware of it. If anyone were to confront her, I guess she would deny it.

If you want the attention of relatives—why not try getting it in a positive way? There are alternatives.

The crux is that if you can deal with your emotions and act from the point of view of the here and now instead of being confined to the past, you'll be a considerably more liberated person. If you're worried about your finances, it's because in your mind you can imagine a huge pile of unpaid bills. The more you think like that, the worse you'll feel. Changing your way of thinking about your personal finances might not pay your bills, but it can—read: should—give you ideas for how you can increase your income, for example.

3

No More Excuses!

An end to all excuses and alibis! They lead nowhere. I wish I could say that I've completely stopped making excuses myself, but naturally that wouldn't be true. Like everybody else, I sometimes fall into the trap and think up excuses for why project Z didn't work out as it should, even though I know that I was the person who did things wrong.

Making excuses is a human trait; it's part of the defense mechanisms that our consciousness uses to protect us from the tough reality we sometimes find ourselves in.

But even though it's a human trait, it's a waste. Excuses never lead you forward; they simply cement your current position. If you're content with that, no problem. But that's rarely the case.

WHAT ARE EXCUSES?

Excuses can be found in any situation in which you point at causes other than yourself. You can't blame unpleasant events on the weather (rainy or cold), on the state of the market (too weak), on taxes (too high), on wages (too low), on your boss (too unfair), on your partner (not understanding enough), on company policy (too easygoing and permissive or too hard and inhumane), on your children (too badly brought up), on your parents (too demanding or too easygoing), on your work tasks (too boring), on school (not interesting enough), on your teachers (not good enough), or on a thousand other things.

But you know what? Setbacks—what we sometimes just call real life—will come your way regardless of the circumstances. Even if all the things just listed were perfect, something would still go completely wrong. And it will always be about you. If you want success instead of setbacks, you need to accept your own role in the whole process. You need to accept and recognize the reality of the situation.

> It was you who ate all that junk food.
> It was you who accepted the job offer.
> It was you who stayed in the same job year after year.
> It was you who chose to believe what they said.
> It was you who ignored your own intuition.
> It was you who abandoned your old dream.
> It was you who bought that unnecessary stuff.
> It was you who didn't take care of it.
> It was you who decided to do everything yourself.
> It was you who said yes to the dogs.
> It was you who thought the thought, who created the emotion, who made the choice, who articulated the words.

And that is why you are where you are right now.

The true measure of personal maturity is to take full responsibility for what happens. And excuses or alibis—they don't belong there.

AN END TO YOUR GRUMPY COMPLAINING

The same thing applies to grumbling and complaints. It's often point-less to criticize the state of things. On the one hand, nobody wants to listen to your dissatisfaction; on the other, it rarely changes the situation.

A person who has made his or her way through the worst life can put in one's path didn't do it by sitting around and grumbling about how terrible everything is. Intellectually, you know I'm right. But you, just like me, are sometimes stuck in the habit of focusing on negative things at the wrong moment.

Complaining about various circumstances is not the same thing as thinking negatively. Thinking negatively is worrying about what is going to happen and painting imaginary, horrifying scenarios.

The complaining that many people indulge in is more of a bad habit than an actual defense mechanism. And it's a habit we've learned at home or at work. There are more than enough people around you who are professional complainers for you to be able to improve your skills simply by listening to them. But that is a skill you really don't need.

There's an interesting psychology in complaining. When you complain about something, it means that you think there is some-thing better elsewhere.

Think about it. If you complain about your boss, it means that you believe there are better bosses. If you complain about the food, it's be-cause you suspect that someone else is eating better. If you complain about your job, it's because you believe that other jobs are more fun.

If you complain about your partner, it means that somewhere deep inside you genuinely believe there are better partners in the world. But I'm fairly certain that if your partner was the last man or woman on the planet, you'd complain a lot less.

When I exhort you to stop complaining, of course it doesn't mean that you should just accept injustices. If you've got problems at home, then it's probably a good idea to raise the issue and try to have an intelligent and constructive conversation. If your coworkers are lazy incompetents, then you need to talk. Naturally, you must be able to give each other some less-pleasant feedback now and then. I'm not talking about avoiding or turning a blind eye to unpleasant things.

What I am against is the sort of complaining that doesn't lead anywhere.

An example: your partner often comes home a little late for dinner. That makes you irritated and grumpy. Perhaps you're the one who has made dinner, and now it's cold. You have a bit of a spat, but then you sit down and eat in silence. The next evening, the same thing happens. But do you ever change anything? Do you try to understand and solve the problem? Why does she come home so late?

Or you complain that you never have enough money. The state raised taxes, so now you have less in your wallet. You're deeply dissatisfied. You talk to everybody and anybody about this dreadful injustice. But, at the same time, you spend at least that same amount a month on lottery tickets or at the casino.

You complain about your poor health, but you don't quit smoking.

To complain is to keep going on and on, "sawing sawdust," as lecturer Jörgen Oom called it. A very fitting expression. What is the point of sawing sawdust? There's nothing left to saw.

Besides, we tend to complain about things that we actually can do something about. That's what is so strange about it. We complain about each other, about ourselves, about the results we achieve. But we have bigger problems. Take, for example, gravity. Everything you let go of, falls to the ground. That's such a pain! But have you ever heard anybody complain about the gravitational force?

To summarize, we often complain about things we could easily do something about but have chosen to refrain from changing.

Why?

Simple. Change involves risk. The greatest risk is being ridiculed by others, to hear that you're wrong, to fail, to need to climb outside your comfort zone. All of those are unpleasant things, so we stay where we are. And complain. Because then it at least feels like we're doing something. But that is a misleading picture of reality.

IF WE TURN THE WHOLE THING AROUND

If we look at the list earlier in the chapter we can actually turn all the sentences around. You could quite simply . . .

> . . . start eating more nourishing food;
> . . . say no, even when some people try to get you to say yes;
> . . . dare to say no to the wrong job;
> . . . leave a job you hate;
> . . . not blindly trust everyone and anyone;
> . . . listen more to your own gut feeling;
> . . . stick with, and work for, your dreams;
> . . . not go shopping with money you don't have;
> . . . take better care of your belongings;
> . . . ask for help;
> . . . learn how to train your dogs;
> . . . read a self-help book and actually try out the ideas.

All of that is in your control, isn't it? You could change everything in just a few minutes, simply by changing you own attitude.

AM I AN OLYMPIC-LEVEL NONCOMPLAINER?

While writing this, I'm on the thirteenth floor in a hotel room in Oslo. I've been here for just over twenty-four hours, because last night I gave a public lecture nearby. My room has been incredibly noisy ever since I arrived—other guests talking, hotel staff wheeling trolleys past my door, the clink of glasses, some unbelievably bad music that never stops. It was after 11 P.M. when I got back to my room, utterly exhausted. I slept horribly. I've rarely been in a hotel room where I heard so much noise.

Now the core of the problem: What have I done to change my situation? Answer: nothing. I only have myself to blame. I could, of course, have gone down to the reception desk after fifteen minutes of noise and requested a better room, one that wasn't next to a busy major road where everyone was driving past as noisily as possible. But I didn't do anything about it. So, no, I'm not free from this meaningless behavior. Instead, I texted my wife and complained about how noisy it was in the hall. As if she—hundreds of miles away—could affect the situation one little bit.

Which leads us to another interesting problem.

WE COMPLAIN TO THE WRONG PERSON

Have you thought about how many people have the rather strange tendency to turn to somebody who is not involved in the situation and who is unable to influence it in any way?

A lot of people turn to their work colleagues and complain about their partners. Then they go home and complain about their work colleagues. Why? Because it's simpler. It's fairly low-risk to complain to somebody else instead of confronting the person concerned. Asking your boss to plan the project better so that you can avoid having to work on Sundays demands more than just raising the same issue with your wife. Asking for a change of behavior at home is a great deal more difficult than moaning about it to your lunch companion at work.

This meaningless complaining is something we should replace with clearly expressed wishes for changes. If you find yourself in a situation you aren't satisfied with, do something about it or get the hell out of there, and do it quickly. Agree to work more on making your relationship work, or ask for a divorce. Make an effort to improve your working conditions, or get another job. Regardless of what you choose, there will be a change.

Yes. It's far easier to say this than to do it. But complaining will get you nowhere. It will only make you bitter.

WHAT DO YOU COMPLAIN ABOUT?

It's useful to look for patterns. What follows is a simple table to help you to identify what it is that you complain about and when you do it. When I did this exercise a couple of years ago, I discovered that it was in certain settings and with certain people—two former colleagues to be exact—that I became a real whiner. We criticized the government, the weather, the economy, the company, the clients, the bosses, the useless organization, the training program, the company policy, and everything else under heaven and earth. There was no end. Ugh. I didn't like what I saw, and I finally broke the pattern.

What the complaint was about	What triggers the complaining?	Can I do anything about the problem? If so, what?
My own pitiful finances	Every time bills need to be paid	Get some extra part-time work, talk to my boss and negotiate a raise, offer to take more responsibility, reduce my expenses

The weather	Every winter morning when the iced-over windscreen needs scraping	Nothing, or move farther south, or build a garage
A persistent stomachache	An hour after every dinner	Think about my diet; perhaps I eat too much of one type of food or have too much heavy food too late in the evening

I realized that this storm of complaint normally took place on Mondays at lunch. So I stayed at my desk on Mondays and took a boxed lunch that I ate at my desk. When colleagues A and B wanted me to come to lunch, I just pointed at my lunch box. And after a few weeks, the pattern had been broken. (I assume they managed their Monday misery sessions in my absence.)

As you can see from the table, the most important question is: What can you do about it?

How Did It Go? What Did You Write Down?

Perhaps it was difficult to think of anything. That might be because you don't reflect on your complaints until you're actually in the act. So pay attention to your own behavior in the coming week. You don't need an app. No excuses (such as not having a pen!). Jot a note on a piece of paper or on your phone when you notice yourself complaining.

The whole point of column three is that if there isn't anything to write there, then *there really isn't anything to complain about.* Just think how much time you saved!

If, however, there's a whole list on the far right, then suddenly you'll have a comprehensive plan of action that will help you actually deal with things that are worth complaining about. A collection of small irritating moments can devour all your energy. You might as well solve all those annoying tiny problems on this list.

At one office I visited, ten people complained that the trash can in the kitchen was placed too far from the sink. But none of them had taken the radical measure of moving it ten feet closer. It sounds utterly ridiculous writing that, but it's an actual example.

If the items on your list are not worth dealing with, then we have a different situation. Because then they're *not worth complaining about.*

Getting stuck in these negative tracks can totally disturb your mental focus and make all the setbacks you encounter feel bigger and more serious. So just drop these little irritants. Easier said than done. Ignore them if they're not worth dealing with. Be a bigger person than the people who complain about utter silliness. Be above that. Move on.

THERE IS ALWAYS SOMETHING TO COMPLAIN ABOUT

Does it even matter if you take responsibility for your life? What difference does it make if some of us complain, grumble, and make excuses? The world will continue roughly the same as usual, anyway.

Uhmm . . . well. If you accept full responsibility from now on and are prepared to behave in a 100 percent adult manner, then an interesting thing will happen: you will become the sole owner of your future. Only you can decide how things will go for you in life. And that's fantastic, isn't it?

Think how wonderful it would be to be independent of others. To not have to make excuses, blame others, point your finger, and name scapegoats other than yourself.

Perhaps you believe that you already do take full responsibility. You look after your family, you keep the flag flying high at work, you look after yourself and your health. I believe you. Absolutely.

But if I could sit on your shoulder for a week, I bet that I would hear you mumble and grumble about one thing or the other and subconsciously blame every imaginable factor other than you yourself. If it isn't the damned traffic, then it's the price of gas. Or the income tax. Or the government. Or the other party. Or it's raining at completely the wrong time. Why is it so sunny? Perhaps you're irritated with your boss. Or the whole company. They're all idiots. You're the only one who understands.

Sure, there may be problems at your workplace, but full responsibility means that you quit finding reasons for why you don't always do the best you can. There are no shortcuts.

Accept that, and arrange your life according to the fact that you own your own decisions. Sure, that can be a burden, but most of all it's liberating. Because now there are no other obstacles than what you can actually influence—yourself. All limitations are gone.

ANYONE CAN OPEN THE MOST COMPLEX LOCK

For the sake of simplicity, from now on I'm going to assume that you really *want* to bring about a change in your life, whatever that may be: your health, your finances, your relationships, your career, your education, your desire to travel, your wish to work as a volunteer, your hobby, or whatever. The fact that you're still reading means you want something more in life.

But remind yourself throughout this book that what you do or don't do is your responsibility. Not mine. Not your mom's. Not that of your boss, husband, wife, or children. Your responsibility.

Remember that nobody becomes successful because of what they know or are capable of or say. It is only the actual *doing* that is going to count.

Somewhere or other I picked up the phrase "Anyone can open the most complex lock in the world; they just have to have the code."

So let's make sure that we give you as many digits as we can.

SUMMARY

Everything you do or don't do is your own responsibility. Being able to take *full* responsibility is the only sign of personal maturity that really counts.

You are also personally responsible for your own reactions to what others do or don't do. Remember that a thought often comes before an emotion, and that emotion comes before action.

The advantage of this approach is that you, if you choose it, will be in possession of your own future. You decide how your life is going to develop. Others will have considerably less power over you.

It's a bit unnerving, in a way. It means that you're going to need to take a few more risks than you would otherwise.

But at the same time, it's absolutely fantastic. Because this approach gives you lots and lots of possibilities. With your new attitude, you can change the course of events and you have an incredible future ahead of you.

If you are going to complain—talk to somebody who can do something about the situation. Even better: if there's something to complain about, try to solve the problem yourself. By all means, tell people around you what you've done. Don't boast about it, but few people are more appreciated than those who solve existing problems.

4

From Minor Problem to Serious Crisis in Three Minutes

Professional problems, hopeless challenges at work, setbacks in your relationships, mess-ups related to bringing up children, personal problems that never seem to come to an end, physical problems, overweight or underweight, financial problems, family and relatives, neighbors, conflicts of every type, plus more—the list can go on and on. Life consists of a whole host of setbacks. Sometimes it feels as if you're surrounded by problems.

Problem after problem, problems that are only interrupted by one *crisis* or another. Problem, problem, problem, *crisis*! I first heard Brian Spencer say this, and it's so true. Everybody you meet has either just gone through a crisis, is in the middle of a crisis, or is on the way to a crisis. They just don't know it yet.

Is this good or bad news?

SO WHAT CAN WE DO ABOUT
ALL THESE SETBACKS?

So what should you do when you crash-land? Pull your hat down over your eyes and hope that everything will simply disappear? Or should you learn how to deal with the mess?

Since it's impossible to completely avoid crises and setbacks, you might as well learn how to deal with them. We have to accept that the world works like this.

What's most important here is that you don't assume the wrong sort of responsibility. Absolutely give others a helping hand with their problems if you can. That will be appreciated, and it will show that you're a good person. But don't assume responsibility for everybody else. They are adults and sometimes need to be responsible for themselves, too. They will learn how to deal with their own setbacks.

ARE THEY REALLY SETBACKS—OR IS IT LIFE?

One thing always bothers me: I'm not sure that we're always dealing with setbacks.

In order to deal with the obstacles of life, it's a good idea to have a strategy, but also be aware that a strategy is not everything. You need to keep track of your own frame of mind. Because often we create obstacles inside our own heads. We build up a mental picture of catastrophe—even though the solution is actually extremely simple. Sometimes all you need to do is pick up your telephone. And realize that it wasn't even a problem at all.

It can be beneficial to have perspective on potential problems. Having the wrong grout color on the backsplash above your kitchen sink is hardly the end of the world. It can easily be fixed, after all.

When I coach people one-on-one, I realize that many of them want to prepare themselves so well that they will completely avoid unpleasant surprises. This attitude often results in perfectionism taking over, and nothing happens. To avoid driving into a ditch, they perfect and polish their ideas for so long that the initial purpose is completely lost.

A farmer prepares his field the best way possible. He plows it, fights weeds and undesirable insects, spreads fertilizer, and sows seeds. He waters and works hard from morning to evening. The crop grows. He follows the crop carefully, waters a bit more. He worries about his crop but watches it grow nevertheless.

The day before he goes to harvest, there is a freak hailstorm that flattens the whole crop.

Everything is destroyed. All his work has been in vain.

Whose fault is it?

Answer: nobody's.

But, you might exclaim, *that isn't fair! The farmer worked so hard!* Yes, sure. It is horribly unjust. Absolutely.

But this is something that all of us are going to meet with— injustices. And that is how things are. How the farmer deals with the situation is up to him. He can choose to roll up his sleeves and make sure that when the next harvest comes around, he will have his revenge against the weather gods. Or he can give up and sell the farm. It all depends on his attitude.

If you want to completely avoid problems and crises and every type of setback, then you'll have to spend the rest of your life hiding in a corner. Pull a blanket over your head and hope for the best.

The rest of us can give you food, we can protect you, we can keep you warm and make sure nothing dreadful happens to you. All you need to do is to stay under that blanket and never leave your comfy corner.

You might well live to be one hundred years old without any major problems. I really don't know.

But what a life . . .

WHEN EVERYBODY NEEDS TO BE PERFECTLY HAPPY ALL THE TIME

Nevertheless, there seem to be many people in our society today who try to protect themselves from everything. Everything, absolutely everything unpleasant must be kept at bay.

We should obviously avoid problems as much as possible. Naturally, we should vaccinate ourselves and make sure that we wear bike helmets. We should use the seat belts in our cars, and we should protect our houses from burning down by blowing out all the candles when we leave the room. Perfectly reasonable measures to deal with life in a cautious manner. The instinct for self-preservation should be there, and you shouldn't take stupid risks.

But in some people I perceive a sort of obsession with getting rid of all types of setbacks in life.

Everybody must like me.

My boss can't criticize me in the least.

If my body isn't exactly perfect, then my life is over.

My neighbor's car is always going to be fancier and nicer than mine.

My children always have to receive top grades at school.

My summer vacation must be perfect, not to mention the holiday break. Everybody must glow with delight, or else it's a total disaster.

My husband/wife/partner must always like everything I
do—all the time.

And I must be happy and carefree from morning to evening,
every day of the week, otherwise life is hardly worth
enduring.

We should love our jobs every second of the day.

Our sex life should always be a heavenly explosion of bliss.

Some of these unrealistic expectations might come from social media infiltrating our innermost emotional life. By scrolling up and down in various feeds on the internet, we're all presented with the perfect lives of other people, their brilliant successes in life, and their wonderful relationships and family life. I doubt anyone exists who is completely immune to that type of input. We forget that nobody posts pictures of the family's squabbles, the burnt Sunday roast, or Uncle George after too many drinks.

THE BENEFIT OF ADVERSITY

It's my absolute conviction that a setback is something positive. It's like a muscle that you want to strengthen. If you put it under stress, it will become stronger. If you never exercise it, it will wither away. To make yourself stronger, you need to push your mental muscle.

One example is of course the pendulum. To make it swing in one direction, you first have to accept that it will also swing in the other direction. You can't make a pendulum swing in only one direction and not the other. It will swing in both directions regardless of what you would prefer. It follows a law of nature.

To make it swing in the direction you want it to, the positive direction, you will have to reckon on the fact that it is also going to swing in the wrong direction, the negative one.

Success demands that you be prepared for the risk of meeting setbacks.

My own theory is that this is what leads many people to give up far too early. They love life when it swings in the right direction, but dread when it goes in the opposite direction. And, as usual, if you want to avoid risks completely, then you're hardly going to get anywhere in life.

If you don't go out hunting for what you want, then you're never going to get it. If you don't ask, then you won't get any answers. If you don't work your way forward, you'll always remain sitting in the same place.

If you don't shoot, you won't hit the target. If you don't propose a business deal, you won't sell anything. If you don't apply for that dream job, it will go to somebody else. If you don't ask that boy on a date, nothing will happen. I know you've heard this hundreds of times, and you realize that it's true.

And yet . . . so many people tend to sit down and bide their time. Wait.

Because it's horrible knowing that something can go wrong. Risks are unpleasant. Ask me. For a long time, I did this myself.

But the people at the top of the mountain, they didn't fall into the trap. They got there under their own steam. Of course, they had help in various ways. But they didn't end up on top by slouching in front of the TV and making other people successful.

WHY DO WE GIVE UP TOO SOON?

Why do you give up? Why do you let go and just float along? You know that nobody is going to leave a treasure chest on your front steps. We know that we aren't going to wake up one morning in April looking good and in great physical condition if we don't do anything.

It depends on us, and only us. We understand that we need to take responsibility for our lives, and we're prepared to roll up our sleeves and do what's necessary. And even so, many fantastic plans just capsize. Why?

There are a lot of reasons for that.

It was too hard. It wasn't worth it. Nobody has faith in me. I don't have faith in myself, either. To be honest, other things seem so much more fun. It takes too long, and I don't have the patience to wait. I can't remember why it was so important. Anyway, it's not important anymore.

It's just too much. Life can't just be work. I don't see any results. What if I'm wrong? Everyone says that I should drop it.

I think that I'm pretending that I still want to do it. And so on.

HAVE YOU EVER GIVEN UP?

Of course you have. A fitness goal you had: losing weight is the most common, but putting on weight can be desirable, too. Building muscle, perhaps.

Learning something new. Golf, Spanish, keeping your desk neat. Getting out of bed in the mornings. Stopping procrastinating. Reading more interesting books. Trying an alcohol-free month. Starting to save money. Spending more time with your children. Refraining from clutching your cell phone every minute you're awake. Taking evening classes so you can apply for more advanced jobs.

It might be a failure in your relationships. Getting your partner to really understand why you say those things. Or getting your partner to read your thoughts. Persuading Auntie Greta to abandon her negative attitude. Convincing your best friend to stop talking about himself or herself. Or finding a partner when you want to have somebody to share your life with.

Why not talk shop? There are lots of setbacks to indulge in at work. Building your own business and earning a pile of money to be able to impress your old pals. Making a career. Doubling your income. Learning a new skill to improve your employability. Starting to take responsibility for your own development. Not whining about your boss when you come home in the evening, because your family just can't face hearing it anymore. No longer using the excuse that you love your job and giving notice to quit and leave your useless boss.

You've tried a whole pile of these things, haven't you? But then stopped. Why did *you* just let it drop?

Deep inside you are the answers you need to dig out and be brave enough to look at.

What would it be worth for you to learn to see why you gave up, and know how you can avoid that next time?

SUMMARY

Setbacks, problems, and crises are everyday fare for most of us. You can always find yourself knocking your head against some wall or other. The more we accept that setbacks are a part of life, the easier it will be to put up with that life. Sometimes it goes well, sometimes less well. It's nobody's fault that this is how the world works. But you need to accept the circumstances under which all of us live.

You can't protect yourself from everything. So training your ability to deal with the hardships of life is the best way forward. Pay attention to your thoughts. Your thoughts govern your emotions, not the other way around.

5

The Four Development Phases: Dodgy Dynamic

Just because something feels difficult, it doesn't necessarily mean that it's a setback. Sometimes it's just a question of different phases in life that we must go through. The realization that ups and downs are there all the time can be liberating. It isn't your fault; this is simply how the world works.

There are a variety of reasons why we sometimes, despite the best of intentions, don't manage to make any headway with seemingly simple challenges in everyday life. It's not always our own fault that the road feels steep. But you can't simply blame the fact that it's tough and give up—that's the complete opposite of taking responsibility. We do, however, benefit considerably from understanding what happens when things go totally wrong. Look at the following image.

This is a model that was originally created by Paul Hersey and Ken Blanchard in the mid-1970s, one that has since spread across the world. They originally examined how children learn new things, and in the process they discovered that adults often acted in exactly the same way.

Hersey and Blanchard wanted to find out how a person progresses from being a happy amateur to a full-blown professional. What

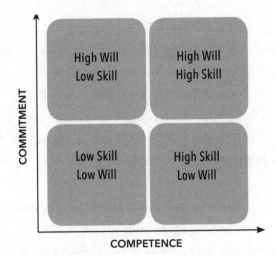

phases does one go through? They, like most of us, had noted that some tasks were more difficult to carry out than others. Even if you started doing a particular task with great enthusiasm, you could find yourself stuck before you knew it. But how does this happen?

They looked partly at the competence of the particular individual—that is, whatever specific knowledge or ability the person has that applies to the situation—and partly at the commitment to a specific task. Commitment was then divided into motivation (do I want to?) and self-confidence (am I capable?).

THE FIRST PHASE—HIGH WILL, LOW SKILL

High commitment (motivation + self-confidence) but low competence (for this specific task).

When You Start Off Full of Energy but Without Really Knowing What You're Doing

When you start a completely new task that you really want to do, you're motivated and you feel very confident about dealing with everything that needs to be done. This is going to be great fun. How hard can it be? Just get going, full speed ahead! Somewhere at the back of your mind you do, of course, know that you've never done this before, which should make you think twice. But even if you're aware that you don't have much competence in this area, that doesn't worry you too much. You just get on with it regardless. Why? You have such a high degree of commitment! Everything feels good, right?

This can be related to just about everything. Finally starting a new exercise class, beginning an educational course, changing your diet, learning Finnish, getting a new job, embarking on that big DIY project at home, planting a hedge, reading an important book that is going to help you make progress in your career.

It's a lovely phase. Everything feels really great, even though you subconsciously might have a creeping awareness of the fact that you don't really know what you are doing. But you just go for it anyway.

THE SECOND PHASE—LOW WILL, LOW SKILL

Low commitment (motivation + self-confidence) and low competence (for this specific task).

When Nothing Works and You're About to Give Up

When you've busied yourself with your task for a while, it's not uncommon to discover that things aren't quite so simple as you previously thought. What should have been extremely straightforward turns out to be more complex. It doesn't turn out like you expected, there are no results, and everything takes far too much time. And it's hard to find the joy in something that isn't going smoothly.

Note that this can be about anything from doing your DIY project at home, to going to the gym, to sticking with your most recent New Year's resolution. What was at first inspiring is now just a burden. Everybody else except you seems to know how to do it. This isn't what you had in mind, and there is no end to the problems.

Most of all, you feel confused. Was this really such a good idea? Perhaps you should return to your usual old routines?

And herein lies the great danger. If you don't know that you now find yourself in a natural but perhaps not especially pleasant phase, there's a risk that you'll simply abandon your big plan. The going is just too rough. And you can add yet another failure to all the others. Not what you needed just now. This is the reason why many gardens are full of unfinished projects, why some houses are "partially" renovated (why some of the baseboards are missing), and why there are so many unused gym memberships in people's wallets (and closets full of almost-new workout clothes).

It's a natural phase, and all of us end up stuck now and then. The challenge is not to give up too soon.

THE THIRD PHASE—LOW WILL, HIGH SKILL

Low or medium-high commitment (motivation + self-confidence) but high competence (for this specific task).

When You Start Seeing the Light at the End of the Tunnel but Still Hesitate

If you keep on struggling—and resist that acute desire to just drop the whole thing and arrive late at work, throw your hammer in the trash can, and burn your Finnish dictionary—you'll notice that even though it's still quite an effort, you are actually, little by little, learning. It's about looking for good news and celebrating small victories.

If you don't give up, it's going to get easier after a while. Keep working at it—going on a run in the morning, studying in the evening, taking on some extra projects at work—and you'll notice how the pressure slowly eases up. You gradually regain your motivation because task after task is going to go more smoothly. Things become a bit easier. You start to see results, even though they're still too small to satisfy you.

Your self-confidence is not yet sufficiently strong for you to be immune to setbacks. There's still a risk that you'll give up, because your self-confidence is not firmly established.

THE FOURTH PHASE—HIGH WILL, HIGH SKILL

High commitment (motivation + self-confidence) and high competence (for this specific task).

When It Finally Looks Like You're Going to Manage to Go the Distance

In the end, it's going to work out. Since you're not a person who gives up easily, you've struggled on through everything as best you could. You've clung firmly to your plan and meanwhile have learned loads about what works and what doesn't work. Your knowledge and motivation have increased—your self-confidence has returned. Now everything feels good again, and you might even find it hard to understand why you were so discouraged before. From this vantage point, it's easier to see that you needed to make your way through all the phases to attain that "flow." Now you have what I call momentum. It doesn't require nearly as much energy to keep on track.

HOW LONG DOES THIS PROCESS TAKE?

No one can say how long it will take between the first and the final phase. This depends on many different factors. But what's important is that you understand that this is a logical process that takes place virtually every time you try something new. Setting off at full speed at the beginning simply indicates keen commitment to the task, and there isn't anything negative about it. One thing or another is going to happen en route, and these things are going to slow you down; this is part of the process.

An important point: there is nothing wrong with you.

You react negatively to setbacks, and that can lead to frustration. As you're learning how to move forward, your commitment will return. You just need to keep your faith that this will happen.

There are studies about this aspect, and it's clear that if you've lost your motivation and perhaps your self-confidence—the second phase—then the next step is to rebuild your confidence. It's hard to feel confident when you know that you lack competence for a particular task. As your skills develop, you'll start feeling better again.

As usual, there's no rule without an exception, but you should also know that if you find yourself completely stalled, the solution is fairly simple: go back to basics, learn the job from beginning to end. Don't cheat. Don't take any shortcuts. Don't ignore the task and dump it on somebody else. You're going to feel much more confident and self-assured once you master this.

SUMMARY

The most important conclusion here is that it's impossible for you to feel the same amount of motivation and self-confidence in everything you do. Even though the model I've just described can vary from person to person, and even though the degree of difficulty of the task you undertake affects how long it will take, you can see how every new endeavor will follow this pattern of waxing and waning confidence and motivation.

We've all been there. On Monday we start off at full speed. Things are going to happen, oh, yes! On Tuesday, our energy level has dropped markedly, and on Wednesday everything is just an impenetrable darkness. But on Thursday, it feels a bit better, things start moving along. And by Friday you find yourself beginning to smile. This is a natural process.

I want to emphasize: not everything you do can be fun and motivating *all* the time. There are many people who only follow their gut feeling and devote their time to what is fun. I'm not saying that you should only do things that are difficult, and force you to struggle 24/7—no, not at all. But if you show interest only in things that feel good and enjoyable, then you are doing things only in the first and fourth phases.

This means two things, both equally bad: if you start new things—the first phase—and encounter a challenge and give up, you will never learn how to master new situations. You will reach phase two, and come to a full *stop*. Then perhaps you'll start something else new—in phase one—which you will in turn drop as soon as the going gets rough. You will simply switch between phase one and phase two. You will add a long row of failures to your mental CV. Not good.

The other thing is that if you want to feel entirely secure all the time, then you will only do things you are already capable of—the fourth phase. In other words, you're never going to challenge yourself by trying something new. Instead of testing slightly new paths in your life, you'll stay in your own comfort zone and continue to do the sort of things you feel good at.

That would put you in an especially unfortunate cul-de-sac. It works for a while, then all development and growth come to a halt.

6

Which Setbacks Are the Absolute Worst?

It's naïve to imagine that life can be perfect all the time. To achieve that, you would probably have to get your very own planet.

In order to get a little perspective, let's make, in a very unscientific way, a ranking scale of the petty troubles in life.

Assuming that the newspapers are right: within fifty years, Earth is more or less going to burn up and all life will die out. If we don't accept the fact that we messed up the world big-time, then it will soon be over. That seems like roughly the worst-case scenario, so let's give the potential end of the world the maximum 100 points on the list of things that can go wrong.

If the end of humanity is the highest rating on the catastrophe scale, how many points would we then give to, for example, the Second World War? The greatest and perhaps worst war in history. Around seventy million or more dead as a result of the global disaster that Hitler caused. That's nowhere near the absolute end, but it is a horrific catastrophe. So how many points do we give to the Second World War? 80 points?

What about the First World War then? However simplistic it may be, we could compare the two wars—so perhaps 70 points in comparison to the Second World War. "Only" ten million dead.

Listing other wars, and in comparison, all of them—regardless of their brutality and evidence of human evil—will probably be ranked lower than the two world wars. But let's give all wars 50 points on the list of catastrophes, because war is always horrible.

What happens if we take a look at other types of catastrophes? Where does the tsunami in Southeast Asia in 2004 land? It was an enormous tragedy. Entire towns were swept away, and houses, cars, people. The number of dead was just over 230,000. But compared with the Second World War, which lasted six years, the concentration camps, the carpet bombing of countless cities, human torture, hideous crimes against humanity . . . should we give 30 points for the tsunami, perhaps?

Nature is nature; we don't control it. But the things we do to each other, we do control those. A person killed by a natural disaster is a different sort of tragedy than one killed by another person.

Corruption, abuse of power, the fact that there are so many psychopaths at the top of lots of different organizations across the world? Perhaps that ranks as high as the tsunami. Perhaps higher, in fact—I think I would give that list 40 points.

And we can go on and on like that.

Compared with the troubles listed above, how would you rank your fiercely held opinion that your mayor is an idiot? Maybe 4 points. That you missed the bus one Tuesday in April doesn't rank at all on this scale.

OUR OWN PERSONAL CATASTROPHE SCALE

Instead, let's look at our own—extremely personal—scale of setbacks. Dying would be just about the worst that can happen to you—90 points. Yes, there are worse things. Your child killed in an accident? That's 100 points. It's hard to imagine anything worse than something happening to your children. Or being attacked and robbed and almost killed in the process. Again, a missed bus scores at a ridiculously low level. But let's put aside the catastrophes for a minute. What should be on your list of trials?

> You are fired from your job.
> Your company goes bankrupt because of the recession.
> You make a fool of yourself because you can't handle
>   alcohol.
> Your car is stolen the day before your family road trip.
> Your garage burns down, and the electricians who put in the
>   faulty wiring didn't have any insurance.

These are examples that we can relate to. These things are unpleasant to have to deal with and yet can happen to lots of people every year.

If you have your own business, bankruptcy is among the worst scenarios you can imagine. You'll have to fire people you like and care about. You're personally responsible for the bank loan. Your bank informs you that they are expecting you to pay them over $100,000.

For somebody who is employed, the equivalent nightmare is losing your job, perhaps in the middle of a deep recession. There are no other jobs available. Your future is looking bleak.

You have debts but no income. You can't pay your mortgage, so you and your family will be forced to move to a tiny apartment. You'll have to sell your private car so that it won't be repossessed. Your company car—that's just history now. Perhaps you have three children who don't really understand why they won't be going on vacation this year. The summer cottage—forget it. You'll have to cancel your gym membership, and none of you will even be able to afford any take-out food for the next three years. Your children continue to grow. Affording new clothes for them turns into a total nightmare.

Then we've got the social "freezing out"—which is not uncommon. You and your family don't fit in with your peers anymore. The other people in your circle of acquaintances won't want to be "infected" by your misfortune, and soon the invitations to dinners and birthday parties have disappeared.

After fourteen years in the banking world, I also know that a dodgy financial situation is one of the toughest factors to deal with in a relationship. Quite often, the relationship will crack after a while, because partners usually end up blaming each other. The frustration has to find some outlet.

So now you're broke, unemployed, have a damaged marriage, and unhappy children. You might start the habit of drinking a little more often that you ought to. Who knows whether your children will even stay with you under these circumstances? You're going to end up severely depressed and might not want to get out of bed again.

At this point, it's best that I explain something: I'm not a horrible pessimist! I do firmly believe in positive thinking over negative thinking, but we definitely need a measure of realism in our lives, right?

HOW MANY POINTS WOULD YOU GIVE TO THE FOLLOWING (VERY REALISTIC) SCENARIOS?

The chain of events described above is far from unique. There are millionaires who have had to leave their homes and lost everything because of poor judgment.

If we consider the scenario of a lost job and a destroyed life to be your personal world war, and rate it at about 80 points on the catastrophe scale, then where should we rank the everyday minor dilemmas, the sorts of things that you have to deal with in an ordinary week? How many points would you give to the following trivial incidents:

- You didn't get your kids to school in time.
- The florists didn't have any pink lilies you had your heart set on. They only had white ones.
- Your neighbor's cat pissed in the kids' sandbox—again.
- A work project means that you have to work late three nights in a row because you wasted time during the day doing completely irrelevant things.
- A rabbit bulldozed no fewer than three gigantic craters in your beautiful lawn.
- Your lying colleagues have been far more successful in their careers than you.
- You messed up a potential business deal with a client.
- Your wallet seems to leak. It looks like you won't be taking that European vacation with the guys next year.
- You're troubled by a bad back despite having done everything the doctor told you to do. Lost weight, started working out, got a massage, etc.
- Your son is not performing well at school.
- Your daughter is being bullied at school.
- Your elderly mother is ill, and you don't know how much longer she has left. This really is hard to deal with.
- Your partner doesn't kiss you good night anymore. He or she might not even love you anymore.
- You might not love your partner, either.
- You have to wait for an agonizing *three* seconds for your favorite webpage to load, rather than the expected *one* second.
- You received paralyzingly few likes on your latest Instagram post.

- Your boss thinks you are an idiot.
- Some days your children agree with your boss.
- You were blocked in at the parking lot and had to wait an excruciating seven minutes before the grade-A idiot came out of the store.

I'm not trying to make fun of these smaller, mundane troubles, but if we don't put things in perspective, we're not going to manage life very well. I don't mean that these small things are unimportant, but in relative terms they are still . . . well . . . small.

On the other hand . . .

EVEN SMALL THINGS CAN CREATE LARGE PROBLEMS

Have you been bitten by a bear? No? I thought not.

How about bitten by a mosquito, what about that?

Precisely. It's the small things that bother us in our everyday life. If we don't learn how to deal with those irritating everyday incidents, we're going to run into problems when we try to tackle the big things. If we can't handle missing the bus without feeling furious, how are we going to deal with a lecture from our most important client? If we lose it when the boss asks us to work a couple of hours extra, how are we going to manage when our children get bullied at school?

In bygone days, an empty gas tank when I was in a hurry to get to the airport could drive me crazy. But I learned that these small bothersome moments serve as a little reminder that life isn't going to be simple—ever. Besides, whose job is it to keep track of how much gas there is in the tank . . . in *my* car? We're back to the question of responsibility again.

The small things are important because they prepare us for the big things. And if somebody has protected you from all those minor irritations . . . well, er, if you've never met with real opposition in your life, then you're going to have endless challenges when real problems do indeed show up. Because they are going to. We can be quite certain of that.

It's like a sort of vaccine. You get a little dose, you learn how to deal with it, and when the proper infection arrives, your immune system is ready for it. Small, everyday problems help us grow strong and resilient for harder things.

THE SPOILED CHILD'S LIMITED POSSIBILITIES TO SUCCEED

People who are frustrated by helicopter parenting often point out that children also need to be prepared for life. They argue that we do teenagers a disservice when we protect them from every unpleasantness in life. In the end, it will rebound and cause trouble: if you're totally unprepared, then the rebound might be especially hard. Because when you get your first job, your mother isn't going to be there to protect you.

But on the other hand, some people argue in favor of the idea that children should be children for as long as possible, and I understand this viewpoint, too. I once wished that I could protect my (now-adult) children from all the evil in the world. The problem is that I can't. The only thing I can do is to try to protect them from the very worst of it, while also letting them confront what I think they can manage on their own. I'm not saying that I was the perfect parent by any means, but both of them seem to manage excellently by themselves, so something must have worked out okay.

Sure, it would be lovely to have a rosy dreamlike existence without any challenges or problems, right? In which everything is great and someone serves you ice cream and fizzy drinks every day without you ever putting on weight. You can have a glass of wine every evening without it affecting you in the slightest. It doesn't matter whether you get anything done at work or not. You get a raise automatically and regularly. The sun shines every day and you're always happy.

I'd also like to live in that fantasy world. It would be very nice.

The sad truth, however, is that such a world doesn't exist. In my opinion, it's pointless to strive for something that is impossible to achieve.

When you think about it, up until now you've actually survived 100 percent of your very worst days in life. You're doing great.

SUMMARY

There are setbacks and there are setbacks. You can deal with them by putting them in perspective. Accept that they come, but make sure that you don't act like you're on the edge of a precipice of despair every time something negative happens.

By stepping back a bit from every situation, you can more easily judge what's right in front of you.

It can be useful to bear in mind the simple "five-plus-five rule": if something won't make a difference in five years' time, then don't spend more than five minutes being upset about it.

7

Your List of Setbacks

Put together a list of your own setbacks. List the obstacles you've encountered in life, so that you have a sense of your own baggage. You don't need to dig too deeply or start obsessing over or wallowing in every trial, but it can be a good idea to know what the situation really is. You might come to the conclusion that your life has actually been rather good so far.

Here is an aid to help you create a simplified table of your setbacks. It's designed help you get a quick overview of your setbacks and things you've experienced in your life so far and to put these in perspective. There's a sample ranking scale on pages 66–67. You can choose what events you list and how you rank them.

Remind yourself of what your life has looked like. The list can have as many items as you want. You could use one hundred, or just thirty things. If you want to list every missed bus since the 1990s, it might be a bit longer.

When you look at this simple list, you may notice something. Look at everything you've managed to survive without giving up. You must be a strong person!

Sure, some things have cost you dearly. Absolutely, you've been knocked around, and it can hurt. I understand. But here you are, nevertheless. And that's fantastic! It can be a powerful thing to remind yourself of the adversity you've already gone through. It's easy to forget.

It's easy to create a list of your own. Write down the obstacles and difficulties that immediately come to mind, using the line that corresponds with a point score you think is appropriate.

My points	Setbacks
100	
95	
90	
85	
80	
75	
70	
65	
60	
55	
50	

45	
40	
35	
30	
25	
20	
15	
10	
5	

THOMAS'S LIST

Strangely enough, my childhood was so easygoing and free from trauma that I'm almost ashamed to admit it. The trouble came later in life. To give you a helping hand, I've created my own list here. Hopefully this will help you fill in your own list. But remember that we're all unique. Things that I consider to be problems and identify as notable obstacles are ones you might laugh at. (Something to note: in writing my list, it turned out that I'd forgotten a couple of major incidents. My interpretation: if something doesn't come to mind, it's likely no longer significant.)

Thomas's List of Setbacks

My points	Setbacks
100	
95	
90	Losing my mother
90	Resuscitating my two-week-old son with mouth-to-mouth
85	Chronic sleep problems for more than thirty years
80	Car crash; I was still inside as it started to burn
80	Came close to being completely burned out—on a leave of absence for three months
75	High-speed car crash; the car was totaled
75	Victim of a psychopathic stalker for six months
60	My manuscripts were refused by publishers for twenty years
50	My books didn't sell particularly well when they were eventually published
45	Second hernia operation, when I almost fell off the operating table in panic
45	Car crash; ended up with a whiplash injury
40	Robbed in a bank and was forced into the bank vault with a gun pointed at me
30	Berated by the CEO of the company I worked for after I wrote a stupid letter to the board
30	Media attack orchestrated by various psychologists because of *Surrounded by Idiots*
25	Allergic to furry animals, dust mites, pollen
20	First hernia operation
15	My daughter's heart murmur when she was a child

15	Car crash, but nothing serious
15	Lost all my friends when I moved to Stockholm
15	My parents' divorce when I was in my late teens
5	My girlfriend dumped me in my first week of military service

As you can see, the setbacks in my life are fairly typical. This very simple technique helps me see things in perspective. I've taken a few hits and have both highs and lows. Knowing that I've survived all these things, I'm confident that I can also deal with whatever else comes my way.

It's important not to wallow in these things or make them the subject of daily conversation.

REFUSING TO BE DEFINED BY OBSTACLES

Peter is a good friend of mine who has struggled with dyslexia his entire childhood and adolescence. Many years ago, he chose to not see it as a shortcoming. It wasn't easy, but now he's written several books, all of them much appreciated by their readers. What did he do? He accepted the fact that it would be harder for him to be an author than it would be for somebody who didn't have dyslexia. He refused to define himself by his diagnosis. He worked hard and succeeded *despite his diagnosis*. Or, as he says, *thanks to* his diagnosis. Without dyslexia, he wouldn't have had anything to battle against.

When I asked Peter how he would rank his dyslexia on the scale of setbacks, he thought it over very carefully. At first he didn't want to put it on the list at all, because the dyslexia has led to lots of good things. But in the end, he allotted it 25 points, because of course it was pretty tough for him at school with unsympathetic teachers who thought he was a bit thick. Nowadays we know better, but thirty-five years ago much less was known about dyslexia.

Peter's reasoning is important. Because, like me, he has always dreamed of becoming an author, the dyslexia was an important motivator for him. It was the thing he was determined to beat. He wanted to prove to himself that he could write, *despite* the dyslexia.

The world is full of such examples. No matter what your situation, if you look around you, you'll certainly find lots of similar life stories.

SETBACKS OR POTENTIAL POSSIBILITIES?

As we think about Peter's example, it's interesting to consider whether what we consider obstacles actually are obstacles. Sometimes we interpret a situation completely wrong. Or our thinking is just a bit too narrow. What one person would call a fantastic possibility, another person would say is useless. But what I would call a setback, perhaps you would see as a possibility. On the face of things, you might see a situation one way, but sometimes it can be a good idea to reflect a little longer on what a particular event can mean.

A good practice—regardless of your first reaction to a particular event—is to ask yourself: What about the situation am I overlooking? Are there any other possible interpretations of this situation? Are there any benefits or positive sides? Of course, there aren't always, but surprisingly often there are positive aspects of a seemingly depressing experience.

Looking at my own list, this is extremely clear. For an author, it's awful to have your manuscripts refused, and I received hundreds of refusals over twenty years. This monumental setback just went on and on, proof that I shouldn't write books. On the other hand, I chose to keep at it because I've always liked writing. In retrospect, I know that those rejections forced me to polish my writing, to develop and become better.

During those twenty years, I didn't think like that; I was just as disappointed and angry as you would imagine. But in retrospect I know that the refusals led to something positive. The first ten books I wrote, which were never published, gave me enough training to be able to express myself so that people understood me. I wasn't published as an author until I was actually ready.

Let's look at some fictional examples.

The Setback

Your boss gives you even more to do. Just piles work on your desk. What a bastard.

The Potential Possibility

Or . . . perhaps she sees that you have potential and is confident in your skills? Soon your career will take off.

The Setback

You miss the bus by a demoralizing five seconds. Now you'll have to wait for nine minutes.

The Potential Possibility

On the next bus you bump into an old friend whose telephone number you've been trying to find for months. Now you spend a great evening together.

The Setback

Your partner wants you to go on a trip together, but you don't want to go. Your first reaction is irritation and anger.

The Potential Possibility

On the other hand . . . perhaps it means you'll get a much-needed break from everyday life, have some time for each other, and enjoy experiences that can boost your relationship.

The Setback

Your son never stops pestering you about the new hockey gear he wants. You can almost see your credit card melting from the financial stress.

The Potential Possibility

But . . . with the right coaching, perhaps your boy will be the next Wayne Gretzky. He'll be able to buy you a new house in a few years.

The Setback

The new owners of the company you work for want to restructure, and you're going to be made redundant after twelve years of faithful hard work. Your career looks bleak.

The Potential Possibility

But . . . the new owners will pay you twelve months' severance when you leave, so you'll have a chance to start up that little business venture you've been toying with. Soon you'll have both the time and money you need.

Of course, you don't need to be naïve. Sometimes bad news really is bad news. If I step into a heap of dog poop on the pavement, my shoes might well be destroyed. If my phone is stolen at the restaurant, that's going to be a headache. But actively looking for potential possibilities even in awkward or undesirable situations leads—more often than you think—to more interesting lessons and new experiences.

What do you have to lose?

A lot of people think that positive thinking is silly, and they don't believe it works at all. But there are useful possibilities and positive outcomes in places we're not used to looking. We just need to step back a bit to see them.

Many of the most advanced inventions we use today have their origins in advanced failures.

Only you can decide how you should react to what happens around you. You already know that, and you've heard it before. I want to remind you that how you react to your situation is your responsibility. Oftentimes, we need to work to put things in perspective. We can accept that sometimes things are going to go totally wrong, but at the same time we can sometimes overestimate the severity of the situation.

So let's go back to your list of setbacks.

Put this book down, and try this:

Look at the situations, one by one. And choose just one to start with.

Go back to that time in your memory and accept that it was an unfortunate experience. Don't focus on the misery, but instead spend a few minutes reflecting on the positive effects of that event.

This is an exercise that I sometimes use when I do one-on-one coaching, and many people just completely dismiss the idea. Getting stuck with a job you didn't ask for can only be negative, they say. There's nothing positive about your child doing poorly in school, they say.

I respect these attitudes. Not all bad things bring something good with them. But more times than you think, they actually do. So add a little realism to your list. Try this exercise for each item on your list of setbacks. I wouldn't be surprised if half or more of your obstacles also moved you forward in a valuable way.

Even really difficult things can create positive effects. A woman I worked with many years ago was devastated by the death of her mother. But after a painful period of mourning, she realized that she wanted to put more effort into her relationship with her father. She did so, and they had a better relationship during his final twenty years than they'd ever had before.

It's easy to sound dismissive or flippant when advising people to look for the positives. But by taking a few steps back and looking at a situation as objectively as possible, we really can gain important insights. This strengthens us and prepares us for the future.

The setback	The potential possibility

SUMMARY

Even though all of us encounter adversity, it's wise to have perspective. Since we're governed by our emotions, we can react more strongly in the heat of the moment than is really justified.

Take a step back and look at each obstacle in turn.

Was it really as negative as you first believed? And is there actually anything positive hidden here?

If you think about the greatest benefit you gained from a seemingly hard situation, is there an element of gratitude for having had that experience in your life? Look at what it gave you.

8

Do We All React to Setbacks the Same Way?

Obviously, different people react in different ways to different types of problems. Besides, we react differently on different occasions. The situation, your mood, and other difficulties or opportunities you may be experiencing at the same time can change how you perceive a situation. People are decidedly different in this area.

What you're interested in, your motivational factors, your driving forces, your unique situation, and more all influence what you choose to consider a setback.

If somebody blocks your car in a parking space when you should be halfway to the airport, I can make allowances for your cursing. But if somebody blocks your car in a parking space when you've just won a huge amount of money on a lottery ticket, then I doubt whether you'll be that put out. The same event, different circumstances. So it's clear, we're never going to be able to completely chart out or predict how we react to trying circumstances.

Just remember one thing: obstacles often bring out our less-flattering sides. Few people look forward to a setback.

Besides, all of us have different experiences. If we compare ourselves with Nelson Mandela, we'll probably look a bit unimpressive when it comes to handling adversity. Spending more than twenty-five years in prison for your political views would have crushed most people, but not him. He was finally released, and he didn't react the way people thought he would. Instead, he turned the other cheek and was elected South Africa's first black president.

THE DISC MODEL

I use the widely known DISC model (dominance, inspiration, stability, compliance) to describe dissimilarities in behavioral patterns. There are lots of other methods, but this model covers most of what you need to know just now. I've associated each of the four behavior profiles with a color—red, yellow, green, and blue—to make the system simple to use and easy to remember.

There are an endless number of factors that affect how a person functions, and in this book I will deal with two of them: a person's behavioral profile and a person's development level.

If you've read my previous book, *Surrounded by Idiots,* you'll soon be getting a short refresher course on the basic behavior types.

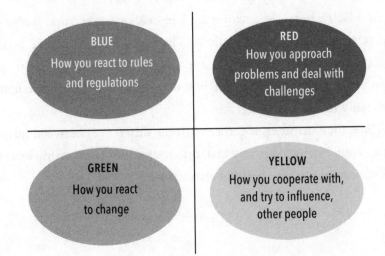

Red, the task-oriented and extroverted color, is governed by an ability to deal with problems and difficult challenges. The tougher the scenario, the better. If something goes a bit too smoothly, the Reds almost become suspicious. What's the catch? Why is it so easy? It should be hard; it should be difficult. You have to put in some work. It might even need to be a bit painful. Pain makes you strong. Reds like a fast pace, action, and having lots of things going on.

If Reds are focused on being active, then yellow, the extroverted and relationship-oriented color, is about integrating. These are the people who always have to convince everyone else to see things their way. They can't leave the room until everybody agrees with them. And they see sunshine even when it's raining. The Yellows also like a bit of action.

Green, the relationship-oriented and introverted color, is about an unwillingness to change. A lot of green in someone's behavior profile indicates a desire to maintain the status quo. Greens won't be in favor of change, even if it's absolutely necessary. These are people who say things like "It was better before," or "The grass isn't always greener on the other side." New ideas are summarily dismissed: everything is working nicely the way it is, thank you very much.

And lastly, blue, the introverted and task-oriented color, is about appreciating rules and regulations. The Blues follow the rule book and always know what is right and proper. They read the instructions before they even open the box with that new IKEA bookshelf. Preferably in three languages.

These four attitudes, together with the differences between introversion and extroversion and task orientation and relationship orientation, lead to certain specific behaviors.

WHAT KIND OF BEHAVIOR DOES THIS LEAD TO?

When we look at how these behavior types play out, we start to see clear differences in every respect imaginable. On the following pages you can see a number of specific qualities relating to a particular color. Remember, however, that there are exceptions. There are always exceptions. It's complicated to understand human beings.

Here are a few points to remember about the DISC model:

- Everything about an individual's behavior cannot be explained with the DISC language.
- There are also other models that explain human behavior.
- There are more parts of the jigsaw puzzle than just "the colors" to map various behavioral patterns.
- The DISC model is built upon psychological studies. It is used across the entire world and has been translated into forty languages.
- Historically, there are similar models in different cultures, e.g., the theory of the four temperaments, which originally came from Hippocrates, who lived in antiquity, approximately twenty-five hundred years ago.
- About 80 percent of all people have a combination of two colors that dominate their behavior. About 5 percent only have one color that dominates their behavior. The rest are dominated by three colors.
- All-Green behavior, or Green in combination with another color, is the most common. The most unusual is all-Red behavior, or Red in combination with another color.
- There may be differences in behavior between the sexes, but I do not focus on the gender perspective in this book.

	RED	YELLOW	GREEN	BLUE
APPROACH	Energetic and direct	Optimistic and spontaneous	Considerate and understanding	Reflective and correct
MANNER	Businesslike	Visible	Sensitive	Formal
WORK STYLE	Hardworking Ambitious Professional Effective Exact	Committed Personal Flexible Stimulating Articulate	Personable Relaxed Friendly Informal Low-key	Structured Organized Specialized Methodical Succinct
WORK PACE	Fast and decisive	Fast and spontaneous	Slow and consistent	Slow and systematic
PRIORITIZES	The task and the result	Relationships and influence	Retaining good relationships	The task and work method
AFRAID OF	Losing control	Losing prestige	Confrontation	Making a fool of oneself
BEHAVIOR UNDER PRESSURE	Dictates conditions and asserts oneself	Attacks and is ironic	Backs down and agrees	Withdraws and avoids
WANTS	Results	Inspiration	Stability	Quality
WANTS YOU TO BE	Straight-forward	Stimulating	Kind	Exact
WANTS TO BE	The one who decides	The one who is admired	The one who is liked	The one who is correct
IS IRRITATED BY	Inefficiency and indecision	Passivity and routines	Insensitivity and impatience	Surprises and whims
WANTS TO HAVE	Success and control	Status and flexibility	Calm and quiet and close relationships	Credibility and time to prepare

	RED	YELLOW	GREEN	BLUE
BEHAVES	Businesslike	Elegant	Friendly	Law-abiding
LIVES IN	The present	The future	The past (when everything was better)	One's own thoughts
RELIES UPON	Gut feeling	Recognition	One's self	Specialists
DOESN'T LIKE	Sitting still	Being alone	Unpredictability	Hurry

- The DISC model does not work for analyzing ADHD, Asperger's syndrome, borderline personality disorder, or other diagnoses.
- There are always exceptions to the concepts I outline in this book. People are complex—even Red people can be humble, and Yellow people can listen attentively. There are Green people who deal with conflict because they have learned how to do so, and many Blues understand when it's time to stop tweaking the details.

WHAT THE FOUR COLORS WOULD DEFINE AS A SETBACK

When we look at the four colors and their interests, we see some interesting patterns.

People who are predominantly Red in their behavioral profile are just waiting for problems, even though they don't know what the problems are. They have a sort of constant battle-readiness, even though they live in the here and now. They don't plan for problems, but they deal with them if they have the audacity to show themselves.

People who are primarily Yellow think a bit differently here. These positive individuals live mainly in the future, where everything is bright and delightful, which means that they can be totally surprised by possible obstacles. They can end up in over their heads. Just like the Reds, they don't really have a plan, because the setbacks were not exactly expected.

Folks with profiles dominated by Green often walk around with a constant ache in their stomachs because they know—from their imaginary experience—that the bubble is about to burst. Somebody is going to mess up, and there will be big problems. This often leads to a certain passivity in order to avoid making things worse, even though nothing has happened at all.

Finally, people who are mostly Blue are risk analysts from birth. They function exactly the opposite of Yellows. Here, the attitude is that just about everything can go totally haywire, so you should use every imaginable safety net and protective measure to keep catastrophe at bay. The result is that they need forever to accomplish anything. It takes time to protect yourself from everything.

But what do they react to? Do the colors get upset by the same thing? How does a Yellow view a setback, compared to a Green? Let's take a look, and see what we can expect from those around us.

How Reds Define Setbacks

It's very valuable to understand what Reds see as setbacks, because that is where they will direct all their energy . . . and it's a good idea not to stand right in the line of fire.

What does a Red person view as an obstacle? Interesting question. For obvious reasons, they don't exactly back away when problems arise, and they're generally well prepared for everything to go sideways. Reds might be the most realistic when it comes to accepting the world as it is. My argument that everyone is affected by problems and crises is nothing new for the Reds. They already knew that.

Since they like speed, action, and to achieve (the best) results, everything that stands in the way of that is a setback.

If a Red boss wants to increase profitability by 2 percent, then too low a turnover and too high costs will be different facets of the same problem.

If a client doesn't want to buy from the Red salesperson, then that client will symbolize the obstacle—not the fact that the salesperson was poorly prepared or not properly updated.

And if your Red neighbor wants to build his garage right on your property line, then your "no" will be a big setback. After all, it prevents him from having his way. *Your* problem is that *you* are now the obstacle to his goal.

Everything that slows down the process is a problem. Everything that means the Red doesn't win. Setbacks are the same as losing: not sealing a business deal, being abandoned by your spouse, having your salary reduced, not being elected as chairman of the homeowners association (loss of power). Anything that means the Red loses control of the situation—their very greatest fear—is a setback.

How Yellows Identify Setbacks

If you remember Yellow behavior, then you'll recall that these people are more relationship-oriented than the Reds. Yellows have an interesting perspective amid all their infectious positiveness. In effect, they see only possibilities and positive outcomes, so it can be a bit of a shock when something goes wrong. What happened? This was going to be a great success!

The most devastating setback is anything that affects the Yellow's ego, like making a fool of yourself in public. Being loudly reprimanded by your boss in front of the whole department might be worse than being quietly fired on a Friday afternoon.

Far-fetched? Perhaps, but Yellows will always be sensitive to events that make them look unsuccessful. Appearances can be the most important thing for them.

Social ostracism. Not being chosen for the football team. Not being invited to the neighborhood's big block party. Seeing colleagues going to lunch together without even being asked if you're hungry. Being left by your partner. Naturally, nobody would think that was ideal, but the Yellow will be destroyed.

Anything negative about the Yellow as a person will be the greatest kind of adversity for this color.

How Greens Recognize Setbacks

Greens can spot obstacles anywhere. They have an introverted side that the Reds and the Yellows both lack. This means that a lot happens under the surface without others perceiving it. Greens consider disagreements and resistance to be setbacks. Any form of conflict is bad news.

This is challenging because conflicts are found everywhere. It's impossible to avoid them. You can't go through life without ending up in conflict with other people or even with yourself. Greens will often be troubled by inner conflict between what they ought to do and what they want to do. Greens don't have the same type of energy as the Reds and Yellows.

When Greens get scolded, they might not react as strongly as Yellows would at that particular moment, but they will remember the injustice for a very long time.

Like Yellows, Greens are relationship-oriented, but a Green lacks the strong ego of a Yellow. This means that Greens can face obstacles in a group setting in particular. Greens won't consider their own personal gain, but will consider the group's success or failure. Team sports work well for Greens because people compete together, but if it goes badly for the team, then Greens will suffer even more deeply than if the failure was theirs alone.

The Blues' Rational Definition of a Setback

When we look at how Blues consider obstacles, we see exciting patterns. As I mentioned earlier, they have their own way of critical thinking, which means that they're not really surprised by anything. When it all goes wrong, Blues will soberly nod and think, *Yep, exactly what I expected*. It will just confirm how they know the world works.

If I wanted to joke about this, I'd mention that old cliché about pessimists being happy when everything goes sideways, because then they're finally proven right. But perhaps it isn't quite that simple.

Obstacles can be defined as everything that doesn't follow the plan. This is slightly ambiguous, because the Blue expects that the plan won't be a sufficient defense against all problems. But when things do start to deviate from the plan, those things become—by definition—a setback.

The Blues love being in control, not of the situation or of other people—that's Red behavior—but they want to have total control over all the details. However, the larger the project, the more unlikely it is that they'll achieve the desired degree of perfection. If they aren't given sufficient time to make the plan so flawless that it would essentially execute itself, well, that, too, might be something they'd consider a trial.

An easily overlooked but important aspect of Blue behavior is that the Blues hate to make fools of themselves. And if they do that by, for example, missing details, being careless, or not having had time for proper quality control, then it's a particularly bad situation. The Blues will go out of their way to avoid precisely that.

Even if they aren't especially relationship-oriented and aren't the most emotional people you've come across, they react strongly to what they see as faults. If their failings are revealed to others, they might not react emotionally, like a Yellow whose ego has been wounded, but they will grind their teeth and be deeply ashamed of their carelessness.

And if you're the one who revealed their mistake, well, then you're the problem in the Blues' book. And that is not good news.

SUMMARY

I'll remind you again that the four colors are a simplification of how we humans behave. We are very often a combination of several colors, but I guarantee that you will be able to use this system in your own life.

9

How Each Color Reacts When Things Go Wrong

Let's have a look at what the DISC model says. As you read, see if you recognize yourself in these descriptions.

THE REDS' REACTION WHEN EVERYTHING GOES DOWN THE DRAIN

Now hold tight! People with a lot of red in their profile—it doesn't have be just red, but could also be red in combination with another color—expect that life is going to cause them problems. As I've mentioned, they have a pronounced competitive streak and aren't afraid of things getting a bit rough. And very often they have more energy than the rest of us.

But naturally things still sometimes go wrong even for these turbo-personalities. The Reds react in two ways when things get tough. They "get to work on it," or they "sneak away from it."

They might sound the trumpet to attack whatever is standing in their way and conquer all opposition. Setbacks in relationships, for example, are often dealt with in this way. They throw out the rule book and will resort to virtually anything when their weapons have been sharpened. It's about winning, about being right, about seeing the other party give up. Because this is about a victory for the Red. Charming? No, but that's the truth of it.

When it comes to concrete issues or problems to be solved, Reds activate everybody around them. There is a battle to be fought! Everyone needs to roll up their sleeves to remove the roadblock in the path of the general progress. Here we have effective project leaders who make sure that everybody has plenty to do.

Being in a bad mood is the rule rather than the exception for Reds. The Red often displays aggression, directed not only at the problem or situation, but at everything and everybody that's in range when things get hot. When the battle is over, there might be little more than splinters left. For the Red, this is of lesser importance; even a scorched-earth victory is a victory.

The other Red response—to "sneak away from it"—is slightly less common, but it happens. It means exactly what it sounds like. The Red simply ignores what has happened and turns to something else. We don't know what exactly triggers this reaction. During all the years I have studied Red behavior, I haven't really succeeded in working out why Reds sometimes just shrug their shoulders and ignore the whole thing. I can't find a clear pattern, beyond the fact that they weren't really interested from the beginning. Like everyone else, Reds can have good or bad days that can influence their reaction. But most likely this is how they respond to things that they feel aren't worth fighting for.

If they hear some bad news at work, something that might affect the Red significantly, but it comes from a complete idiot, they can ignore it without the slightest difficulty. Reds have the ability to ignore things that they don't think are worth wasting energy on.

Obvious strengths: the Reds are fairly tough and can deal with adversity well. They see it as a true challenge, and they are willing to fight to the bitter end because they don't particularly care what everyone else thinks of them.

THE YELLOWS' REACTION TO
A DEEPLY UNFAIR EXPERIENCE

The Yellows have an especially positive basic attitude that is a very good defense against all injustices in life. When yellow is combined with other colors, this applies to a varying degree.

One of the Yellows' keys strengths it that they are always looking for possibilities. There is no opening they don't find to help them negotiate their way through an obstacle. If there is an exit, they will find it. But they also have well-developed defense mechanisms that shield them from the harsher blows of life. If, for example, a client doesn't want to put in an order, they can quickly explain it away with the rationalization that it was the wrong client anyway. Even a direct insult might be brushed off as the other person's problem: they didn't know any better. The Yellow shakes off defeat as easily as you change your shirt.

Besides, they will—as usual—share the burden with others, since they never stop talking. Everybody around them is going to know what is going on.

Relationship problems are often handled with the Yellows' dubious gift of the gab. They are sparkling communicators who can turn any conversation to their own advantage. And it's going to sound good, too. (It's not a coincidence that many salespeople have a lot of yellow in their profiles).

What's interesting about Yellows is that they can react extremely strongly once the bad news hits them. For a moment, they'll feel awful, especially if somebody else witnesses their difficulty. Sure, they can go around with a collection bag to gather all the attention and sympathy they're owed, but if the situation looks really bad, it will damage their egos. Not good. And then they'll feel like shit. In the days following the setback, the Yellow will "rewrite" the experience in his or her head so that it isn't quite so bad. This, too, is a defense mechanism that helps for the time being, but it doesn't solve the problem in the long term. If a really Yellow person gets to ponder a problem long enough, then the setback will eventually be rebranded as a victory.

The Reds' desire to fight through a problem isn't as pronounced in Yellow behavior, which can limit Yellows' development in the long term. They struggle on and have lots of energy, but on the whole they are more sensitive than the Reds. It depends somewhat on their individual driving forces, but the Yellows might very well give up if they think it isn't worth the struggle.

The Yellows' strength in dealing with setbacks is their unbroken positive way of looking at the world. They will always find something to laugh at, which cheers them up and helps move them along.

THE GREENS' WAY OF DEALING WITH THIS COLD, CRUEL WORLD

The Greens—depending upon how much green there is in their profile—tend to struggle with setbacks. They might not be natural fighters, and they function better when daily life moves at an ordinary pace. They can become extremely worried by seemingly small things. They view setbacks as a part of life, but they are extremely exhausting for people who only want a bit of peace and quiet. This often leads to a Green's passive behavior. After all, there's less risk of being knocked around if you stay at home and pull the curtains.

They are (just like the Yellows) fairly sensitive to major setbacks when they encounter them, but (unlike the Yellows) they don't forget as easily. They simply have a better memory than the Yellows. Negative experiences, like getting a reprimand from the boss, or being obliged to work late when you've planned a relaxing evening in front of the TV, or finding that the bill from the mechanic is not going to be cheap can whirl around inside the Greens' consciousness for months. They tend to brood, until the problem has grown into an enormous obstacle.

As for relationship problems, the Greens are actually extremely good at dealing with these. They are, after all, natural relationship types, and are very good listeners as well. However, their fear of conflicts can sometimes lead to difficulties. If they are caught up in a difference of opinion, it can be very difficult for them to deal with. It's harder for Greens to handle setbacks in which others are involved than it is to manage problems that only affect them.

As Greens are fairly natural introverts, a lot of their energy comes from within. Unfortunately, this includes both positive and negative energy, so when a bad experience whirls around inside their heads it is continually intensified until things look absolutely hopeless. A serious adversity, like being fired or losing a close friend, can lead to burnout. This means that Green people might need help to get themselves back on track.

On top of it all, Greens tend to view everything as a setback. It doesn't need to be anything more serious than an empty toothpaste tube in the morning; the day is wrecked. What a Red or Yellow person would never perceive as a problem can completely paralyze a Green individual, leaving them anxious 24/7.

The Greens' strength in dealing with adversity is that they're good at getting others involved. They get help and make sure that they have support from important people in their lives.

THE BLUES' ANALYSIS OF INEVITABLE SETBACKS

The Blues have an interesting approach when it comes to obstacles. Since they are brilliant risk analysts, they will (as I've mentioned) likely have foreseen most things before they happen. All that a major setback actually does is confirm that the Blue was indeed right. *This project was doomed to failure. Why did we even start this adventure in the first place?*

Blue people are perceived as pessimists for a reason. They are forever looking for things that can go wrong, and when things finally do go bad, they're almost happy to have been proven right.

It may seem contradictory, but they often react very calmly to most things, even when there's been a major snafu. Blue people try to actively distance themselves from their emotions—even though no one is completely emotionally neutral, they do it better than the other colors—and look at the situation. What has actually gone wrong? How did it happen? Who is responsible and what does the presumed solution look like? Sorry, that should be *solutions* (plural), because Blues need at least three different alternatives to decide among.

They tend to solve all problems and setbacks in the same way, even when they concern relationships. In that regard, they're seen as somewhat "clinical" by those around them. They create lists of what has gone wrong and see everything in terms of "facts," because that feels logical. The problem is that more emotional individuals think that the Blues are idiots who can't handle emotions.

That is a misconception. The Blues understand emotions, even though they camouflage their own, and they will definitely remember every individual's different reactions. But they will argue logically, even when confronting relationship issues, which more often than not makes things worse, because they have little respect for touchy-feely stuff and general yammering. It will make them withdraw completely. And more than any other color, the Blues like their own company.

It's simpler to deal with task-oriented issues. These can be broken down into their constituent parts and analyzed. This takes time, but Blue behavior does lead to a brilliant problem-solving ability. The Blues' stamina is fantastic, and if they've decided to cross a mountain of resistance, then they are going to do it. The only real risk is that they'll run out of time.

Since they are masters at making plans, they're going to draw up long lists with next steps. Just like with Red behavior, the Blues consider it natural to meet with opposition, but whereas the Reds try to destroy any obstacles in their way, the Blues will methodically pull every obstacle apart bit by bit.

Yet (and this is something to consider when you have a Blue person in your vicinity) Blues are more interested in the process itself rather than in achieving a goal. The path itself is going to be more important than the destination. The Blues' extremely long-term perspective can mean that they consider setbacks interesting problems in themselves, which can be resolved when they get there by way of something on their list.

In short, Blues' strength in dealing with setbacks is that they analyze objectively and don't get too emotional. They take the time necessary to turn the ship—even if it is going to take a very long time.

SUMMARY

How we behave in the face of setbacks is contingent on the particular situation as well as other personal qualities. Driving forces, development levels, mood, competence, general motivation, and self-confidence all influence how we confront and manage problems when they arise. The DISC model—like all other similar models—has its weaknesses in giving a 100 percent accurate description of how a particular individual functions under stress. But it can help us understand the most basic constituents of someone's behavior.

I am fairly certain that you recognized a couple of examples in those descriptions. And they can give you some clues as to how you should consider the setbacks you will encounter.

My own experience is that it's possible to learn to deal with setbacks. One of the best pieces of advice I've ever received is to try to look at the situation as it really is. Not to make it bigger or smaller based on an emotional response, but to simply consider what happens as neutrally as possible.

Easy to say, but not so easy to do. It's easier for the task-oriented profiles, the Reds and the Blues, than for the Greens and the Yellows, who are more person-oriented. There is no value judgment in this, but Reds are often successful because of their resilience in the face of adversity.

Every setback you've had in life is feedback from the world you live in. You need to learn to see how useful that is. Take it for what it is. Always learn from your mistakes. A cliché? Perhaps it is. But you can learn from other people's mistakes, too. Realize that you are not the center of the universe.

10

How Does the Author of This Book Deal with Setbacks?

As you've already seen, I've met with some daunting obstacles in life. I've encountered everything imaginable, from burning cars to media storms. The ranking I listed in chapter 7 shows how I felt about each of these various situations. On the whole, setbacks that are personal and related to relationships were much more difficult for me than things that were connected with my work. The same might be true for you.

A REALITY CHECK

So am I good at dealing with setbacks? One of my methods for handling setbacks and adversity is to accept that they are a part of life. I know from my own experience that it's impossible to escape them totally, so I've stopped even trying. I do the best I can as an author, lecturer, husband, and dad. I don't count my blessings in advance. But I also don't plan on negative experiences. If they come along, then that's that.

I've found it valuable to distinguish between situations that I *can* influence and stuff I *cannot* influence. When it comes to taking responsibility for myself, I practice what I preach.

Things I can influence include:

- what I do;
- what I refrain from doing;
- how I react to what I can't influence.

As an example, we can consider the media storm that my book *Surrounded by Idiots* caused at home in Sweden in 2018. The book was about the basics of the DISC model, the four colors, and served as an introduction to behaviors and everyday psychology. I wanted to spark people's curiosity about these subjects, because I believed that there were far too many unnecessary conflicts in our everyday lives due to ordinary, simple misunderstandings. So I used a suitable model and wrote a book. That seemed fairly low-risk. After all, the DISC model had existed and been used the world over for more than forty years. Something like fifty million analyses have been carried out in about forty languages. Regardless of what you think of such a method, it was out there. And many people had used it.

After the book had been on sale in Sweden for almost four years (and sold close to one million copies), some people had become so irritated by it that they decided something had to be done.

A handful of my competitors—lecturers, authors, and consultants, many with training in psychology—did their very best to publicly attack the book and me personally. There weren't many detractors, but they were impressively loud.

Of course, that wasn't enjoyable. Like everyone else, I prefer it when people like and appreciate what I do.

On the other hand, the criticism was not unexpected. *Surrounded by Idiots* had become so popular that criticism was unavoidable. The book was everywhere. The critics were harsh: the book was stupid, meaningless, a waste of paper. As for me, I was a fraud with limited intellectual capacity who didn't know what I was talking about. Why didn't I just go away?

So how did I handle this?

My Responsibility: What I Did

I took action where I could. I read the criticism until I understood what the heart of the complaint was. Via several newspapers and radio shows, I presented my own arguments and rebuttals. The critics were right on a couple of points. In the early editions of *Surrounded by Idiots,* I had been a bit careless with some of my wording, and that could lead to misunderstandings, so I corrected that for future editions. But we talk about details.

That was all I could do. I also continued to work on new books and on my lecture material. I continued to spread knowledge about behavior and everyday psychology. My calendar was so booked up with speaking engagements, I couldn't do anything else.

My Responsibility: What I Didn't Do

I also got to choose what actions to avoid. When more critics joined the chorus of complaints, I was aghast. But since I couldn't do or say anything to change their opinions—they, of course, had every right to their own opinions—I simply did not respond. And I stopped reading what they said. That was my way of dealing with what I couldn't influence.

My Responsibility: How I Reacted

I could also govern my own reactions. I chose not to react to what certain aggressive critics said. Since I have experienced major crises in life, I wasn't extremely affected. The positive reactions from my readers easily outweighed the voices of a few critics. My inbox almost exploded with supportive cheers that drowned out any criticism.

Obviously, I wasn't completely impervious. Sure, it was unpleasant to have others put words in my mouth, but I saw no reason to correct all these fantasies about me or my books. People who want to find fault will always look for it. The same people will, incidentally, be reading these words, too, and be sharpening their pencils to hack away at this book as well.

While certain critics became more and more irate, I reminded myself of why I do what I do. I want people to explore how we communicate with one another, and be curious about acquiring greater self-awareness.

But, and this is important: I don't have any ambitions to convince people who aren't interested. I don't force my opinion onto anybody else, nor should you. If people don't want to listen—then simply walk away. If you think a book is bad—put it aside and pick up another one.

My message to you is: try to establish a levelheaded response to things you can't influence anyway. It takes too much energy and focus to worry about what other people might think.

As Winston Churchill said, "You will never reach your destination if you stop and throw stones at every dog that barks."

LEARNING FROM LIFE

You can gain important insights from your setbacks. When people attack you instead of disagreeing with your message, when they demean themselves with a personal attack instead of having an objective discussion, then you know that their position is rather weak.

You don't need to worry about it. It says far more about them than about you.

MY COLOR PROFILE

As I write in *Surrounded by Idiots,* people with different behavioral profiles react to bad news in different ways. Reds tend to not listen until the end, get angry, and then launch a counterattack.

My red column is high. Very high. A lot of people don't realize it, because I know how to keep it under control when necessary. That requires active effort, and sometimes my control fails when I let my emotions gain the upper hand. Ask anyone who knows me well. I'm not always super-nice to deal with. But that's also one of the main reasons why I've learned to think before I speak or react.

The Yellows are quick to feel insulted, and become dejected in response. Getting personal criticism can hurt a Yellow person badly, because it goes right to the heart. It doesn't look good; What is everyone going to say? Falling off a pedestal is probably the worst thing that can happen to Yellows. Their egos suffer quite the blow. Luckily, the Yellows have well-developed defense mechanisms, so they brush off most stuff fairly quickly. And within a couple of weeks, everything is back to normal.

My yellow column is also quite high. I recognize myself in the description of how criticism can sting, but only if it comes from people I care about—basically, my family. That can hurt. And sometimes I take up a defensive position and try to make myself look better. Immature. Yes, I know.

Individuals with a lot of green in their behavioral pattern are very sensitive to criticism and take almost everything personally. It's easy to crush a Green person if you're really nasty. Greens are offended by almost everything, and often are hard on themselves without any external help. Also, they have an irritatingly good memory for injustices.

My green column is, on the whole, nonexistent. My apologies.

Blue behavior is interesting because the Blues simply distance themselves from the matter. They are task-oriented analysts who are fully aware of facts and details. They can stare at you with a completely blank face while you rant and rave. Then they'll ask you to put that in writing, because they want to go through what you said in peace and quiet. That way they can break down your arguments to bits.

My blue column is just as high as my red column. This is the behavior I lean on when people around me rush ahead and don't know what they're doing. Some people have learned to appreciate this, but others think it's a real pain that I remember every single word from the last meeting.

SUMMARY

Again, this is not an exact science. People are complex, but even with as simplified an analysis as this one, you can begin to understand more of your own reactions and perhaps find explanations for why you feel a particular way.

Remember that even though you're not responsible for what others say to you or do to you, you are responsible for how you choose to react.

I suppose that was my way of saying, *Think positively.*

But what if it's just not possible to think positively? What do you do then? You'll find the answer in the next chapter.

11

Our Tendency to Focus on
the Negative

Let's reflect for a moment on why so many of our life experiences can be perceived as obstacles.

We've all been there. You might be driving in the car somewhere and suddenly everyone slows down. For reasons unknown, you find yourself in traffic, and it is not moving. You can't see an accident or anything causing the problem. You're stuck there for an hour. Suddenly the line starts moving. Slowly, slowly you crawl along, swearing.

When you reach the place where the traffic jam started, there's still nothing there. No broken-down car. No fallen branch. No explanation. Except for one thing . . .

. . . The most beautiful sunset you have seen in all your life leaves you, and thousands of other motorists, speechless.

Unbelievable, isn't it?

Unbelievable is putting it mildly, because that is never going to happen. There is never going to be a sunset so beautiful people stop their cars. On the other hand . . . if there had been a major car crash, then we'd certainly slow down and have a good long look. *Is that a leg that's sticking out? I think I saw some blood.*

HOW OUR BRAINS ARE PROGRAMMED

If we ask neuroscientists, they'll explain that it's how we're wired: we're forever looking for problems and risks, because that increased our chances of survival once upon a time when we were living in the wild. The short version is that our consciousness is always on the lookout for things that have the potential to go wrong. There's nothing wrong with you. Your brain is programmed to function this way. If it hadn't been, perhaps mankind would have died out long ago. If we hadn't seen the danger lurking around us forty thousand years ago, we might have been a very short-lived species.

Nowadays, there are fewer benefits to this problem-spotting behavior. But we do the same thing regardless. That is one of the reasons why the media works the way it does. It shocks us with huge headlines proclaiming this or that catastrophe. Good news hardly has any place in today's newspapers. Why? Because doomsday headlines generate more clicks online than good news. Writing about war, murder, death, climate disasters, and catastrophes catches our attention far more than reading that the sun shone and somebody got a new job.

I was something of a news junkie for many years. After listening to several news reports in the car on my way home from work, I simply had to get home before six o'clock to watch the news on TV. Then the other news program at seven thirty. After that, a break until the longer news show at nine o'clock. Just before going to bed, I filled up with the late-night news. By the time I got into bed, I was updated on murders, terrorist acts, wars, conflicts, economic crises, fraud, and natural catastrophes.

In retrospect, I don't have a good explanation as to why I sucked up so much (bad) news. I was stuck in a habit. In the end, I succeeded in breaking the habit, and that is one of the best things I've done.

Nowadays, you have to have an almost inhuman focus in order to avoid getting caught in a negative spiral. After surfing the internet and completely losing your faith in humanity, you have to drink a bottle of wine and munch a box of chocolates to reacquire a degree of hope.

Not watching the news was a way for me to keep my mind clear and unmuddled. If something really serious happens, I hear about it one way or another.

MORE ACTION = MORE MISTAKES

Our own mistakes can create painfully negative thought patterns.

If we consider the most successful people we can imagine, they're all extremely action-oriented. Many of them hate small talk; they don't want to hear delightful plans or talk about everything that *might* happen. They want to know what *is* going to happen.

So they act. Shoot first, ask questions later. That leads us to an interesting observation.

Even though some people take action more quickly and more frequently, it doesn't always end up for the better. Of course not. Sometimes our reactions are both quick and wrong, to put it mildly. The speed of the decision alone means that these doers make more mistakes than other people.

They will sometimes be scorned for this. The psychology is interesting here, because making mistakes and making a fool of yourself is viewed very harshly today. Everything must be perfect; nothing must look bad or careless. Perfectionism has spread.

Making mistakes is, of course, a pain. It can create setbacks and leave you sick to your stomach. But it's also unavoidable to sometimes make mistakes; this is part of a learning process. Mistakes and errors are simply feedback that tells you this particular thing didn't work, try something else.

Never making mistakes means very little learning of new knowledge. There is almost nothing that teaches you more about a particular thing than doing it wrong from the start. And yet many people are hesitant.

You shouldn't risk your job or your marriage in the name of making mistakes, but accept that mistakes are a necessary obstacle you can't avoid.

WHAT ARE YOUR WORST MISTAKES?

Time for a little exercise. Write down your worst mistakes in life, the times that you really made a fool of yourself or perhaps did something shameful. Not your setbacks, because those can be things that were unrelated to your own actions. No, this is about choices you have made yourself—a list of mistakes.

You don't need to show the paper to a single soul. You don't need to post your list on a billboard for all to see. But describe your own behavior fully and in detail. Be really honest about it. It's not enough to just think about a particular situation, because your brain is going to protect you from the unpleasantness and will conjure up lots of defense mechanisms.

As an example, you could write:

I was going to ask this girl to dance, but I was so bowled over by her and extremely nervous, I had a few drinks before I did. Unfortunately, it was more than just a couple, and when I finally got up the courage to talk to her, she noticed my breath and said no thank you.

Now you can write down what you learned from this:

Drinking alcohol is not only good for your self-confidence, it's also effective at frightening away girls with good taste. I'll have to find another way to build up my courage next time.

Another example might be:

The boss asked at the morning meeting if everybody was satisfied with the new organization system, and then (in front of the whole group of twenty-five people) I chose to complain about the negative aspects of the new system and criticize the boss for certain decisions. Unfortunately, afterward I was called up to his office and was reprimanded, my judgment was questioned, and now I realize that I've ended up on his shit list.

So, what did you learn from this?

I learned that even when the boss asks for some honest feedback, I should express myself carefully and respectfully. Considering his ego, I should always give negative feedback when it's just the two of us, instead of doing it in front of the whole team.

So, what do you say? Shall we try it? Devote a few minutes to this before you go on reading. I guarantee that you'll find useful insights when you consider the lessons you can learn.

My mistake	What I learned from it

As you can see, making mistakes is not all negative. There's a lot of knowledge to be gained here. Once you discover that you've made a mistake, big or little, you'll find that this is an opportunity to learn new things, to adjust your behavior or change your attitude, or whatever it might be.

As usual, this is easier said than done. You need to train yourself so that you consciously improve your ability to approach mistakes in this way. It might take a while before it comes naturally, but that doesn't mean you should stop trying. Just like learning to drive, it's difficult at first. But after a while you don't even think about everything you do behind the steering wheel. You just do it.

Don't let a fear of mistakes paralyze you. That would be the very worst mistake of all.

12

Welcome to Laterville!

Imagine that you've had a phenomenal idea. You've thought up something truly valuable. Perhaps it's a business idea; perhaps it's something that could jump-start your career; perhaps it's as simple as starting that DIY project you and your partner have dreamed about for so long.

STARTING . . . SOON

This idea is so brilliant and so urgent, it's so important and so critical to your future . . . that you simply have to think it through just one more time.

You need to wait for the right opportunity. Maybe the weather could be better. Later on might be a good time to roll up your sleeves. When you feel stronger, more rested, more motivated. When the planets are aligned or when the recession is over. When taxes are lowered or prices raised. Yes, soon . . .

So you put this brilliant project aside for future use. Now and then, you'll remember your idea, but it never feels like the right moment.

Or you don't have time. Or it's hard to determine whether it really is a good idea or not.

And after a while, you don't think about it anymore. Now it's gone. It has disappeared into eternity and gone to the graveyard of good intentions.

You don't even notice that you have moved to a place called Laterville.

WHERE IS LATERVILLE?

Laterville is inside every person. All of us have an address there. We run away to Laterville when we should do a particular task but don't feel like it at the moment. This is where we wait, waffle, plan, think. And remain passive.

In Laterville, everything looks just great on the surface. Everything more or less works as it should, and nothing really seems to need to be changed. There is a deceptive calm. There is no hurry, no stress. It's where you can be yourself awhile. Nothing is especially important here. You have what you need and you're not living a bad life. On the contrary, you're comfortable, really comfortable. So there's no hurry. Everything is going to happen—later. The problem with Laterville is primarily that you feel satisfied here.

WHO DO YOU MEET THERE?

The other inhabitants of Laterville, of course. They don't think that there's much of a hurry, either. They agree that it's time to take things easy and reflect on life before you throw yourself into something you don't even know much about. They, too, have ideas and ambitions. Drawers stuffed full of them, in fact. They are not shy about talking about their grandiose plans. They're absolutely going to use all those wonderful ideas. But later. Much later. In Laterville, everybody speaks the same dialect. And it is a very disheartening tongue.

That great idea I had in May, I'm going to write it down—later.
Yes, sure it's time to start visiting the gym—later.
I'm really going to start putting some money aside for that
*   project—later.*
That training course sounds interesting. I'm going to apply for
*   a place—later.*
At last, my dream job opened up! Of course I'll call the boss of
*   the company—later.*
Now I really am going to visit my mother—later.
We should start having date nights, my partner and I—later.

The problem with Laterville is that it's an incredibly large town. A gigantic metropolis. In fact, Laterville is almost unnaturally overpopulated. The majority of all the people you've ever met have an address of their own there; they often visit and meet in gardens, at cafés, at lunch spots, or at home with each other—and discuss everything that they are going to do later in life. They sit and dream awhile.

I'll do it later.

Always later.

Later.

Later.

Later.

Often they don't even do that. They just do what they've always done. And that's why they get the same results that they've always gotten.

But not you. Oh, no, you have ambitions. You want more.

IS IT POSSIBLE TO GET AWAY FROM LATERVILLE?

If you want to move away from the paralyzing situation in Laterville, you need to sell the house you have there. Put it on the market. But that's the least of your problems. I promise you, the house isn't going to be on the market long before someone makes an attractive offer. Because a lot of people want to live there. They really like it in Laterville. It's an insidious place and far too easy to be drawn to.

Few of the inhabitants in Laterville are ever going to succeed at anything extraordinary. That doesn't mean that there aren't any honest taxpayers here, certainly not. A lot of them work hard, don't fool yourself. And there's nothing wrong with working hard. But their true ambitions and even their dreams are hidden under a sluggish, indifferent veneer of imagined satisfaction. Once these people have moved to Laterville, they behave as if they've left life behind them. Some are just waiting to retire.

This isn't about folks who have been physically exhausted from manual labor or years of hard work; that's a different situation, and as a society we should support them.

I suspect that so many look forward to retirement because they don't *want* to work. But why don't they? Because they don't feel like they're doing anything meaningful. Their present jobs don't give them anything. Their workplaces are dysfunctional, their bosses are bastards, and their coworkers are (to be honest) not much better. Why would anybody want to keep working there? Or maybe they only stay because of their coworkers, but the work itself is meaningless.

You might as well just buy a ticket to Laterville, where you can sit at the latest trendy café and grumble about the government, taxes, prices, companies, immigration, the weather, football, TV, or whatever you want as long as you don't need to take responsibility for your own situation.

WHAT IS LIFE LIKE IN LATERVILLE?

Slow. There's a striking fact about Laterville: leaving this place is not something you do just like *that*. You've surrounded yourself with people who support you in doing absolutely nothing. Otherwise you'd disturb things far too much. It's fine for you to be yourself, but if you stand out too much and give the impression of being unique in comparison with the rest of the inhabitants, then problems will come your way.

This is where you'll meet people who think it's way too wasteful to spend extra money on fresh produce, but who don't think twice about spending the same amount on snacks and beer.

Saving a hundred dollars a month is unthinkable for your neighbors in Laterville, but drinking or smoking up the same sum every week doesn't present a problem.

Fifty dollars month for a gym pass? Forget it. Sixty dollars a month on cable is, however, perfectly acceptable.

This is where you'll also find folks who think it's a waste to spend money on a weekend seminar or an educational program to help them grow and build their future, but who strangely enough buy the latest Gucci belt for three times as much.

In Laterville there are block after block of people who would never invest in their own businesses, but who would gladly pay that amount for an iPhone 88, or whichever version we're on. Because, you just *have* to have one.

But there are other priorities, too. Time works the same way here as it does everywhere else. Even here, there are twenty-four hours in a day.

In Laterville, you have neighbors who never have time to go to the gym. Because three to five hours a week is actually a lot of time. Nevertheless, they manage to fit in three hours of TV—every day.

In Laterville, you'll bump into acquaintances who think it's a hopeless project to find time to read, but who, for some reason, manage to squeeze in a couple of hours on Facebook, Instagram, and YouTube—every day.

Unfortunately, we also have parents who think it's too expensive to put aside some money for their daughter's college fund, but who can afford to travel to Thailand every year—on credit, with 20 percent interest.

If you ask your neighbors how to achieve your goals, the majority will have nothing to say. Goals? What do you mean? Walk up and down the street. Knock on the doors. Ask everyone who opens, *What are your goals in life, and what are you doing to get there?* They probably won't even understand the question. Let alone have an answer.

To put it bluntly: in Laterville, everyone is on their way to . . . nowhere.

I realize that this can sound elitist. But remember: I'm not saying that the inhabitants of Laterville are less worthy or important. That isn't what this is about. All people are important. It doesn't matter who we're talking about. Everybody has the same right to everything in our society. I am not saying this as a cliché, but because that is what I truly believe. Everybody should have the same opportunities.

But I am saying that their attitude to the world around them and to their own possibilities and goals is not going to help them move forward in life. They are missing the opportunities in front of them.

Do you really want to live in Laterville? Forever stuck in an environment where all that counts is the here and now, where future possibilities make up a cloudy vision that nobody really thinks about?

No, you don't want that. Because there are alternatives.

YOU'RE JUST AS WELCOME TO WINNERVILLE

Ah! Winnerville! This is a place with considerably fewer inhabitants than Laterville. And that means the prices are much higher, but oddly enough, there is always a rapid stream of people who move in here, too. And anybody is welcome to build a house here in Winnerville. Because there is lots of open land here.

People who live their dreams reside in Winnerville, people who make an incredible effort to realize their visions and who dream big. Who aren't afraid of all the work that is involved in realizing their dreams. Who, when their neighbor buys a nicer car, immediately go across and congratulate them on the purchase and ask to go on a test ride with them. And think to themselves that perhaps they, too, ought to work hard so that they're able to afford such a nice car.

Here you are inspired by the success of others instead of intimidated by it. You would never scorn somebody's dreams or ambitions to go further. Instead of explaining why an idea won't work, your neighbors in Winnerville will immediately say, *Great idea. How are you going to make it happen?* And they will often offer to help you.

Here people see possibilities. They dare to believe in change, but accept that you must work for it. They realize that a serious plan for the future needs to involve more than five lottery tickets every Saturday. Everybody in Winnerville has worked to get there. Nobody got there via an inheritance, or won their way in by chance.

In Winnerville, they know that not only millionaires are self-made. They understand that everybody is self-made. But only the successful ones admit it.

WHAT DO THE STREETS OF WINNERVILLE LOOK LIKE?

Winnerville is where all the successful entrepreneurs live. The elite athletes. The managing directors and authors and doctors and lawyers and businessmen and everyone who has been successful in their particular spheres. The best in any field you can think of all live here.

But the single nursing assistant who—despite the fact that she must support her ailing mother—manages to put aside a little for the future also lives here.

The refugee who refused to give up after his job application was rejected 784 times and who now works at the local bank lives here as well.

The person with dyslexia who, after being labeled as stupid during twelve years at school, now runs his own business with two hundred employees has also built a lovely home here.

In Winnerville, amid the new IT billionaires, you will find the author who, after a half lifetime of refusals, managed to get published.

You'll find the swimmer who won the local championship despite the fact that she has no arms.

The woman who after years of abuse found the courage to report her husband to the police and who is now brave enough to leave the house after it gets dark—where does she live? In Winnerville.

Anybody could be your neighbor in Winnerville—from the person who was refused a bank loan to start his business and instead got an extra job as a cleaner at night to save enough money and now owns a chain of thirty gyms with one hundred employees . . . to the cancer patient who was told she had no chance of survival and five years later is busy training for the New York City Marathon.

THIS IS WHERE ALL THE PEOPLE WHO BELIEVE IN THEMSELVES LIVE

In Winnerville you'll find everyone who has chosen to believe in themselves rather than listen to others. Those who refused to believe that it was impossible, and now stand there stronger than even they themselves dared hope.

Winnerville is a wonderful place to be. When folks get together in the evenings, they don't talk about other people. They don't gossip about who said what about this and that, who divorced whom. They talk about ideas, possibilities, and they always have the future in clear focus.

They don't talk about problems and they don't complain very much. Instead, they discuss how things could be improved.

Naturally some worries are aired, and in Winnerville you can often find people who have suffered adversity in life. But the interesting thing is, since they live in Winnerville and not Laterville, they always get up again when life knocks them down. That might also be why they ended up in Winnerville. They don't carry all the world's woes on their shoulders. They accept that sometimes they're going to lose, and they learn from their mistakes. Instead of banging their heads into the bricks that are thrown at them, they build staircases and bridges.

And they don't laugh at others who've met with misfortune. Instead, they give them a helping hand, because they know that the next time it might be them who are in need of help.

To put it briefly, in Winnerville people are happy, quite often just as happy as in Laterville. And I wouldn't be surprised if they actually feel a lot better.

IDEAS IN WINNERVILLE

Imagine the following scenario: For several years you've observed that your department is lacking in certain ways. This or that system doesn't work perfectly, and you've talked endlessly with your colleagues about why nobody does anything about it. A lot of time has been wasted debating the problem, particularly whose fault it is that the situation came about in the first place.

But one morning you wake up with an idea. Suddenly you see the solution! Why didn't you think of that before? Of course, you don't have all the details completely worked out quite yet. You're not sure how to go about it. But you feel in your whole body that you have just stumbled across something very important. But how do you launch the whole thing? Start something on your own? This is new territory for you.

Imagine that you raise the question with a good friend in Winnerville. Perhaps a neighbor. You describe the whole situation, share about your idea, and voice your justifiable fears.

Your neighbor is going to say that you should give it a try. It sounds like an excellent idea. When you say that you've never done anything like this before, he'll point out the obvious: nobody who tries something for the first time has done it before.

When you say that you're worried that you don't have enough money to move forward, he talks about how he started his own business. For three years the family didn't have a car, he says. Now they have three cars, and all of them have British names. They didn't go on vacation, they didn't even go to the movies. But today he runs a flourishing business with lots of employees. He lives in the prettiest house on the street, and his children see him more than ever because he can afford to be at home three days a week. And they travel wherever they want, when they want.

Perhaps you mention to this successful neighbor that you don't know how you will find the time. He asks you how many hours a week your ordinary job takes. When you say forty, he'll laugh and say, *Well that's excellent—you're free Saturday and Sunday! Not to mention all your weekday evenings. And with less time in front of the TV, you can always start on a small scale. Just go for it,* says your friend.

But what if it goes completely sideways? you say.

Yes, that could happen, says your friend. *But then you'll have gained experience if it does.*

Besides, since he knows how hard it can be to build your own business, he offers to help. He encourages you to ask whatever questions you might have. If he can help you, he'll be happy to. Because however busy he may be, he can always find a little more time. Your friend in Winnerville knows how to handle time.

That's another thing about the people of Winnerville. They help one another. They don't sit and smolder enviously about their neighbor's new car. No, they understand that it's important to build networks. Who knows, perhaps you will repay the favor someday?

Try it! What's the worst that can happen?

. . . AND IN LATERVILLE . . .

What would happen if you woke up that same morning in Laterville? Same company, same background, exactly the same irritation at the failings in your workplace. And the same brilliant idea has just appeared in your head.

Full of energy, you describe this business idea to your friend while you drink your Friday beer. Because it's finally happy hour and he wants to unwind, he listens with only half an ear. But once he understands—perhaps you work together—that you have a good idea, he says helpfully:

But you're not an entrepreneur! You work in the office/storeroom/ outdoors.

But it's a great idea, isn't it? you counter. He immediately wonders how you're going to finance the whole thing. It sounds like you will have to invest lots of money. Your own money. Waste of time asking the bank. They don't lend money to small businesses, anyway. Everybody knows what the banks are like. Damned bloodsuckers. You can lose everything. Have to sell your house. Think about your family. Don't do it.

Now you'll have to listen to a story about somebody's brother-in-law and a terrible interest rate, but after that you try again.

Your friend insists that it isn't going to work, because if it had been a good idea, then somebody would already have done it. Ergo, it must be a bad idea. Now let's have another beer.

Your buddy confides in you that you need to have contacts and connections to get anywhere. Without the right network, the project is doomed. Who do you even know? While you search for an answer, he blurts out, *Somebody has to actually buy what you sell. Have you sold anything before?* No? Just as he thought.

Now you, too, start to think that the idea sounds stupid.

But your friend hasn't finished with you yet. He gives you the coup de grâce.

How would you find time to do all the work required? You already do some overtime, and you need to give yourself a bit of free time. If you insist and say that you think it would take five years to become really successful, he's going to laugh his head off.

Five years! Are you crazy? Then you'll be five years older than today!

The fact that by then both of you will be five years older regardless of what you choose to do with your time doesn't bother him. He doesn't think that way. He is too problem-oriented. He can't see the goal. There is no vision. His thinking is far too narrow.

Instead of supporting you and helping you think up solutions, he tells anyone at the bar who will listen what an idiot he works with. By the time everyone has finished laughing, you'll regret that you ever mentioned that stupid idea.

They're right. Since you've never succeeded before, what makes you think you'd succeed with this project? What were you thinking?

Note: Your friend at the bar in Laterville might be intelligent, friendly, a good dad to his children, hardworking, a well-educated fellow, and a faithful taxpayer. That isn't what this is about. It's about his narrow thinking. His attitude is wrong. He sees only problems and doesn't want you to succeed.

He restricts you and provides all the arguments you'll ever need to put off your brilliant idea.

The next morning, your idea is put aside and forgotten.

But . . . two years after the thought: *Shouldn't somebody do something about this problem?* flitted through your head, you see an advertisement for exactly that same thing. Somebody has solved the problem exactly the way you imagined and is now in the process of building a future for herself based on that one idea.

And then you are going to regret not going ahead. Oh boy, are you going to regret it.

All of this might sound a bit harsh. I realize that. And perhaps I've really annoyed you now.

Good. Because I want you to react. And keep on reading.

Because I have a confession to make: for many years, I lived in Laterville.

13

My Life in Laterville

I had a big house in Laterville. A posh address. A typical Laterville neighborhood. No one in the family was suffering. We were doing okay. But not much happened. I rarely thought about the future. Instead, I acted based on what would happen next week or possibly next month. And, sure, it worked. We had food on the table.

What's really unnerving about this is that I don't know when I moved into Laterville. I don't have any clear memory of how I ended up there. When—after a series of random events—I finally moved out, I realized the truth. I turned around and looked at the place where I had spent the first forty years of my life.

Everyone who's known me for a long time knows that I've always worked a lot. Worked hard. I've never had an issue with that. I'm happy to arrive at work a bit early and stay at it past working hours. Work the odd Sunday now and then. That never bothered me. It was about taking responsibility and doing what was right. Everyone who knew me in those days would probably say that Thomas Erikson worked hard. But did he work smart?

When I think back to how many years I wasted working without any clear direction, I can get really angry. At what, you may ask? At myself, of course. It's no one else's fault that I ended up in Laterville, where life is on cruise control and ordinary is good. I moved there of my own free will.

Or, to be more specific, the lack of my own will.

Perhaps I wasn't actually unhappy in Laterville. I just . . . was.

There's no one to blame other than myself. When I try to figure out what I was thinking, all I can say is that I probably didn't think at all. I didn't have a plan for anything. In fact, I didn't take any responsibility at all.

Although that's not right, either, when I think about it. Just like most of my neighbors in Laterville, I planned my vacations in far more detail that I planned my career. Or my life, for that matter.

Let's look at that sentence again:

I planned my vacations in far more detail than I planned my career.

WHAT HAPPENS WHEN YOU DON'T PUT ON YOUR THINKING CAP

I'll avoid saying something clichéd, like, *You have lots of vacations but only one life,* but you know that's true.

Why didn't I take life more seriously? There's no intelligent answer to that question. In some moments, I think back to my childhood, and, God help me, my friendly and totally supportive parents were simply . . . too kind. Sometimes I wish that they'd given me a kick in the pants and demanded a little more.

But it doesn't make a difference how it happened that I worked hard year after year without a larger plan or any true direction. I suspect that I did it because everybody else did it. My parents did it, all my relatives did it. Everyone I ever knew did exactly the same thing. We were busy working without thinking about the future.

During my adult life, I've had lots of brilliant ideas, thousands of sparkling fantasies and possibilities. But I never picked up the shovel and started to dig to see what was there.

Because that wasn't what you did in Laterville. You just worked, picked up your kids from school, ate dinner, watched TV for a while, and then went to bed.

Good night.

I didn't have any goals for myself. If anyone had asked me where I planned to be in five years, I would have laughed and just waved the question away. Five years, are you crazy? How could I possibly know that?

Because in Laterville they never ask questions like that. They look sideways at everyone who doesn't stick to the norm. They call entrepreneurs "workaholics." People who stay in good shape and go running every morning for an hour are "gym freaks." People who say "no thanks" to an extra glass of wine are "killjoys." They glare at anybody who stands out and has a good career, or who earns a lot of money or rises in status.

How do I know all this? Well, I did it myself.

THE ANNOYING EXAMPLE OF THE
SNEAKY SOCIAL CLIMBER

Once one of my neighbors replaced his car at the same time that he bought a huge new motorcycle. A Harley-Davidson to be exact. It must have cost him a ton. Rumors around town also said that the whole family had gone on a Mediterranean cruise. How disconcerting! The family lived in a house roughly the same as the one we lived in. They had led a completely normal life up until this new state of things. And I suddenly noticed that he irritated me when he waved cheerfully from across the street. Didn't he suddenly look a bit stuck up? My own smile was definitely pasted on.

Why was that?

The guy could now afford nicer things. And, in secret, that disturbed me. I'm not proud of it—it makes me look like an envious bastard—but I did compare myself to him.

Over dinner, we speculated resentfully about how it had happened. How could the neighbors suddenly afford both a new car and a motorcycle? And how come they were off on vacation all the time? His wife hardly ever left the house! How was all of this possible?

I guessed that his windfall was probably inherited money. If it wasn't an inheritance, it could only be a lottery prize. What other explanation could there possibly be? Because he couldn't have earned it, surely. Not with the way he looked. Or with the education he presumably had. And since I'd talked with him, I knew that the guy wasn't particularly smart. He had a bit of a one-track mind, even though he wasn't exactly stupid.

Is there anything more irritating than a person who you know is less smart than you does better in life than you? It's infuriating.

Then they moved away.

Phew!

What a relief it was when I saw the moving truck pull out of their driveway. At last I could relax a little. Soon, the balance in the Laterville district was restored. A different, ordinary—and hopefully deep in debt—family moved in. Life returned to normal. Those happy, lucky social climbers had only made people feel bad.

Later I learned that the wife had started an online business and sold dog food. That was probably where their extra money came from. That was in the days when the internet was fairly new, and nobody really knew where it was going. But instead of thinking *Aha, that's the explanation,* I found it even more annoying. I'd thought about starting a business on the internet. Only later.

My frustration wasn't about them, not really. While I burrowed deeper into the bedrock of Laterville, this family pushed its boundaries. And managed to do well enough to upgrade their lifestyle a bit.

What did I do? I was thinking. Waiting for the right time. I wasn't exactly planning, but I put all sorts of ideas neatly on a shelf where I could look at them when I had time. I was so smart that it was bound to work out. As soon as the right opportunity turned up, I'd be on my way. Everything would sort itself out—later.

This family had an idea, put it into practice, and found success.

And here comes an important insight: The universe couldn't care less who intends to do what. All that counts is what you actually do.

The most complicated combination lock in the whole world can still be opened by someone. You just have to have the right code. If you have the combination, your background, your last name, or your education doesn't make any difference. All that counts is what you *do*.

In Laterville, there's far too little constructive thinking. Life just trundles along. And when somebody does do something, the rest of us try to explain why they probably should have refrained from doing it. If they don't listen, and they end up in the ditch, then we can point a finger at them and say I told you so. And if they, to everybody's dismay, become really successful, then we hope that they move the heck out of here as soon as possible.

WINNERVILLE OR LATERVILLE?

The great thing about your future hometown is that you are in charge. The decision to test your wings is entirely in your hands. It's up to you. And you know it.

You can choose how you will see the possibilities that are right in front of your nose.

If you don't want to tell me or anyone else just now, put down the book and go into the nearest bathroom. Look at yourself really closely in the mirror and say out loud in a firm voice:

I choose to live in Winnerville.

That's it. Now you've made a decision that I want to congratulate you for. From now on, nothing is going to be like it was before. The world is at your feet.

You can, of course, also say to yourself in the mirror, *I choose to live in Laterville.* That's fine by me. What's important is that you make an active choice and don't just let things fall where they may while you surf the internet for the latest football scores.

What's so great about *that* Laterville decision is you can now close this book and save several hours of your time. This book is written for those who want to get away from Laterville and find a nice place in Winnerville. Give the book to somebody who wants to get somewhere.

Or keep on reading and see what can happen when you actually pack your boxes and move from one place to the other.

A shark in an aquarium will never reach its natural size. Its growth will always adjust to the environment it's living in. If you release the shark into the sea, it might not grow into the size of the one in *Jaws*, but it will get a great deal bigger than in the aquarium.

The same thing applies to you and me. If we change our environments, then we can grow much more than when we're surrounded by the wrong people.

SUMMARY

Sleeping your way through life is comfortable, but it doesn't work well. Or, well, I suppose it actually does, which is the very kernel of this problem. Shutting your eyes to real life does work.

But is it the best life you can experience?

No. There is always more to see and do: more things to experience and great things to achieve if you don't just wander along. But this demands that we actively think about our situation and sort out how we want to live.

It's not a failure to live all your life in Laterville. But think about it: if you could drive a (fill in your dream car) instead of your ten-year-old (fill in what you have in your garage right now), wouldn't you like that?

If you'd rather spend your winter vacation with your family in (fill in your dream holiday) instead of staying at home with Auntie G—wouldn't you like that?

If you could sleep well at night instead of waking up virtually every night worrying that your marriage might be falling apart—what would you choose?

If you could avoid that sinking feeling every month when the bills arrive, and instead could be blown over by the wonderful thought that you can put some money into the kids' college funds this month—wouldn't that be great?

If, instead of looking away when a homeless man asks for a few dollars, you could donate monthly to a shelter—wouldn't that feel better?

Even if you live a perfectly okay life today and nobody in your family is suffering—what would it be like to explore your real potential?

14

(Not) Working Smarter

One of the big problems in Laterville is that a lot of people there live with the delusion that there is an endless amount of time. The problem: there isn't. Time is the most limited resource you have. It's the only resource that can never be replaced. Nobody can get more time. Nobody. Let's look at the effects of wasting your time.

We often assume that success involves working harder. Much harder. Harder than anyone else, in fact.

Sure, it's hard to become phenomenally successful by being completely lazy. Very few success stories have been written by sitting on the sofa and scratching your head. Laziness is hardly the key. But the solution? Is it really to work harder than everybody else?

Hmm. There's nothing wrong with working hard, but I am convinced that you know lots and lots of people who work extremely hard—you might even be one of them—but they don't get anywhere. They just stay where they are, treading water, doing the same job year after year. They've found their spot in life and now they devote all their energy to it. And that's perfectly alright. But as I wrote in the introduction to this book, I assume that you're reading this because you want to grow and move forward.

It's about working smarter.

The key is what you do with your time. It's almost guaranteed, if you handled your time better you could be enormously more productive than you currently are. Time is the golden variable that you need to learn to master.

THE MOST IMPORTANT FACTOR FOR SUCCESS: STOP SQUANDERING YOUR TIME

There have been so many studies on our efficiency that we're all sick and tired of hearing about them. We don't need yet another scientific report to tell us what we already feel with our whole body: most of the time we are not efficient.

But success is fundamentally about using your time to do exactly the right thing. Because when that time ends . . . there is no more time.

My advice is: don't squander your time!

Nowadays, I am incredibly careful about how I spend a day. With whom and why. My mailbox is forever full. The telephone rings; social media sometimes boils over; all my channels of communication are filled with demands on my time.

There are studies and statistics that say that really successful people say no to virtually everything. Interesting, isn't it? Warren Buffett, one of the richest men in history, evidently says no to 99 percent of the opportunities he is offered.

THE EASIEST WAY TO LOSE FOCUS

You open your web browser to check something quickly, a little detail connected with a job you're working on right now. Unfortunately, your home page is some news website, and it is amazing at concocting snappy headlines. You get ensnared in a fascinating article about Kim Kardashian's backside, something that, naturally, *has* to be read immediately. This links to another article, one about her sister's new Mercedes. This tempts you to look at cars online. Soon, you know all about the latest, fabulously expensive Mercedes. This reminds you that you need to take your own fabulously inexpensive car in for an oil change. But where's the best place to go?

You start looking at different mechanics nearby to see if you can reserve a time online, which means checking your calendar and realizing that you probably can't get the oil change done during work hours because you have so incredibly much that you have to get done. This reminds you of a deadline that is threateningly close. Now your thoughts are back on your work, but not at all on the task you were originally working on.

And as if by magic, you've wasted half an hour of your day on . . . nothing. If you're the average person, you will probably feel a bit sheepish at this point. You might even feel a bit guilty. You don't get paid to read up on the Kardashians. But this is how our brains work, and some of us have chosen to take advantage of that.

You don't need to take my word for it. Read the work of Swedish doctor and brain researcher Katarina Gospic. She knows about these things.

A lot of our time is spent surfing the internet, but that is far from the only thing that steals time from what you should be focusing on. Below is a list of possible time thieves in your life, which will use up altogether too many of your (approximately) seven hundred thousand hours here on planet Earth:

- all social media—no exceptions
- everything on TV, on every channel day and night— including the news (especially the news)

- video games, computer games, phone games, online casinos, and online poker
- commuting—traveling, i.e., not the destination
- bad planning, your own or somebody else's
- partying too late the night before
- sleeping too long the day after
- only reading for pleasure
- drinking coffee and chatting with your colleagues instead of working
- virtually every meeting you are going to participate in—ever
- sitting in your yard all summer, drinking beer and complaining about the government

There is nothing wrong with any of the "activities" in the list above. But if you want to achieve something specific in life, then these activities are not going to get you there.

However you define success—inner harmony, a stress-free existence, economic independence, a strong body, better health, a loving relationship, wonderful children, a brilliant career, a spiritual experience, saving enough money so that your children won't have to take a loans out for college, being debt free—these things aren't going to get you there.

SO WE DON'T GET TO HAVE ANY FREE TIME?

As you've seen, a lot of what I consider time thieves are actually forms of entertainment. TV shows, listening to music, reading books, surfing the internet. We need to allow ourselves recreation and entertainment. We need to rest and do things that are just for fun. But when you lack a deeper meaning in your day-to-day life, you often distract yourself with simple, short-term entertainment. Unfortunately, such pleasures can leave a bitter aftertaste. The challenge is to amuse yourself "just enough"—i.e., take time to rest and have fun, but don't let these things mindlessly consume your life.

There is evidence that we truly do need to take breaks, get an energy boost, or rest awhile. But resting is, as I see it, a way of finding the strength to go further in the direction you want to go. Rest is not a goal in itself.

This is a critical insight.

REST IS A MEANS—NOT A GOAL

Neither our bodies nor our brains function at their best when at rest. Nature never intended us to sit on a sofa and stare at a screen, no matter what may be on it.

Nature designed us for activity! Especially physical activity. If you are physically active, you function better mentally. There's no doubt that the physical and the mental are connected. Of all the successful people I've met, the vast majority have been physically active. They go to the gym, they run, play tennis, go skiing, and do all sorts of other things. Body and mind undoubtedly belong together. Don't you believe me? Read *The* Real *Happy Pill* by Dr. Anders Hansen.

If you want to achieve something that is important to you—build your own company, train your body, educate yourself for your dream job, make a career, find your dream house, renovate a summer cottage or that vintage car you've always dreamed about, make a fortune, or get your children into the right schools—then you have to take action first. Make a list of what needs to be done, and work your way through it.

Once you've started and are working toward your dream, you can take a bit of time off. I'm definitely a fan of treating oneself. But like in every job, you don't get paid if you don't do the work.

Accomplishment first, reward afterward.

Do the job first, then rest.

Could it be simpler?

The frustrating truth is that it is that simple. And yet we don't always manage to do it.

DO YOU GET PAID BEFORE OR AFTER THE PERFORMANCE?

When I hold certain types of workshops, I ask the group what they would pick if they could choose between two alternatives:

1. To be paid on January 1 (in advance) and then work for the whole year
2. To get paid on December 31 the same year, that is, in arrears, or after the work is done

Naturally, everybody answers January 1. We don't like waiting. The problem is, of course, once I've been paid I don't really want to do the job. What happens then?

Imagine a one-hundred-meter sprinter who starts a world-championship sprint with a victory party. She's carried into the arena on a throne, wrapped in her country's flag—before the final race. The crowd cheers! She's lifted up on the podium and receives her gold medal. The sponsorship contracts are waiting in her hotel room. When she steps down from the platform, she puts on her running shoes and stretches. She lines up with her nine most fearsome competitors from the whole world. They glare at her. Now there is just one tiny detail left—to actually win the race.

You might be thinking, *What an idiotic example!*

Are you sure about that?

WHEN YOU REST FIRST

Imagine that you run a little business with a handful of employees. They arrive at work at eight o'clock in the morning, and the first thing they do is drink coffee and chat for fifteen minutes. Then half of them go out for a smoke. Then it's time for lunch, followed by a coffee break. Then they need another smoke break, right? After that, they make some private phone calls, check out some vacation cottages on the internet, check up on the sports results, and wander around in the building for a total of half an hour hunting for a missing stapler.

You observe this bizarre scene with a mixture of fascination and horror. At half past four, when you ask them what they've been doing, since they certainly haven't done a bit of work all day, they answer:

It's no problem! We just like to get paid first. We're going to work really hard from 11 P.M. to 5 A.M.

The psychology is exactly the same as for the hundred-meter sprinter. It looks crazy when you think about it.

A Really Stupid Example

January begins with everybody taking a full holiday for five or six weeks. Then they combine all the rest of the free days (all the weekends, holidays, and a bundle of sick days). In Sweden, we end up with something like 135 days per person. If you—the employer—aren't already having a breakdown due to the stress, you'll welcome your employees to work sometime in May—135 days into the year.

The same psychology again, but on a larger scale. And when this interesting group of employees eventually comes to work, they'll have to have coffee and lunch first, of course. Because they want to do the fun stuff first.

Why Not Take It to the Extreme While We're at It?

Let's assume that you live to be 80. We won't count the first twenty years, because you were in school. But once you start at your job when you are 20, you'll immediately ask for and take those 135 free days per year, up until you plan to stop working at age 67. That means . . . that you don't need to physically present yourself at your workplace for another 6,345 days, i.e., when you are 37.4 years old. Unfortunately, now you're in for a serious amount of work and no breaks whatsoever. Just work until the very end.

I know. Nobody does that.

That's an extreme example of trying to get your reward first. You can't build a society on that mentality, but nevertheless we both know that many people find it hard to do the work because they're looking for quick rewards.

So when do you need to put your boots on and get the work done? That's the question we all have to ask ourselves. It's better to wait for the reward than to enjoy it in advance.

SUMMARY

How much time do you waste? You can't re-create time. When it's gone, it's gone. Time is your most limited resource. Every time you use an hour on the wrong thing, you're squandering your most valuable resource.

People who learn to handle time so that time itself works for, instead of against them, are going to be successful. Regardless of how they choose to define success.

But a person who never has control of his time is never going to be fully successful. That person is going to meet setback . . . after setback . . . after setback . . .

15

Dare to Notice What Doesn't Work

In order to avoid setbacks, we need to take a look at what doesn't work—the small warning signals that I touched on very briefly in chapter 2. If you notice them in time, they might only indicate slight bumps on the journey to success, little setbacks rather than big ones. If you wait to address them, the problems can grow until they're too large to solve.

If you consider your situation (for the moment it's irrelevant whether you live in Winnerville or Laterville) and you notice something is off, that might be a warning sign.

And there are a lot of them, once we start looking.

For example, let's think about your job. If it's Sunday afternoon and you start to feel irritated, tired, or just sick, it says something about your attitude toward your job. You might not hate your job, but these bodily reactions signal that something is wrong. According to international studies, most serious heart attacks in the West happen in the mornings. Mondays are also the worst day. The second most common is evidently Sunday evenings. Why is that?

Is it because you're actually working in a poisonous and aggressive environment? Or is your boss a bastard? You might say that there aren't any other job openings available, and while that might be true, it still won't help your physical and mental health. It might only make the matter worse.

Your work environment is just one of the areas we need to take a good look at.

If you run your own business, do you accept that your profits have gone down by 30 percent, or do you pretend that everything is just great?

If you don't feel well physically, have you done the work to discover why?

Relationships are particularly difficult.

Some people make excuses for a dysfunctional marriage. They don't want to see their partner's negative behavior in the light of day. They shut their eyes to how their teenagers speak to them. They have a good friend who's in the process of wrecking her own life, but they keep quiet because they convince themselves it's only a phase.

They mean well, but sometimes it all goes very wrong. And then you have to do something instead of continuing to live in denial.

HOW DO SUCCESSFUL PEOPLE DO IT?

Few individuals on this planet are more closely scrutinized than successful people. Shelves have been filled with books about entrepreneurs, athletes, best-selling writers, top bosses, investors, spiritual leaders, and anyone else who has achieved some sort of success. At the end of this book, there's a list of books you can read to find even more inspiration.

One thing is clear: these people encounter just as many problems and obstacles as you and I do. More, perhaps, because they very rarely sit still. The difference is that they don't deny what is happening around them. They don't shut their eyes and ignore trouble— regardless of whether it's a major problem or a little inconvenience.

Keeping track of obstacles is one of the things that made these people successful. Instead of pretending that a problem will soon pass, they start by trying to understand it, and then they work on solving it. And it doesn't make any difference how challenging or exhausting it is; they do it anyway.

The advantage of this attitude and behavior is obvious: by acting early when something is going off the rails, you can reduce considerably the negative consequences of the problem.

BEWARE OF YOUR OWN DEFENSE MECHANISMS

You'll remember the warning signals I mentioned earlier—small things that indicate that something isn't quite right. Your teenager comes home late again. Weird messages in your work inbox. A strange comment from a neighbor or friend. Somebody you care about smells of alcohol and it isn't even noon.

All too often we choose to pretend to be stupid or blind and ignore everything. We sweep all those unpleasant signs under the rug. This can be an effect of the defense mechanisms that our psyche uses to protect us.

All people have defense mechanisms when the pressure is too overwhelming. This often happens automatically. Defense mechanisms can be functional and, to an extent, beneficial, but there are also some tendencies that are unhelpful.

Functional defense mechanisms give us continued access to emotions and impulses. Sometimes, however, emotions and ideas and the consequences of our own actions completely pass us by. This can lead to serious problems if we're not attentive.

Different people use different types of self-protective mechanisms and may have several to choose from or only a handful. Relying on the same defense mechanisms, regardless of the situation, is not functional.

Repression quite often means self-deception. You try to repress unpleasant experiences from your conscious thoughts. However, you may find that you still feel anxious and worried even as you've made yourself ignore or forget the real reason behind your worry.

Intellectualization or *disassociation* happens when you observe a threat without involving your emotions. That way, you avoid worry and discomfort.

Rationalization involves attempting to justify an action or inaction as appropriate regardless of whether it actually was. Few people like to admit to failure, so they often respond by rationalizing and blaming the failure on external circumstances that they can't control. This can also often manifest as attempting to justify irrational behaviors.

Projection means that you unconsciously shift feelings and qualities onto others. You don't want to take the blame for what has happened, so you find other scapegoats. This also happens on a collective level and can be used by various types of leaders to demonize their opponents, for example. History is full of shocking examples.

Displacement occurs when your own worry, or perhaps anger, is transferred from the real cause to somebody else who gets the blame. Displacement is reminiscent of projection, but whereas projection is unconscious, here the person is (in a rather obscure way) aware of the process.

Humor can also be a defense mechanism. It helps reduce anxiety to be able to laugh in stressful situations. Thanks to the release of hormones, we feel physically and mentally better when we laugh, even though it still doesn't solve the actual problem.

Denial means that you reject the reality of the risks in your surroundings. You simply shut your eyes to a situation that is fully visible right in front of you. The everyday term for this phenomenon is "ostrich behavior."

WHAT DEFENSE MECHANISMS DO YOU USE?

Confronting things that don't work often means that you need to do something uncomfortable. You might need to build up your self-discipline; confront somebody who doesn't like you or whom you don't like; accept that there are going to be people who aren't going to like you or what you do; ask for something you need from somebody who has it; or demand respect instead of being trampled in a relationship.

But since you're an ordinary person, the last defense mechanism on the list, *denial,* is going to prevent you from acknowledging the truth. It's going to tell you that there isn't really a problem. And you'll do nothing to fix the situation, because it's not a problem. So let's take a look at the effects of denial.

SO WHAT DOES DENIAL LOOK LIKE?

You'll probably recognize most of the responses on this list, since you've heard and said them a thousand times:

- Teenagers these days are impossible to control.
- That has nothing to do with me.
- I mind my own business, and you should do the same.
- Don't rock the boat.
- That's how it should be; leave it alone.
- Everybody has credit-card debt.
- That's never going to happen to me.
- If I say anything, I might end up in trouble.
- In California, marijuana is legal.

- Meh—it's just a phase she's going through.
- I can't sleep without a glass of red wine.
- It's impossible to do everything in normal working hours.
- Keep quiet, and it will blow over.
- He said he would pay me back.

Sometimes, we make up reasons why something didn't work, instead of admitting that the situation wouldn't even have happened if we'd dealt with the warning signs in time. Being proactive when something starts going wrong is always better than "wait and see."

You don't need to feel like a failure if you've done this, because everyone else has, too. But you do need to change the way you handle certain situations so that you can avoid unnecessary setbacks. It's cheaper, simpler, and involves less conflict. You'll be a great deal more satisfied with yourself if you confront things as soon as you realize that something is off.

Success here would be to calmly observe a situation without making light of it or seeing it as worse than it is. Just evaluate what's happening and think of it as an opportunity to learn something.

In the business world, some companies are led by people who, instead of making the annual returns look better for the board of directors, actually find out why the sales figures for their biggest product have gone down the drain. They really do want to know why customer satisfaction has tanked. They're always asking which advertising campaigns are performing the best, and they're prepared to take a hard look at rising costs.

They approach things rationally and logically, not hiding or explaining away what happened. And that's totally different than searching for scapegoats.

DENIAL IN EVERYDAY LIFE

In 2019, an American study showed—brace yourself—that 75 percent of all employees hate their jobs. Do you have your dream job? If you do, then I want to congratulate you.

But if you don't have your dream job, what are you currently doing to get it? Or are you living in denial? Are you one of those people who go around singing the praises of your own job and praise your employer every time you get the chance? And if you are, is that genuine, or are you trying to ignore the fact that you would rather do something completely different?

Workaholics often live a lie. An extremely packed calendar doesn't work out well for anyone in the long term. But this gang often justifies it by saying that they earn loads of money, that the company demands it of them, that everybody else works just as hard, or whatever—anything so long as they don't have to question their own lifestyle.

Getting out of denial is tough. If it was simple, they'd have done it long ago.

DENIAL IS BASED ON FEAR

Often, denial is about the fear that something else could be much worse. If we act, perhaps everything will crash down around us. So it would be better to pretend there is nothing wrong.

While I wrote this book, I interviewed some psychologists who work in clinical psychology. Several of them said that they had clients who were masters at denying reality. Even if there was clear evidence that their partner was having an affair, they refused to confront the partner. They didn't want to accept the fact that the relationship was over. It was simply too much to contemplate.

Think about your own life. What situations are you reluctant to deal with? Are there examples on the list below that frighten you?

- Your boss always leaves work early but is happy to dump lots of last-minute projects on your desk.
- You have a business partner who doesn't seem to be really committed to the business.
- Your monthly bills are starting to add up to more than your salary.
- Your teenager smokes or uses drugs.
- Your aging parents need to be looked after.
- It hurts every time you pee.
- Your partner has started to withdraw and has become more condescending toward you recently.
- You never have time for things that you would like to have time for.

YOU DON'T NEED TO MOVE HEAVEN AND EARTH TO SOLVE THE PROBLEM

Some things are easy to deal with; others, not so much. But remember that the situations you've ignored up to this point don't necessarily need a radical solution. If you have problems at work, perhaps you don't need to change jobs. Sometimes it's a question of addressing a particular issue with the right person. If there are problems in your relationships at home, talking them out is often a big step in the right direction.

My point is that if you deal with these types of situations as soon as you see them, and *don't wait* for them to disappear of their own accord, then dramatic measures are rarely needed. Most of the time, ordinary, simple methods are perfectly adequate.

But it starts by accepting that some situations aren't working. See them for what they are. And then act.

I'll say that again.

Act.

ACT NOW, NOT LATER

Make a concrete list of things that you have ignored/denied up until now. Write down three things you know need to be dealt with, but that you've chosen not to pay attention to.

Pick the simplest. (It's better to start with something small, like finally touching up that scuff on the living room wall, than with something big, like asking your thirty-six-year-old son to finally move out.)

Then write down three actions for each problem that will help correct the situation.

I asked my old friend Stefan, from the far north of Sweden, to help me with examples. He definitely tends to put things off. He's a great guy, competent and ambitious, but he has a pathological pattern of waiting things out when something isn't working right. This is what he wrote:

What I Tend to Ignore

My boss has started to hover around my desk and ask when I'm going to finish one of the projects I'm working on. I know this is because I virtually never make my deadlines. It's always been like that, and I hate talking about it. That's just how I am.

What I Need to Do to Deal with the Problem

1. I need to talk to my boss. I need to admit that I'm aware of the problem, but that I've been avoiding it for years.

2. After that, I need to ask her to help me keep to my deadline by taking a few things off my plate so I can focus undisturbed on the project. I'm easily distracted by everything else that happens and often lose track of big goals in favor of smaller tasks.

3. Then I need to talk with somebody who is good at meeting deadlines and ask if he or she can show me how to approach the projects.

These are all things that won't get anybody fired. And if Stefan follows his extremely simple plan, he'll avoid a lot of headaches and anxiety. The challenge here is Stefan's Yellow behavior. He finds it hard to stick to a plan, regardless of how good it is.

Now it's your turn! Be honest with yourself. There's no point in trying to fool yourself. The only person who suffers from that is you.

What I Tend to Deny

What I Need to Do to Deal with the Problem

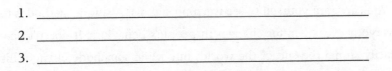

1. _____
2. _____
3. _____

It doesn't have to be any more complicated than that. Make sure that you really define the problem and that the steps you list actually solve the problem in question. Then make sure you carry out the first step on the list. Write it down in your calendar. Right now. I promise you that you're going to feel relieved, satisfied, happy, and proud of yourself when you've done what you need to do. Then deal with number 2, and once that's done, move on to number 3.

Break the bad habit of letting denial be a part of your everyday life. Choose to act, and then just do it. Once you've created the habit of action, possibilities that you can't even imagine will open up for you. That's a promise.

I had to pep Stefan up a couple of times before he found the courage to go to his boss, clutching the sheet of paper. Instead of saying what he came to say, he simply handed the sheet of paper to his boss. She read through it all carefully, got up, and gave him a big hug. She was happy to not have to raise the problem herself with Stefan. She congratulated him on his self-awareness. Together, they solved the problem one step at a time. Of course, Stefan still sometimes procrastinates on difficult tasks, but not to the same extent as before.

SUMMARY

We all have things we know we need to do, but we hide behind various rational and irrational reasons for avoiding them. Sometimes, they're ordinary defense mechanisms. By learning to recognize the type of defense mechanisms we use, even very difficult things can become much easier.

You can train yourself to see warning signals. A simple method is to have your eyes open for changes in people's behaviors. It doesn't necessarily signal the end of the world, but when somebody changes his or her normal behavior, it might be a good idea to take a closer look.

If it turns out to be a false alarm—so much the better! Now you've saved yourself many sleepless nights!

In order to solve the problem, you often have to do something you're not accustomed to doing, which in turn means that you need to be willing to leave your comfort zone.

16

Leaving Your Comfort Zone

I just mentioned that behind denial there is often some sort of fear. Fear governs us more than we're aware of. Oftentimes, the greatest setbacks are those we've imagined inside our heads, typically because we are afraid of something.

Fear can paralyze us. It can create a kind of passivity that can't be broken. Fear is dreadful, yet we all have fears. Most things outside our comfort zones make us uncertain, worried, and even afraid. What's interesting is that all of us have different-sized comfort zones. They are completely unique to the individual.

A while ago, I met Jeanette, who has been a security guard and bodyguard in extremely risky environments for more than twenty-five years. She has no problem stepping straight into potentially lethal situations in the middle of the night with who-knew-what kind of terrifying people hiding in the shadows. She has been, in countless times doing her job, threatened by every imaginable type of weapon. Not a pleasant work environment. It would scare most of us to death.

But Jeanette just shrugged her shoulders at that kind of fear. Just another day at the office. So she must not have been scared of anything, right?

In personal situations, however, she was afraid of saying what was on her mind. It was frightening to challenge people in her immediate vicinity, people she liked and met every day. But never wanting to leave your comfort zone, or only doing so with extreme reluctance, is limiting. The only way to grow or develop is to step outside it.

What about you? I'm sure that you've heard this before, so I won't elaborate too much. But in order to avoid unpleasantness, many people choose to stay in their comfort zones. It feels better there. Safer. Fewer risks. But at the same time, there's an almost total lack of development. It's a permanent move to Laterville.

And Laterville is where dreams die.

IS PESSIMISM ALWAYS BAD?

Mark Twain is reported to have said, "I am an old man and have known a great many troubles, but most of them have never happened."

If you aren't much of an optimist, then it sounds crazy to hear somebody chirp out, *Think positively!*

A few years ago, psychologist Mattias Lundberg and comedian Jan Bylund wrote an entertaining and illustrative book called *The Happy Pessimist*. To very briefly summarize, the authors have a thesis that for certain people it's actually better to think negatively, because that ensures that they will never be disappointed by the results. Even though that's not my personal attitude, I respect the fact that there are some people who think like that. The delightful thing about us humans is that not everything works for everybody.

CAN WE REALLY PROTECT OURSELVES
FROM EVERYTHING?

There's a strange attitude in society today that seems to prioritize avoiding potentially messy or troublesome situations above all else. You can't take risks, no matter the context. I touched on this earlier, and it's certainly no fun to experience fear. That's why many people protect their children from everything bad. Of course, I don't mean that we should subject our children to unnecessary risks, but to protect them from absolutely everything is simply not possible.

I don't mean to downplay the struggles of those who have experienced true suffering in life. But the expression "What doesn't kill you, makes you stronger" does indeed have some truth to it.

You remember the long list of my own setbacks in chapter 7. Besides the simple fact that, in retrospect, I couldn't have done much about many of the incidents on the list, they've also given me something. I have a certain sense of strength and protection against future setbacks that life might throw at me.

Trying to eliminate all potential future threats just doesn't work.

As a child, when I stood on the lowest diving board at the swimming pool and was about to jump a whole three feet, I was terrified. Why, I don't really know.

You can never get rid of fear. You've been in situations when you were genuinely afraid. And a well-meaning person promised you that there was nothing to be afraid of. Right? The problem is, there is. There are lots and lots of things to worry about, to be afraid of. And those things are always going to be there.

WHAT AM I AFRAID OF?

Personally, I always observe myself carefully when I realize I'm hesitating in the face of things that shouldn't be very complicated. These can be minor things, like making a particular phone call, or discussing something at home that might involve potential conflict, or spending money on a consultant I'm not sure of. When I feel reluctance about something, it's often because there's a difficulty somewhere, and it isn't always easy to see what that is.

None of these fears are particularly serious. Just like on the personal-setback ranking in chapter 7, you need to put things in perspective. Work-related things I feel nervous about are hardly deadly.

But fear, pure and simple? Well, I'm afraid . . .

> . . . that something will happen to my children: that they will get sick, lose their jobs, lose their faith in the future, or have their hearts broken by some bastard;
> . . . that something terrible will happen to my sister, despite her rock-solid positive view of the universe;
> . . . that I will get sick or too stressed or just such a pain to those around me, and my wife will leave me, and so on;
> . . . that I will never be able to finish another manuscript;
> . . . that my published books will never reach any readers;
> . . . that the app and the web courses I've produced will be gigantic wastes of time and money;
> . . . that I will be suddenly gripped by stage fright and never be able to give a lecture again;
> . . . that I will lose faith in what I do and never want to leave my house again;
> . . . that I've wasted half my adult life on the wrong things;

. . . that all of humanity will die out during my children's
lifetimes.

These are just off the top of my head. Why ever get out of bed again?

On the other hand . . . most of the things on this list are totally outside my control. But the fear is real nevertheless. So I try to stay realistic and keep moving forward.

Even though he's in great health for his eighty-seven years, my beloved father is still getting older.

Even though I can't control whether U.S. readers are going to love or hate my book, I still need to send it out and let the market take care of the process.

Even though three hundred Swedes died in traffic accidents last year, I'm still going to drive my car.

There is nothing to fear but fear itself.

But the feeling of being afraid is there, regardless of how illogical it is. Everyone experiences that now and then. All you can do is accept that bad things *can* happen. The risk is there, but we can't let this fact paralyze us.

It's possible to learn how to handle your fear. And it's almost ridiculously simple.

FEEL THE FEAR, AND DO IT ANYWAY

All you need to do when you are faced with a situation that frightens you is to identify the fear, accept that it is there—and do what you need to do anyway.

Perhaps the best book in history about dealing with fear is *Feel the Fear . . . and Do It Anyway* by Dr. Susan Jeffers. It became a monumental best seller many years ago, thanks to its incredibly simple message: even if you're afraid of something, the fear isn't going to disappear until you've learned to handle it. Jeffers says that fear is always going to be with us, and that sometimes you need to deal with it head-on.

I read the book some years ago, and I can't express how much it has helped me. It helped me out of a very destructive relationship. Now I very rarely back away from conflict, and that's largely due to my experience in that relationship.

After I read Jeffers's advice and prepared myself well, I took the bull by the horns and said exactly what I thought: "This isn't working. What you do to me is not acceptable. It's going to stop, and it stops here." After some very intense moments, I was suddenly free. And stronger than ever before. I felt the fear and did it anyway.

FACTS ARE ONE THING; RELATIONSHIPS, A COMPLETELY DIFFERENT STORY

Do you want to live your life on your own conditions or on somebody else's? One of the challenges when you want to grow as a person—whether it be building your self-confidence, getting into shape, earning more money, or building a company—is that the people around you may not like this change. Very often, people feel threatened and start to oppose you.

This is problematic. When people around you don't support your growth, then you must choose: the relationship or your dream.

This kind of obstacle is extremely frustrating and hard to understand. Why would a person who insists that he or she loves you stop you from achieving your personal goals? This is often related to how hard change can be. But it might also be jealousy. Or simply a threat to the person's status within the family.

A man I met at a dinner many years ago said that he left his wife because she'd gone and gotten a better education than he had. I was flabbergasted and wondered what he was talking about. Remarkably, he thought that it was completely natural to specifically look for a woman who was less educated than he was. It was his task to support the family, and he was the alpha male in the family. If she was suddenly more educated, she could potentially get a better job than him, and he found the idea totally impossible to accept. What can you even say to that?

And that might be our greatest fear of all—to be forced to deal with these painful situations.

WHAT ARE YOU AFRAID OF?

Put the book down for a moment. Think about what limits you. What makes you hesitate and even refrain from doing something that you hope could lead to good things?

Take a pen and paper. Write down three things you feel fear, worry, or unease about, but that you know that you should confront. It doesn't have to be shipping off to a war zone. Or putting the family's life savings in a high-risk investment fund. It can be something as simple as going across to your neighbor and asking him to stop smoking on his balcony because the smoke goes straight into your bedroom.

Write down your three points now.

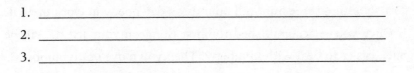

1. _____
2. _____
3. _____

Your list could include things like this:

1. Asking your boss for a raise
2. Asking your spouse to spend more time at home
3. Starting that fun project in your free time that you've been thinking of for a while

When you think about starting that project, perhaps you mainly feel excitement, but at the same time you feel daunted thinking about all the extra work it will entail. And the stress that might follow. And what your partner is going to say about it.

When you think about asking your spouse to spend as much time with the kids as he or she does with coworkers, perhaps your pulse races a bit.

If your boss is the tough type, perhaps you'll get stressed even thinking about asking for a raise.

Sort the list from the easiest to the hardest. Perhaps your list would look like this instead:

1. Starting that fun project in your free time that you've been thinking of for a while
2. Asking your spouse to spend more time at home
3. Asking your boss for a raise

You can now see that the least scary thing is to start that fun project. You can now get right to it, even though you feel some butterflies in your stomach.

Because this is what happens: by doing what feels the least uncomfortable, and succeeding in that, you build up your strength. Your fear tolerance becomes higher. Just like at the gym, you don't start squatting three hundred pounds on day one, you work up to it.

Once you've accomplished the first thing on your list it, will be much easier to deal with number 2. Then you move on to number 3.

Does that sound simple? That's what's so brilliant about it. It's so simple, it almost feels unreal. Simple if you *do* it, that is.

By not pushing against your fears, you're depriving yourself of a future that could be magnificent. You lose the possibility to really live the life you've imagined.

Do you want to govern your fear, or do you want the fear to govern you? Only you can answer that.

17

Fear and the Four Colors

Not everyone is afraid of the same things or feels discomfort about them. Of course, a lot depends on what you experienced as you grew up and what you've been through in the past. Yet there are certain patterns that can be worth pointing out. Patterns linked to our basic behaviors can teach us something. And even though the four colors in the DISC model are primarily focused on communication, we can find some interesting clues here.

AFRAID THE RED WAY

If you're mainly a Red, then your greatest fear is losing control. You want to have control, and losing it can be really frightening for you. You want to have control of the situation and what others do or don't do.

It's perfectly alright to feel that way, but you need to think about how you're going to handle it. The person with a dominant red streak prefers to make all the decisions and steer others. The problem is that this doesn't always work. If you're the boss or the head of the family, then it might be simpler. But your need to always feel like the alpha can be a serious limitation.

My recommendation is that you accept that the world is complex, and you can't have control over everything, no matter how hard you work.

The Solution

Hand over some of the responsibility and control to others. See how it goes. Give a helping hand if necessary, but learn that things can happen without you. When you become accustomed to this way of behaving, you're going to feel stress release its grip on you. This is how a Red person can step outside his or her comfort zone.

It's not a sign of defeat to give up control. On the contrary, it's a strength that is gradually going to improve your efficiency and results. If you want to go really far, you need to learn to accept and use the energy of those around you. And accept that you don't have all the answers. Nobody does.

UNPLEASANT FOR A YELLOW

Yellow behavior includes a very deep-seated fear: losing your prestige and sinking in status. Yellows are very sensitive to what people around them think of them. Being in an elevated position suits a Yellow very well. Yellows really love to be in the limelight. And the risk of descending to the same level as the rest of us simply scares them.

You might not admit that even to yourself, but, with sufficient self-awareness, you know it's true. If you've always been the one people come to and ask questions about X thing, then you'll find it very painful if somebody else outcompetes you. It will go right to your heart, and you might find yourself completely paralyzed.

Relying on a gut feeling is very natural for a Yellow, but it won't help you. You need to accustom yourself to not being the center of attention at every meeting.

The Solution

Trust that everyone else is not going to forget you just because you're not in the limelight every second. You're already an interesting person—you can adopt a more laid-back position. When you realize that there's a lot to learn from listening to others, you'll feel more comfortable biding your time a little. This is the Yellows' way of stepping beyond their comfort zones.

A person who listens and lets others into the fold is going to be extremely popular with the rest of the group. You're going to feel their appreciation.

GREEN ANXIETY IN EVERYDAY LIFE

Perhaps you're primarily a Green, and it's perfectly obvious—both to you and to others—that you're afraid of conflict. You don't just feel uneasy when people raise their voices and make a bit of noise, even a dirty look or ambiguous comments; irony in general, and sarcasm in particular, can unnerve you.

You want to be a friend to all, but since that isn't really possible, you struggle to protect yourself from a merciless world. You try to be gentle, friendly, and always behave in a nonthreatening way. The problem is that many people aren't going to understand where you stand on certain issues. Which can be exactly what leads to raised voices and dirty looks.

You need to find a new approach here, because it's not helpful to go around being terrified of what might happen in the next meeting.

The Solution

You need to become a little clearer with your true opinions. Dare to express a distinct point of view and see what happens. Some people are going to agree with you; others are going to disagree. But you can improve your ability to listen to the opinions of other people without taking them personally. Remind yourself that people don't think about you as you might believe. Most people think more about themselves than anything else, which makes the risk of conflict rather small. If you, as a Green, really push and go outside your comfort zone, you're going to discover that it isn't so dangerous after all.

Try it on a small scale. Notice what it feels like. Realize that nothing terrible happened. And move on. For your own sake, you ought to stand up for yourself and say what you think, instead of forcing others to find out afterward. That, my friend, is in fact often the issue behind these conflicts. The clearer you are early on in a process, the less bickering there will be later on.

FEAR FOR THE BLUES

Even though you Blues are task-oriented, there's something that really frightens you: making a fool of yourself. Supplying the wrong information, incorrect data, or coming to unsound conclusions— terrible! Everyday life contains unlimited possibilities to make a fool of yourself and have your mistakes revealed to one and all. But this fear limits the chances for those around you to see you for the true professional you are.

Nobody thinks that you're infallible. There are no perfect people, even though there are many who try to be. And Blues are the ones who try the hardest. Your nose for perfection might sometimes be an advantage, but the only way to entirely avoid mistakes is to lock the door from the inside and throw away the key.

You need to find a more logical method of attack. That's how the real professionals work.

The Solution

Let go of this need to appear perfect and the fear of making a fool of yourself. Accept that you are an ordinary living human being who, like all of us, is sometimes going to be wrong. It is not going to kill you. That's what it feels like to leave your comfort zone.

I am not suggesting that you start being careless. That doesn't do any of us any good. But you can let go of some tasks sooner than you normally do. When you think you've achieved 90 percent, you'll still have gone much further than other people would have. Be satisfied with your achievement (unless you're a brain surgeon; then please hold out for 100 percent). Accept that you've done your part, and move on. If—and it's highly unlikely—somebody should find some mistakes, don't see it as a defeat but as a good opportunity to learn new things. Because you like to improve your skills, right?

SUMMARY

Being afraid is completely natural, and nobody totally escapes this. Even the most successful people you can imagine have a particular comfort zone. Only psychopaths and narcissists never experience fear or stress. The only way to get around this for the rest of us is to push directly against the fear—and just do it anyway.

Even though the fear is real, we sometimes tend to exaggerate it.

Don't do that. Don't picture worst-case scenarios in your mind. But don't underplay anything, either.

Once we act despite the fear, we often discover that the feeling was exaggerated.

Look at what you are afraid of. It's okay; it only makes you human. But act on what you see. Start with smaller things to build up your confidence. That will strengthen you for bigger tasks.

Okay. Now it's time to look at a serious setback and see how to tackle it piece by piece.

18

The Harry Case, or How to End Up in a Ditch

A man who is definitely past his prime—let's call him Harry—is fed up with his beer belly and his poor health. His eyesight is not what it was, and he doesn't feel particularly strong. Over the last twenty years, he established bad habits like eating too much junk food and snacks, and drinking too much beer and "diet" soda (thinking it's not unhealthy). He hates walking for more than a short distance, he takes his car everywhere, and hasn't seen the inside of a gym for fifteen years. He persuades himself that he has some sort of innate basic fitness because he played football in high school.

We don't know anything about Harry's colors or driving forces, but we do know Harry sits in front of the TV in the evening with his hand in a bag of peanuts, watching meaningless reality series. His favorite shows are the ones with dysfunctional characters, since they make Harry think that his own life isn't so bad after all.

He might end the evening with the late-night news and all the depressing updates it contains.

He fills his mind with negative thoughts and then goes up to bed. Of course, he sleeps badly and finds it hard to get up when the alarm clock rings at six thirty. He feels more dead than alive at work until lunchtime, which means he doesn't get much done. His body aches and he can't concentrate.

Between you and me, it doesn't look good for Harry.

But something suddenly causes him to wake up. It might be a friend who died young, an old flame who has gotten back in touch, a comment from one of the kids, who is genuinely worried about him. It doesn't matter what sparked the change, but now things are going to happen. He is going to be a new man!

And that's great. Sometimes you need that aha moment to say, *That's enough! I don't want to live like this anymore!*

He gets a gym membership, buys some new workout clothes, pumps up the bike tires, and throws away all the junk food he has in the pantry. He promises to go to bed by 10 P.M. every evening so that he can go for a run at 5 A.M. the next morning. He solemnly swears to his wife that things are about to change.

HOW YOU START A HEALTH JOURNEY

Harry starts a health plan that would make the producers of *The Biggest Loser* green with envy. From now on, he is going to bike to work. He will visit the gym six days a week. He is going to steam with sweat. No TV and peanuts or beer in the evenings.

Two months have passed with six days a week in the gym—we will assume that our friend Harry actually does work out at the gym (obviously not everyone does)—and now he has aching muscles he didn't even know existed. He pulled at least three muscles, because the first thing he did was put too much strain on his body. He's beginning to worry that he's done serious damage. He's already fed up with a diet of boiled cod and broccoli. When he bikes to work, it rains three days in a row. His butt is sore, and he has aches and pains all over.

Every time he steps on the scale, he's worried. Nothing has changed. His jacket is still as tight as before.

Sometimes he forgets to pack his gym bag, and he finds it hard not having cream in his coffee after lunch. He's had cream in his coffee for at least twenty years, after all, and is well aware that it is not exactly beneficial for his weight.

Then there is a happy hour at work.

Everybody nags Harry: Can't he just take it easy? There are several couch potatoes in this gang: Roger and Freddie, for example, are even worse off than Harry. At least one of them will have serious heart problems soon.

And Harry resorts to a tactical defense mechanism called rationalization. He really does deserve a couple of beers and some fries, since he leads such a healthy lifestyle these days. For God's sake, it's possible to live a good life without having to exist solely on kale! So he goes *all in* this Friday night—beer, whiskey, and every kind of snack you can imagine—and wakes up the next morning with a hefty hangover, a headache that eclipses the sun, and a stomach that is desperate for a really oily pizza with extra cheese. After a party like this, his body is screaming for liquid and fat.

NOW HERE'S A REAL SETBACK

Is all hope lost? Or was that just a little relapse?

Well, it depends. Mainly on Harry, of course, but also on those around him. There is a risk that this might happen:

All the good habits are abruptly broken after an evening out with his workmates. If you've cheated once, then you can cheat again. Besides, Harry's wife doesn't really like how Harry goes to bed earlier and earlier. She misses his company in front of the TV in the evenings. And when she takes an extra cinnamon bun, his good eating habits make her feel bad. So he starts listening to her when she encourages him to ease up on the restrictions a bit.

And the fact is that after another couple of months of intensive training, he starts to hesitate: Why is he actually doing this? What was he thinking when he first started? Was he really in such bad shape? His goal seems to be more distant than ever. He's not going to lose thirty-five pounds in the immediate future.

Bit by bit, Harry goes back to his earlier life and soon makes up for everything he missed during his health kick.

Six months after his aha moment he weighs even more than he did before. And he feels even more tired than ever. His body is screaming after all this mistreatment, but that isn't the real problem.

Now he feels like a failure, too. And he's in a worse place mentally than he was before he started.

He had such high hopes and did so much right. So how did it go so wrong?

THE SETBACK BROKEN DOWN IN EIGHT PIECES

Why did it go so totally wrong for Harry? Why did he end up in a ditch despite the fact that he had both the desire and the commitment?

If you knew why Harry failed, what conclusions do you think you would draw? Would you be able to make use of that insight in your own life?

How fantastic it would be if you could be certain that you would succeed at whatever you set out to achieve.

I pulled a muscle. Became allergic to kale. My shoes were no good. The gym was too far away. I had too much to do at work. Beer just tastes too good. Those are just meaningless excuses. You know that. I know that. And I bet that that Harry knows it, too. You either have results or you have excuses. You can't have both of them at the same time. And very rarely is there just one single cause for failure.

Harry's problem can be listed in eight points:

1. He didn't know *why* he was doing all of this.
2. His goal was far too *vague* and *fuzzy*.
3. He took on *far too much* at the same time.
4. The results were initially *invisible*.
5. He lacked *persistence*.
6. He underestimated the difficulty of *breaking old habits*.
7. He *surrounded* himself with the wrong people.
8. He drifted . . .

Let's have a look at each separate point.

1. He Didn't Know Why He Was Doing All of This

If there isn't a clear, sensible reason to change a particular aspect of your life, then it isn't going to work. Why suffer through nights of salads and mornings of running if there's no rational explanation?

Harry wanted to get into better shape. That was a good idea, of course. But why did he want to do that? Was it for fun? Did he want to impress somebody? Did he simply feel bad when he looked at himself in the mirror? If he knew exactly which *problem* he wanted to solve, it would have been much simpler. You need a more specific motivation than simply thinking *Now's the time!*

The answer to the question *why* identifies the specific problem. We don't take an aspirin if we don't have a headache. If there isn't an identified and accepted problem, there's no need for a solution.

If Harry had identified that he couldn't go on long hikes with his best friend like he used to, perhaps he would have been motivated to stick with his health regimen. Without those hikes, he rarely saw his buddy.

If he knew that it was starting to be hard to make it through a regular workday because his body was so sore and stiff, he might have had a proper reason. If you can't do your work well, you risk being criticized, demoted, or perhaps even laid off the next time the company reorganizes. Serious concerns.

If he genuinely missed his sex life with his wife because he was often too tired to even think about it, perhaps something would have made him stick with the exercise program. Is that a problem or not? Hard to say.

Perhaps if his *why* had been admitting to himself that he wanted to impress that new pretty woman in the department, things would have gone better. I just made up Harry, so I can't be entirely certain. Sometimes it isn't a problem that needs to be solved, but a possibility that could be opened up. But there are worse reasons to get into better physical shape.

None of his goals will succeed until Harry has established the real reason why he needs to get into better physical shape. That is what keeps him going. That's what provides the basis for all motivation, that subtle and—admittedly—elusive ingredient. It's what really drives him forward, even when the going gets tough. It's what gets him out of bed in the mornings when it's raining, that helps him to say no, thank you to a piece of cream cake (even though cream cake is the best). It makes him sweat on the step machine, instead of bingeing peanuts.

A Hair-Raising Example of Denial

A few years ago, American researchers carried out a so-called screening study. They wanted to find out more about people who were at higher risk for a specific type of cancer. They placed ads designed to appeal to the demographic in the risk zone and offered them a free screening test. Thousands responded. Some of them turned out to be predisposed to this form of cancer. Then one thousand of these people were offered free advice about their lifestyles to minimize the risk associated with this cancer.

How many of them dropped out of the program, and how many stuck with it?

Of the *one thousand* people who voluntarily contacted the study—i.e., acted on their own initiative—*nobody* accepted the free advice.

Think about that for a moment.

The number of people who wanted to avoid dying of cancer: zero.

Even though they now *knew* that they were at a higher risk of becoming seriously ill, nobody wanted help. How could that even be possible?

It is easy to laugh at this depressing example, and think, *What a bunch of idiots!* But before we do that, are we certain that we would make a more rational decision if we were in the same position?

It's hard to change yourself. It requires a very strong reason, a purpose, a cause—a powerful *why*—for a person to deny him- or herself obvious pleasure in favor of a long-term reward.

2. His Goal Was Far Too Vague and Fuzzy

I need to get in better shape. Can you get much vaguer than that? Even though it sounds like a brilliant goal, Harry needs to ask himself this question: What does that mean? *Get in better shape?* What sort of shape are we talking about?

If you and I were to try to picture somebody who's in good shape, would we see the same image? I know what I would see in my mind's eye, but is that what you would envision? And what does Harry think of?

Perhaps he has a vague idea of a (twenty-year-younger) fitness guy in fancy shorts with the flattest stomach you can imagine. Perhaps it's somebody with enormous biceps. Maybe all of this, or none of it. The risk is that his mental image of what he wants to look and feel like doesn't exist at all. It could be a vague desire that things should be different. All Harry knows is that he's unfit, and that's *not* what he wants to be.

But where does he *want* to be? Without a more concrete goal, there will be no results.

Some People Completely Lack Goals

And perhaps that's the main problem. The majority of us have virtually no goals.

For years, I've wondered why so many people are resistant to setting goals. And I have an idea why that is.

To know who won the football game, we need to keep track of the points. And if somebody wins . . . then it means . . . that somebody else loses. That, I think, is where people get nervous.

Nobody Wants to Lose

We don't all have a need to win. But nobody wants to end up last. Nobody wants to hear that they failed. And if it feels so bad to lose, then it's actually better not to know. The resulting logic is:

If I don't set any goals, then I can't fail to reach them. If I don't have any goals, then nobody can judge me by them. Not me nor my colleagues nor my boss. On the surface, everything is going to look fine no matter what, right?

The problem isn't that you aim too high and miss. The problem is that you (to avoid leaving your comfort zone) aim too low . . . and hit the target. Then you stay there. You're satisfied with something mediocre, because you at least got what you aimed for. And who can argue with that?

What Do the Experts Say About Taking Risks?

Our brains aren't designed to make us feel good. They're designed to do everything necessary for us to survive, regardless of how bad it makes us feel. Our brains would prefer that we survive, even in total misery, rather than risk that we die happy.

What's the consequence of that impulse? Don't take any unnecessary risks.

Setting tough goals is a way of taking a risk. You can fail. Horribly. Once upon a time, failure meant a threat to your life. If you took a wrong step in the jungle, a tiger could eat you. If you lost your bearskin during the winter, you might freeze to death. If you stay where you are and keep your head down, then you're going to survive. Don't challenge anybody, don't stick out. Don't be different. You won't be kicked out of the group, which could be deadly. Your brain is going to try to resist all such ideas.

Think about it: When you set a really challenging goal and achieve it, what do the people around you say? A few, the people who really care about you, are going to be pleased for you. Those closest to you. Your mother and a handful of others, perhaps. But make no mistake about it, most people won't be pleased by your success.

The majority probably won't care at all. They couldn't care less. But many people around you will be surprisingly pleased if you fail.

That's the sad truth. It means that their own efforts don't look so bad.

Why Lottery Winners Go Bankrupt

Nowadays, we don't risk our lives in the same way. Nobody is going to bar you from the tribe to die in the wilderness, but social exclusion is still a risk. It's a basic need to feel socially accepted. Being rejected by the group is a uniquely painful experience for any person.

There have been studies in the United States in which million-dollar lottery winners were interviewed. A lot of them became depressed after they won the money. If you live in a particular socioeconomic class and suddenly you find yourself sitting on a pile of money, then you're undoubtedly going to stick out from the group. And nobody is going to love you for it. Quite the opposite: a lot of people are going to resent you. Some are going to hate you. You don't fit in anymore, because you have a new car and nobody else has one.

Nor can you just get up and move into a so-called affluent area, because everyone there will know instinctively that you haven't earned the money yourself. They know that it's just a lottery win. You don't fit in there, either.

So where do you fit in?

Perhaps it is easiest to just spend all the money quickly so the problem disappears. This presumably happens unconsciously.

Indeed, it is more common for lottery winners in America to declare bankruptcy than it is for ordinary Americans. Approximately a third of all lottery millionaires (according to the National Endowment for Financial Education) go bankrupt within three to five years. Before you think, *That's because they haven't learned how to look after their money*—I agree that can be one reason, but lottery winners' brains can mess things up for them. The mind quickly reverts to its earlier situation: being broke. That has become a sort of default position.

The best salesperson is praised by the management at all the sales meetings. But all the other salespeople say rude things about her behind her back. The person who has the nicest house on the street gets smiles from his neighbors. But that person is probably not invited to many spontaneous backyard BBQs. The person with the fanciest car might be suspected of shady business activities. There might be something not right there. Illegal gambling on the internet? Narcotics, perhaps?

Besides, this doesn't have anything to do with money; it's about what you make of yourself. If you win the lottery—which is extremely unlikely—and suddenly have millions of dollars, then you'd better become a millionaire mentally, too, and fast.

With the wrong mindset you'll soon be back where you started. Subconsciously or otherwise.

Unspecific Goals Rarely Lead Anywhere

Let's say you want a higher salary. The annual salary discussions are coming up soon, and you hope to get a share of the pie this time. You go in to your boss's office and tell her about your desire to get a salary increase.

Sure, says your boss. *You can have ten dollars more a month.*

Are you satisfied now? No.

So you try again.

Okay, let's talk about it, she says. *How much more?*

If you start stammering and can't answer, this is not going to go very far. And you should not ask her how much she's willing to give you. The risk is that she will answer, *Nothing.*

Conclusion: goals need to be so clear that people can understand them.

3. He Took On Far Too Much at the Same Time

How do you write a book? Answer: One word at a time.

How do you walk coast to coast? Answer: One step at a time.

How do you build stronger muscles? Answer: One push-up at a time.

How do you eat an elephant? Answer: One bite at a time.

How do you acquire better eating habits? Answer: Start by drinking an extra glass of water.

The problem is that these things take time. But bad habits have been built up over the years, and you won't be able to get rid of them in just a few weeks. You need to accept this simple fact. Harry started doing everything at the same time. Working out, eating better, not drinking alcohol, getting up early, and going to bed early. The complete opposite of his previous lifestyle and daily rhythm.

If Harry hasn't taken care of himself for years, it's going to take time to remedy that. But regardless, he can't do everything at once. That is an unreasonable demand. And if it doesn't work, he'll soon meet new setbacks. Failing with a workout routine, or with a diet, or with sleeping habits, or with a active lifestyle, or whatever it happens to be is discouraging. This is only going to add fuel to his this-isn't-working bonfire.

There are inspiring public speakers who say that you should aim high! *The sky is the limit! You can do whatever you want!*

Absolutely. You should dream big. Then these same big thinkers say that you should repeat to yourself your (typically) unrealistic goals as often as you possibly can.

- I'll be ready for Mr. Universe next year!
- I'll be the CEO!
- I'll spend all my time with my children!
- I'll visit ten countries in the next three years!
- I won't work a single hour of overtime next year!
- I'll be financially independent in two years!
- I'll live in a country mansion by a lake!

All of those are excellent and honorable goals, but the risk is that it's too much to bite off in one go.

Let's take the question of money, because it's so easy to do the math.

I shall be 100 percent debt-free next year!

Great! But if you have just taken out a $350,000 mortgage on your house, have no savings in the bank, but still have an ordinary salary, then it isn't realistic. What would be realistic, would be to say to yourself, *This year, I am going to pay an extra 10 percent over my required payments toward my mortgage.* (Don't bother working out how many years it will take; that isn't the point here.)

The following year, perhaps you pay an additional 12 percent off. And after that 15 percent more. Suddenly it becomes manageable.

Harry needed to have a much more detailed, gradual plan to be successful. He needed to start on a smaller, more manageable scale. Instead he ended up creating even more painful obstacles.

4. The Results Were Initially Invisible

The worst part about setting goals and starting to work toward them is that, at first, you will hardly see any results at all. What Harry had forgotten was that it had taken him perhaps twenty years of neglect to get where he was.

Question: How do you put on thirty extra pounds?

Answer: By one bad decision at a time.

It would be much simpler if after the first mouthful, you immediately put on thirty pounds and started having heart problems.

If you wolfed down a bag of potato chips and immediately found that your pants were four sizes too small . . . how many more bags of chips would you have that week?

But the process doesn't work like that. It's slow, long, and drawn out, and the pounds sneak up on you without much fuss.

The crazy thing is that it works the same way in the opposite direction.

If you change your diet, you can't expect those thirty pounds to disappear by the next weekend.

The same applies to smoking. If, after smoking your first cigarette, you suddenly had a terrible hacking cough and woke up the next morning connected to a ventilator, with graying skin and feet you can hardly feel because of poor circulation, then you'd understand immediately how bad smoking can be.

And when you stop smoking, it takes up to a year before you notice what your food actually tastes like. Yes, that's right. If you're a smoker and you think you know what food tastes like, then you have a surprise in store. When you finally stub out your last cigarette, it will take six to twelve months for the poison to leave your body.

If you run on autopilot at work too long, perhaps your new boss will finally notice and nominate you to be the next in line to try out those nice unemployment benefits. It won't happen the first week, but after a month or so of being lazy, someone will notice.

This is how the world works. Even if your actions don't result in any visible effects at first, they will in the end. And, yes, sometimes this planet is an unfair place to live.

The same thing happens in a relationship. If you have an argument—when you refuse to admit that you're wrong, you make a scene, rush out of the room, and slam the door behind you—and come home from work the next day and find signed divorce documents waiting for you, then you would immediately know that you were out of line. But it might have taken twenty years to build up to that scenario.

Think about what happens when you plant a seed. Some seeds will start to germinate in a few days, others will take months. There is a Chinese tree with seeds that can take up to five years to start germinating. And you have to tend it, water it, and add nutrients, even if you don't see any immediate results. If you stop tending your completely invisible seed, well, it will die down there in the soil.

Harry gave up because nothing happened right away. The results were invisible.

The Richest Man in Babylon

Here I'm going to condense a whole book into four sentences.

In the book *The Richest Man in Babylon,* by George Clason, we learn that the path to becoming rich is so simple that the majority of people miss it. All you need to do is put aside 10 percent of your net income every month. The fact is that rich people save first and consume afterward, while less financially successful persons consume first and then save what might be left over. Then it's simply a question of mathematics and time that determines when you'll consider yourself to be rich.

Simple, right?

I once went to a financial freedom seminar. A money guru stood on the stage like a glowing ball of energy, and his first promise to us was this: *Everybody here is going to double their income.*

A murmur passed through the lecture hall. Each and every one of us leaned forward. He definitely had our attention.

Then he said, *The question is: How long is it going to take?*

What a disappointment.

As usual, we wanted a quick fix. Sure, sometimes somebody might achieve "overnight success," and, sure, people do make a huge amount on the stock market. But if you plan your future on those odds, then you'll almost certainly die destitute.

You don't expect your children to turn into adults in a single day. You don't say to your six-month-old daughter, "Now you need to pull yourself together and start walking on your own. This is taking forever. And why are you still crawling around?"

You would never shout at a tree to make it grow quicker. It is going to take thirty to fifty years to reach maturity. The same applies to physical training, your career, building relationships, or creating a profitable business.

If you have a conflict with someone and that person finally apologizes for what they have done, that's good. But it's going to take some time before you fully trust him again.

At first you won't see any changes in your relationship. Building trust definitely takes longer than apologizing. It can take years.

Even if the results aren't immediate, we sometimes need to trust that we're going in the right direction. If you've set a good goal and identified the right steps to take, then you're doing it correctly. Have faith in the fact that you're on the right track. But accept the reality of the world we live in.

5. He Lacked Persistence

The next problem in Harry's case was his persistence. Or rather, his habit of instant gratification.

Now, Harry is not unique in the least. We want what we want, and we want it now. Waiting is not something for modern man. Harry gave up because, despite his considerable efforts, the mirror showed no proof that he was on the right path. Despite his weight lifting, his muscles hadn't gotten bigger. Despite his morning runs, his beer belly hadn't disappeared.

This isn't a book about the best way to get into good physical shape, but what we do know is that your body, which is governed by your brain's striving to survive, is going to resist change. Your body is not going to let go of fat just like that, because that is valuable energy it has been carefully storing for years.

Remember, your brain couldn't care less what you look like on the beach. It only cares about one thing: that you survive.

That makes it easier to build muscle. And, paradoxically, the more muscle you have, the easier it is to burn fat.

But how do you keep going when you don't see results?

Imagine a tasty slice of hot juicy apple pie made from fresh apples. The pie is still warm from the oven, steaming and golden brown with a crunch of caramelized sugar on the outside. Every mouthful melts on your tongue. And it's topped with a magical vanilla ice cream. Perfect. It's a flavor orgasm.

Now imagine a glass of water.

What do you get here?

Nothing. Absolutely nothing.

We'll go through it again: apple pie = heavenly delight.

Water = nothing.

For the first year at least. Perhaps even for the first three years. After that, the glass of water will win by a mile. And after twenty years of apple pie, your regret will be deeper than the Mariana Trench.

This is one of our great challenges. The right choice—the water—gives no immediate gratification. The incorrect (over the years) choice—apple pie with vanilla ice cream—gives an instant payoff.

Harry was wandering through a minefield of temptations every day. Ads for easy pleasures are everywhere. Food, sweets, drinks, TV, apps, games—all sorts of things that give us short-term enjoyment at the cost of the long term. The world happens to be full of temptations.

Here we have a problem.

Life has two types of hardships: either we live with the restrictions of discipline or we suffer under the pressure of regret. Discipline, however, is light compared with the burden of regret.

Short-term pleasure often leads to long-term pain.

But short-term pain often leads to long-term pleasure. Patience, durability, persistence, determination, stubbornness, obsession. Or a passion for change?

6. He Underestimated the Difficulty of Breaking Old Habits

We've all made this mistake, particularly when it comes to our health. Change is going to happen now! But bad habits that have taken years to build up won't disappear that easily.

The old line *I've had a drink every day for forty years, but I haven't made a habit of it* is, of course, amusing, but there's a treacherous psychological truth here. We are always going to stop/start in the future. That sounds logical, because in the future we're going to be delightful people with perfect self-control. We fool ourselves that we can stop bad habits whenever we want. And start with the good things. Later.

But this is where our brain plays a major trick on us. Change can be a threat to our survival, so we don't have any built-in support system. Which means that we have to summon almost inhuman willpower to do what's necessary.

Your Active Choices Govern Your Results

Of course, there are people out there with wills of steel. The people who can just decide and then go and do something. I've met some of them, and they are nothing but impressive. So there are exceptions, and perhaps you're one of them. But those are exceptions.

Habits are about choices—the choices you make, things you choose to do or not to do.

Everyone can choose. All the time. If Harry's choice for the last fifteen years has been to hit "snooze" three times then fall out of bed, flop into his car, and buy a cinnamon bun and a huge caffe latte with extra everything on the way to work, then we know just how difficult it will be to jump out of bed at five o'clock to put on his running shoes and run for half an hour before he's even eaten. And then to celebrate his run with three boiled egg whites and a glass of water. That, too, demands an active choice.

To spell it out: the solution to Harry's problem is still to do it right. But the path to creating the new habit is not straightforward. Say that Harry was sitting at a restaurant because that particular day he forgot the lunch he packed. The kale-and-sweet-potato salad is still at home, in the hall. Now he's sitting with a menu in front of him. There's good food on the menu, but there is also not-so-good food on it. Because a menu is just one long list of possible choices.

Perhaps he will choose the salad. If he does that, then it's okay. But if he chooses the hamburger with fries? *One hamburger doesn't make any difference,* thinks Harry, and he chooses the hamburger.

But how did he end up so unhappy with his health?

Answer: One hamburger at a time.

As I mentioned earlier: he didn't put on thirty-five pounds after the first hamburger. It probably took a couple of thousand hamburgers to get him to where a daily salad would never have taken him.

He can also choose to fool himself. If he takes the hamburger and fries, that just means ninety minutes on his exercise bike tonight. So he *could* actually order the hamburger. But speaking of choices . . . tonight, perhaps, he skips the exercise bike and chooses to catch up on the TV show he has missed, and now watches three episodes in a sitting.

That sort of choice is not going to help his plan to get in good shape.

If he and his wife usually end every evening in front of the TV with something tasty and a couple of shows on Netflix, then it's going to require an enormous effort to skip that and simply go to bed. And do that without staring at his cell phone for an hour, too, because that effectively sabotages his night's sleep. Google it!

Harry's wife is still going to want to have him on the sofa, otherwise she'll be on her own in front of the TV. That's *her* choice. *Her* habit.

Good habits can be difficult to build, but they are easy to live with.

Bad habits are easy to create, but difficult to live with.

What Is a Bad Habit?

A bad habit is something you do that goes against your larger goals in life. This is important, because it means that whether a habit is bad or good depends entirely on the person.

If you drink energy drinks by the bucketful, but your goal is to be best at *Fortnite*, then it doesn't make any difference. If, on the other hand, your goal is to be slim, then the energy drinks are not going to help you.

If you usually work late in the evenings, that's a good habit if your goal is to boost your career and move up in the company. But if your goal is to spend more time with your kids, then overtime is a coup de grâce.

If your goal is to save enough money for a down payment on a house, then it's a good idea to put aside some money every month. If you regularly empty your bank account thanks to your shopping habit, then there won't be any house. But that won't make any difference if your goal is to build muscle.

Your Goal Is the Deciding Factor

You need to focus on your goal. Any habit that prevents you from reaching your goal is a bad habit.

Example: Your goal is to fit into your wedding suit on May 1, 2022. You should go downstairs and pedal away on your exercise bike for sixty minutes every morning before you eat breakfast. Which means that watching yet another episode of *The Big Bang Theory* at eleven o'clock the night before is a very bad habit. Why? You don't put on weight from watching TV. That's true, of course. But if you stay up too late in the evening, then you're not going to manage to climb out of bed in the morning.

Here's another example: You want to become the boss of your department within the year. You should focus on your primary work responsibilities and attend all the leadership courses you can find. Also, during the year you intend to read at least ten books about leadership. What does this mean? That whenever you waste time on the wrong things during work hours or listen to podcasts on other subjects—regardless of how fascinating they are—instead of reading those books, it's a bad habit.

Or another: You've made it clear to your family that you need to stop wasting money because it's difficult to cover all your expenses. You and your partner are completely agreed about this (but perhaps not your teenagers). It's essential that you pay down your debts faster rather than continue to spend at the same pace. When your partner signs up for an upgraded cell phone account or even more TV channels . . . and you, also stuck in your old ways, don't protest, then your behavior is an extremely bad habit. You need to establish another way of reacting.

This isn't easy, but even small things are important if you want to start a new life.

7. He Surrounded Himself with the Wrong People

Everybody loves a winner!

That's bullshit. Everybody definitely doesn't love a winner.

Some will love him or her, sure, but many more will want that person to fall from the pedestal, never to be seen again! In her book, brain researcher Dr. Katarina Gospic describes this phenomenon perfectly.

Again, it's about survival. But survival forty thousand years ago was, as I mentioned earlier, something different from what it is today. If we wanted to survive, it could be valuable to spread distrust of the strongest member in the group. It could potentially strengthen our own status. If, for example, a popular person falls into disgrace, the collective is often quite ready to drag the former hero through the mud.

Why?

Well, if we diminish the person we previously worshipped, then we can shine a bit more. Perhaps we might become the star ourselves? The more we shine in relation to others in our social setting, the more we increase our chance of survival.

"That's why we like it when stars fall," writes Gospic.

We feel smug when things go poorly for somebody else. The most extreme form of this eternal competition and comparison is extremely unpleasant.

With weak self-esteem, you risk being tempted to diminish

somebody else to make yourself seem bigger. It feels good, and it does actually work. For a while. Then the novelty fades, and you need to think up new nasty things to make yourself feel superior.

I don't really know what the solution to this pattern is, except that the more self-esteem you have, the less the rivalry between individuals. So, in simple terms, we need to build up everybody's self-confidence so that they don't feel threatened. The path to get there might be a difficult one.

The people around you aren't necessarily on your side. Some of your seemingly strongest supporters dream of kicking you down again.

So you need to surround yourself with the right people. Before you rely on your gut feeling and start thinking that there aren't any "wrong people," I want you to hear me out. Okay?

To Succeed, You Need to Surround Yourself with the Right People

The wrong people will pull you down quicker than the right people will be able to lift you up.

If you've found an important *why;* if you've succeeded in formulating a clear and exciting goal; if you've prepared a plan and broken everything down into manageable steps; if you've learned what persistence means; and if you're in the process of building new, better habits that will take you to your goal—people are still going to tell you that you are doing everything totally wrong.

Unhelpful people immediately compare themselves with you. If you do something that is a bit too good and a bit too ambitious, they'll appear less successful. It's best for another person's self-image to persuade you to abstain.

But Who Are the Wrong People?

Living in a context where you're surrounded by the wrong people can be so toxic that you won't be able to achieve anything at all.

Envy, jealousy, laziness, comfort, ignorance, unwillingness to listen, their own failures . . .

You remember what it was like in Laterville. That's where these people mainly live, the people who don't see success as something important and worth striving for. They would rather watch soap operas and laugh at some fictional characters than go to a symposium and be inspired by new ideas and ways of thinking. The wrong people are the type of friends who only see risks in every opportunity and immediately ask you to sit down and stop rocking the boat.

The wrong people are those who are perennially negative and look for faults in others.

The wrong people live for drama.

The wrong people are like shadows that disappear as soon as the sun stops shining on you.

But the wrong people are also those who effusively praise everything you do and never, ever give you any constructive feedback. That is also a form of deception.

The wrong people are those who regularly say one thing but do another.

The wrong people stubbornly maintain that you need at least a PhD if you're going to accomplish anything at all. The wrong people confuse education with intelligence. It's perfectly possible to have a shiny college degree (or several) and still be a blockhead.

The wrong people talk about you behind your back. Listen to what they say about your shared acquaintances. If they talk badly about your other friends in front of you, then you can be pretty sure they're doing the same thing to you with someone else.

The wrong people pay lip service. They do the right thing only when somebody is watching. But wrong is wrong, even if nobody sees you. Just like right is right even if nobody sees. Right is right even if nobody does it. And wrong is wrong even if everyone does it.

They're going to drag you down and poison your air quicker than one can say schadenfreude.

Was Harry Surrounded by the Right People?

What support did Harry have from those around him? Did his family support him? His wife was hardly going to say that it would be better if he stayed in bad shape. She would certainly have said that getting into good shape sounded like a great idea. But then what?

If she still wants to drink wine and eat sweets in front of the TV in the evening—what are his chances of breaking this habit? If she mentions that his alarm clock, which rings at five o'clock every morning, disturbs her because *she*, of course, isn't going to get up at that ungodly hour of the day—what will that do to his motivation to crawl out of bed? If she complains that he leaves sweaty clothes lying around, or insinuates that, wow, there are certainly lots of women who go to his gym—how is that going to affect his desire to work out?

What about Harry's friends at work? That gang that still drinks gallons of beer every Friday and Saturday night as if their lives depend on it, who smoke and eat a pizza for lunch—what kind of support is he getting from them? After all, they're going to be frustrated if he—against all odds—succeeds with his ambitions to get into shape. Many of them simply want him to fail. If he succeeds, they'll be forced to see themselves in a completely new—worse—light. So what do they do? They pull him down.

Come on, Harry, man, just one beer. You're no fun.

Surrounding yourself with wrong people is like breathing poisoned air. It only leads to new setbacks.

8. He Drifted . . .

The most subtle difficulty that Harry found himself in, in this series of blunders, was that he simply drifted away from his path. He probably wasn't even aware of the fact that he gradually fell off the wagon. For various reasons, he lost his focus, started easing up on his good intentions, didn't get up at the crack of dawn, started taking a bit of cream in his coffee again, ate fistfuls of peanuts here and there, and so on. Bit by bit, he stepped off the straight and narrow and fell back into his usual behavior.

Sometimes everything is just how it should be. You know why you decided to do a certain task. You've set a sensible goal. The plan is realistic and sound. All the right components are there. You're aware of your bad habits and have actively started to exchange them for new, better habits, in terms of your health, career, relationships, money, home, or whatever. The negative heckler types among your circle of friends have been exchanged for enthusiastic supporters.

And nevertheless . . . you wake up a year later in a completely different place than you'd intended. Oops, how did that happen?

This can happen for a lot of reasons, but based on my own experiences, somewhere along the path you might encounter a distraction that puts you off your intended course.

It can be the tiniest thing that steals your focus—a meeting, a trip, a friend, new demands on your time, some other problem, a conflict at home, a crisis in your immediate vicinity. Or nothing special at all.

You don't even notice it. It just happens. Your focus slips away.

And everything returns to what it was like before.

There is a well-known trick—you might have seen it before—but when you interlock your fingers together (i.e., interlace your fingers as in prayer), either your left or your right thumb comes out on top. That's how your hands settle, and that's what feels right. If you now open your hands and adjust your grip so that the other thumb ends up on top—how does that feel?

Test it yourself.

You'll discover that it feels weird. *Wrong*. It isn't really you.

Now go back to the "right" grip.

What do you notice now? Oh, much better!

Precisely. It's more comfortable like this.

And herein lies the danger. For various reasons we tend to strive for comfort. And we don't even notice when our ancient instincts pull us back to the old, established ways. It just happens.

There are several ways to avoid this, but it can be really tricky. It's so unbelievably subtle. First of all, you need to see it. Then you can think up a solution.

The reason Harry fell back into his usual pattern was probably a combination of several factors, but it ended the same way. One of the major issues was that he simply drifted off . . . to Laterville.

SUMMARY

It's obviously impossible for me to know how many of these obstacles you recognize in yourself. Perhaps you've tried something similar to what Harry did, and actually succeeded. Or you got further than him, and yet still ended up on the rocks. But what I want to emphasize is that it isn't just one thing that prevents us from reaching our goals. It's several factors that work together, and that's why it's deceptive when you try to understand what went wrong.

It's simplistic to bring out the usual list of defense mechanisms and rationalizations.

- It was Steven's fault for not supporting me.
- It was that sprain in my right ankle that did it.
- If it hadn't been for all that overtime I had to do last fall, it would have worked out.

It's rarely that simple.

The fictive Harry didn't lack the willpower to come to terms with his life. He understood that a change was necessary. What he lacked was insight about how difficult it is to change yourself.

It's about starting in the right place. Starting with *why*. That's where you need to begin to avoid being pulled down into a swamp of poor self-confidence, disappointment, and, in the worst case, self-pity.

Ten years ago, the American author, lecturer, and philosopher Simon Sinek made a name for himself across the world with his book *Start with Why*. He was later accused of simply repackaging old information. But I think that completely misses the point. It makes no difference whatsoever if we've already been told what we need to do in order to change. If we don't do it, if we haven't done it, then we need to hear it again. And again.

But Simon Sinek was completely right. Important change rarely occurs without having a really good reason behind it. Without a powerful reason, it simply won't happen.

Now it's time for you to take in that message and find your *why*.

19

Adapt or Go (Extinct)

If you really want to avoid setbacks and obstacles in your life, you will have to accept change. Before we deal with concrete solutions, I want you to get accustomed to the idea that if you want new or different results, you are going to have to change some aspect of your approach.

Things weren't always better back in the day; a lot of things were simpler. The measure of success wasn't complicated. Work hard, play by the rules of the game, keep your head down, don't ask too many questions, follow the leader, and become the expert nobody can survive without. Stay where you are.

But the building blocks of success have changed: work hard, break all the rules, keep your chin up because optimists always win. Question everything. You can lead yourself. Take initiative.

What's the measure of success?

Interesting question. These days, nothing is certain anymore. Nevertheless, expectations are higher than ever. When I asked an old acquaintance, in the middle of her career, for her opinion, she explained that she works as hard as she can, while at the same time doing all she can *to look as if she's hardly working at all*. Sure, she asks questions, but she doesn't really expect anybody to have any answers.

We can't influence most of what happens around us. That doesn't, of course, prevent us from being shocked by misery, injustice, or violence. But sometimes you don't have any choice. You're simply obliged to accept that the world looks the way it does. And adapt to that reality. That's part of taking responsibility. Observe what's happening around you, but don't get stuck in it.

There are different theories about what creates success. They range from the idea that you need ten thousand hours to master something, to the thought that you simply need to work harder than everybody else. Maybe it's the ability to think positively or the ability to control your emotions.

All of that is probably important, and I wouldn't disregard any of these skills, but as I've said earlier, I suspect that people have varying abilities to handle setbacks when they arise.

Which brings to mind an interesting theory.

The ability to adapt.

Everything changes all the time. Darwin talked about natural selection, or as he also expressed it: survival of the fittest.

A lot of people have interpreted Darwin as meaning that the strongest survive, but that isn't quite correct. It's about the ability to survive in your particular environment. There were bacteria back in the days of the dinosaurs. They adapted; the dinosaurs did not. Bacteria have even adapted to our very best antibiotics; they seem to have an ability to mutate and adapt endlessly.

And a lot of really successful people have the same ability. They can see the same situation that everyone else sees, but nevertheless respond in a completely different way than everyone else. That's an example of adaptation.

There are so many examples of companies and organizations that refused to adapt and are now extinct, that it's pointless to list them all. So I'm not going to even mention Kodak.

In modern times, there are lots of examples of the exact opposite: companies that actually have adapted—and survived. And not just survived, but prospered more than ever.

I was astonished when I heard that Netflix began its business by mailing DVDs to people's mailboxes. Then they saw what was happening in the tech world, did their homework, and adapted. I think you could call Netflix a fairly successful company.

What does it look like for you and me? Have we chosen to adapt? It's an active choice. When was the last time you had to adapt to a situation that was the last thing you wanted?

Every time you move to a new "environment" you need to adapt. All of us have moved environments, and we need to learn to adapt to new situations. We have the ability. But how do we use it?

ACCEPT THAT THIS IS HOW THINGS WORK

There is an enormous difference between accepting the possibility of something and living in fear of it. We could suddenly find ourselves at war. We are privileged to live in a part of the world where that hasn't been the case for many years, but it's still a possibility. But despite knowing this to be true, most of you haven't gone out in the last fifty years and built a bomb shelter in your yard or sat up at night keeping a lookout for airplanes.

If you mess things up at work and risk hearing some sharp words from your boss, you know that the risk of being reprimanded decreases when you do better work. So you do the best you can, deliver the best you're capable of—but you don't sit there and worry about the possibility that your boss might be in a bad mood that might result in you bearing the brunt of her annoyance.

You do the best you can, then you move on. You adapt as best you can. When the time comes, you'll find out whether it worked or not. If it didn't work, then you need to adapt further. And move on. But you always need to look at the results and let them determine whether you're on the right path or not.

Because results do not lie.

If you've lost your keys in the dark, it doesn't matter how long you look for them. However much you crawl around in the gravel, you won't find them. More of the same doesn't work.

If you want to win over a client from your most successful competitor but the client isn't impressed by your proposal, then you'll have to try something else. More of the same doesn't work.

If you want to lose weight, and your morning walks don't have any effect, then you need to try something else in your exercise and training routine. More of the same doesn't work.

If your children refuse to do their chores, then you'll have to seriously think again whether your chore chart with stickers is really motivating them. Try new methods. More of the same isn't going to work.

It's always a bit of risk to use yourself as an example, but I'll stick my neck out again. As I've said before, I wrote for twenty years without being published. So the question is: Is that really a success story? Well, it depends on how you look at it. I wrote a bloody horror manuscript in 1991 and sent it out as soon as I finished it. No revision, no editing, nothing. I was surprised and a bit offended that nobody wanted to publish the masterpiece. If I'd continued to do the same thing, I still wouldn't have had any books published. But I changed my strategy, changed my style, content, genre, got some help, and practiced lots of different skills. And now you're holding my tenth book in your hand.

WHAT ADAPTATION IS REQUIRED TO WRITE A BOOK?

Writing a book is a surprisingly good metaphor. It's a difficult project. You have to put in at least one thousand hours per book and do it without being paid. And that demands an almost inhuman degree of adaptation.

Deciding to write a book that might take six months of work without knowing if you're even going to get it published . . . that's a crazy project. No reasonably normal person should take it on.

Authors who have sold millions of books have no guarantees of anything. Nobody knows whether the next book is going to take off. Not the author, not the editor or publisher, not the marketing people, not the readers. Nobody knows.

Writing a book gives you no guarantees. The entire work is a gamble, pure and simple. And yet there are thousands of crazy people like me who just can't stop themselves.

For all of us, it starts with a *why*. Writers *want* something. We don't all want the same thing, but we want *something*.

HOW A BOOK ACTUALLY COMES INTO BEING

First you have to have an idea. Then you need to develop that idea and try to write it down so that it becomes comprehensible, at least to you. If you can convince others that the idea is going to work, even better.

Then you'll have to set aside sufficient time (one thousand hours is probably not enough) so you can work on the project. On top of all the normal things you must always do. Most authors have a day job, too.

Then you start writing.

And then you should keep on writing. And you don't know if you'll get anything for doing it.

This demands enormous adaptation while at the same time you make sure that the rest of your life is functioning properly.

ADAPTATION IS THE KEY

Once you get started, you need to keep up the pace so that your self-confidence doesn't have time to completely erode. More than once, you're going to question your own ability. If you aren't accustomed to working with mental brakes demanding that you stop every second, then you'll be forced to adapt to this new frame of mind. And when you've eventually written the whole book, it will be time to rewrite it. Everyone has a different process, and only a handful of rare people can hand over the first version of the manuscript to their publisher and say, *Here you go. It's finished now.*

No, no, no. Even the best authors are obliged to rework their manuscripts many, many times.

Then your manuscript can be sent to a publishing house, which, hopefully, will accept it. I don't know what percentage of books sent to publishers are accepted, but it's some depressingly small fraction of a fraction of 1 percent.

The publishing house will then want to make more edits and changes. Now we're really talking about having to adapt. However good you think your book is, they'll want to change it. And all you can do is hang on. All my books have been revised several times, even well after the point when I considered them to be perfect! But in every case, they've become a great deal better once the professionals have had their say. You just have to get used to it.

Then it starts again.

A new round of editing. One, two, three, four, five times.

And still none of the people involved really know whether there is a guaranteed market for your book. In the 1980s, people said that you just had to "accept the situation." I heard that so often that I started to detest the phrase.

So instead I say, adapt. That's how it works.

AM I JUST TRYING TO GET RID OF FUTURE COMPETITION?

Absolutely not. If you have a good idea—then go ahead! Go for it! You can write a book, too. That's what I did, and it's been a fantastic experience. But my point is this: trying to do everything right away is not going to work. You need to accept that it's an enormous project that you have to approach step-by-step. What you can do is sit down and sketch out your idea. Then start jotting down whatever comes into your head. And while you're on this journey, you'll discover loads of things you didn't have a clue about. As you learn, you'll have no choice but to adapt.

Now imagine that along with your book project, which still requires a thousand hours of your life, you're going to be taking a leadership course, and you'll be putting in a few extra hours at work to ensure your career stays on track, and that you're also going to transform your body from head to toe. All at the same time.

No, no, no.

Remember Harry. He tried to do everything at once. Working out at the gym and trail running. Changing his daily schedule. Overhauling his diet. Giving up alcohol.

It's too much. Think of this as another form of adaptation. You need to adapt your life to move the focus from many different things to pursuing a single important dream, whatever it may be.

Time is the limiting factor you need to consider. Everything that is worth doing is going to take time. There are no shortcuts.

But use your time well. Make it your friend. It isn't too late.

Henry Ford started the Ford Motor Company when he was forty-six years old. The rest is history.

Small steps are the way forward. You don't need to turn your whole life upside down. You don't need to revolutionize the world. You can get where you want to go with very small changes. But how?

20

How Do Your Colors Affect Your Ability to Adapt?

Your color(s) definitely influence your ability to adapt successfully. To understand how your behavior is affected, you first need to understand the strengths and, even more importantly, the weaknesses of your profile. All behavioral profiles have their strengths and weaknesses. The strengths are, of course, more fun to talk about, and they'll get you started on your way. But not all the way. Later on in this book, I discuss how we can't become successful by building only on our strengths. We also need to be aware of our weaknesses, and that's where the most adaptation is required.

Let's turn it all around. How does each color need to adapt in order to achieve success and reduce unnecessary friction around them?

THE STRENGTHS AND WEAKNESSES OF RED BEHAVIOR

Red individuals might not love change, but they accept it and push through as long as the change leads to results. They are fast movers. Thought and action are almost the same thing. They'll move forward efficiently and rapidly, however tough it looks. They're goal-oriented and really do love to win. They're often competitive people.

Another one of their obvious advantages is that they're task-oriented. Why is that helpful? Well, they often manage to put their own feelings to the side in tough situations. They look at the actual issue and try to find a solution to the problem in front of them. The fact that they're not primarily relationship-oriented makes it simpler for them to appraise a person's virtues, instead of only considering (like many people do) who they are as individuals.

All of this is positive. It's best for the Reds to continue down this road. But these strengths have a flip side, too, and there are failings in Red behavior.

The greatest problem is also their greatest strength. The tireless Red drive is a headache for many of the people around them. They're seen as aggressive because they'll look virtually anybody in the eye and aren't afraid of raising their voices if they want to get their own way. As a result, Reds can step on people's toes and make enemies. They might not always care about that—they're not relationship-oriented, after all—but it does become a problem when they need help.

In the heat of the battle, Reds often forget that they can never achieve their goals entirely on their own. Nobody can succeed by themselves. The only way to achieve real and long-term success is to adapt to your surroundings.

How Reds Should Adapt

Reds need to be sensible and slow down the pace a bit. They need to actively avoid behaving too dominantly and authoritatively toward those around them. Since nobody likes to feel controlled, the Reds can learn to back away a little and let go of some things. But, as we've seen before, this is one of the things that the Reds hate most: losing control.

But this is an extremely important adaptation for them to make.

If you have mainly red in your behavioral profile, you don't have to let people walk over you or stop being committed to your work. But you do need to let others have a say. You can't succeed entirely on your own, however much you would like to.

You also need to show that you care about others. Simply asking questions and finding out how people feel is greatly appreciated by almost everyone. Except other Reds, since they think that you've just wasted several valuable seconds on nothing.

You should also be aware that your feeling of urgency sometimes creates a situation we call "fast and wrong." Accept the fact that speed is not everything. That's one of the most important changes you need to focus on: slow down and reflect a bit more.

THE STRENGTHS AND WEAKNESSES OF YELLOW BEHAVIOR

Yellows love change. They're bored with anything they've already done three times. Time to think up something new! The result doesn't matter, because change itself is fun! Does this mean that Yellows are the best at adapting?

There isn't really an answer to that question. Yellows are good at seeing possibilities, at finding new paths, at thinking outside the box. They're rarely limited by tradition or convention. They don't think that things were better before. Rather, their focus lies somewhere far in the future.

They're also graced with creativity. They answer questions that nobody has ever asked and solve problems that nobody has considered. Through their incredible imagination, they have the capability to see the invisible. And they can also explain what they mean in a way that others will appreciate and enjoy. Yellows often speak in metaphors. The pictures and worlds they conjure are amazing, which means that you're excited and want to join them in creating something brilliant.

The flip side of this is that a lot of people perceive exactly the same qualities as dreamlike and frivolous. They talk too much, and when they open their mouths, they haven't thought through what they're going to say. Long soliloquies of unprocessed thoughts pour out of their mouths. Since Yellows often smile, laugh, and joke about everything and everyone, they're not taken seriously. Their tendency to avoid details often leads to an enormous mess. Because they can't keep track of their own work and find it hard to be punctual, they can cause problems both for themselves and for those around them.

Yellows need to realize that they are far too focused on themselves. Their ability to continually place themselves in the center of everything can really get on people's nerves.

How Yellows Should Adapt

What you, as a Yellow, need to do is to sit down and exhale slowly. Put your cell phone down, and put on your thinking cap. Look around you and notice the fact that there are lots and lots of other people in the world.

If you're the only person talking, then you'll only hear things you already know. But, regrettably, that won't lead to any development or growth. Your tendency to put yourself first is not appreciated by other people. You definitely need to tone things down a bit. You don't have to start wearing gray clothes or take a vow of silence, but you do need to work on your ability to listen. You need to do this very intentionally, because you don't focus on what others say.

You should also realize that however incredible it may seem, other people also have ideas that you'd be smart to consider.

Finally, perhaps the greatest change you need to implement is to start focusing on facts and details. Right now you're far too broad in your assumptions, and you need to make the effort to acquire a more thorough understanding of the situation and the details involved.

THE STRENGTHS AND WEAKNESSES
OF GREEN BEHAVIOR

Greens are often allergic to change. Especially rapid ones. That kind of change is decidedly unpopular. Even if it may lead to results. Greens can find it extremely difficult to adapt in general.

It's not all doom and gloom, however. Green behavior usually includes a friendly and accommodating attitude to most things, as well as to most of the people the Green meets. Like the Yellows, they are relationship-oriented, and they'll often go out of their way to accommodate and agree with those around them. They're generous to others and are actually the best listeners of all four colors. Their genuine interest in their fellow human beings is also reflected in their behavior.

On the whole, Green people are also reliable. They try to do what they've promised, and in general they behave fairly considerately toward their fellow human beings. They don't forget to ask how you're doing, and if things aren't going well, they'll take your suffering to heart.

The flip side of this Green behavior—and what you as a Green need to be aware of—is this aversion to change. Since Greens are governed by emotions more than by rational motivations, it can be particularly difficult for them to adapt.

This can sometimes lead to others perceiving Greens as stubborn. Even if the proof is there in front of you, you're not going to want to change.

Another weakness is your inability to handle conflict. There aren't many people I've met who enjoy conflict, although some probably do, but Greens avoid conflict to an absurd degree.

Greens tend to agree rather than oppose, no matter the situation. If somebody says "Let's go right," the Green will say yes. If someone else says "No, let's go left," then the Green will say yes again. It's easy to see how that's going to go wrong.

How Greens Should Adapt

If you have a lot of green in your profile, then you probably already know what you need to do in order to adapt to those around you. It's just that you don't want to do it, right? Sometimes you wish that the world worked differently and that you didn't have to continually change yourself.

Try it on a smaller scale. Make some small adjustments, a little bit at a time, and see how you feel. Don't think like a Red or a Yellow, who love to make big, dramatic changes. No. Baby steps. Then you'll feel more in control of the process.

If you always plan your work projects the same way every time, or work with exactly the same coworkers all the time, try changing something in that well-worn methodology. There's a good chance that you'll discover things you like.

Since you're aware of the fact that you can be fairly passive, you should—for your own sake—challenge yourself by climbing out of your comfort zone.

THE STRENGTHS AND WEAKNESSES
OF BLUE BEHAVIOR

Blue people don't have any issue with change, but the change must be based on logic and designed to improve results. The best changes are ones that are backed by comprehensive studies and a clear understanding of the problem being addressed. If there isn't a problem, then there's no need for a solution.

Other people might have a gut feeling that it's time for a change, but Blues will see that as frivolous. Feelings are not a necessity and should not be part of decision-making. We're talking about facts and concrete information. It's a bit of a paradox, but Blues are actually extremely likely to follow new rules and regulations, i.e., to adapt, but only if they understand and accept their utility.

They'd be happy to put together the new guidelines themselves, and they'll follow them to the letter.

The flip side of this is obvious. In situations where their high standards aren't being met, Blue people will block everything and will refuse to play along. They stop listening and continue to do things as usual, following the same familiar path. Whether this path is right or wrong is of less importance. It's the proper route, so they'll follow it off a cliff if they have to.

Unfortunately, people around them will react rather negatively to this. Blues need to learn that they're dependent upon others and that if they see only risks and problems, they will repel certain people. It's not possible to work entirely on your own, isolated from other people. Blues are sometimes obliged to adapt their speed to that of the majority.

How Blues Should Adapt

To adapt to new circumstances and conditions, you need to be well informed. Okay, we get it. But you should remember that a dozen trains have left the station while you've been weighing the merits of sixteen different alternatives. You should, of course, gather information and look for the best options, but you also need to realize that this can go too far. When the people around you tell you to stop digging, then you know it's time to stop digging.

Write down exactly what you need to know. But don't make the list too long. And promise yourself that you will jump into action when the facts are there in front of you. Distance yourself from that sometimes paralyzing passivity you experience that says you should sleep on it one more night, think a little longer. No, no. You need to get your boots on and make some decisions.

Why not work with some Reds and Yellows? You could complement their energy with your focus on detail and create a really winning team.

SUMMARY

If you want to change and adapt, it's a good idea to know exactly where to begin. The greater your self-awareness, the better you will know where you stand—and the greater the likelihood that you really will manage to make the necessary adaptations on your path to success.

Now it's time to move on. Toward the bright future. Are you going to come along?

PART II

Creating Lifelong Success, or How to Win Every Time

. . . .

21

The Three Coworkers

Let me introduce you to Lena, Karin, and Mari. These three women are friends who've known one another quite a long time. They work at the same firm and are in their forties. They've perhaps become rather settled in their ways. But one of them, Lena, by chance, puts together a plan to shake things up and find greater success. Keep an eye on her as you keep reading.

THE FIRST MONTH

Lena has worked at the same company for several years, and she thinks things are beginning to stagnate a bit. She works in sales and is quite a good salesperson. She's been given a ticket to one of those inspirational seminars that's being hosted in town. Karin and Mari will also go to that event.

Have you ever been to this sort of seminar? Lecturers and inspirational self-help coaches try to convince the public that they should aim high and build a brilliant future. They might focus on health or education or leadership or personal development.

A bright, sunshiny person will tell you that if you only do this or that, then your whole life is going to change. Your world will be transformed in ninety days. Except that after ninety days, nothing's happened. So you and I dismiss those stupid ideas, because we must have missed whatever magical thing would have changed our lives.

During the seminar, the three friends all have slightly different reactions to what they're hearing.

Lena feels positive and tries to actively absorb what she hears. She feels she might as well try to learn what she can from the speaker while she's here.

Karin makes some sporadic notes but mainly just listens, because she thinks rather highly of her own memory. She thinks the speaker says a lot of sensible things, but nothing so revolutionary that she couldn't have figured it out by herself.

Mari, on the other hand, doesn't listen at all. She mainly just occupies herself with her cell phone. She doesn't even know why she agreed to go.

How will these different attitudes and reactions affect the friends?

Lena

Lena is influenced by some of the advice from the seminar, and starts to implement it bit by bit. One of the things she does is to start reading inspirational books instead of just watching TV. For half an hour every day, she reads an interesting book and gets new ideas about how she can improve in her career.

She also listened to the health advice she heard during the seminar. She's not in bad shape, but she has put on a few extra pounds that she doesn't really want. So now she starts biking to work on the days when it isn't raining. It's only a few miles, and it gives her some much-needed exercise without taking up too much extra time.

The sales office is on the fifth floor, and instead of using the elevator, she now walks up the stairs. On the food front, she makes just one little adjustment. Instead of coffee and a couple of sandwiches with cheese, she starts making scrambled eggs for breakfast. Not a big deal.

As for her relationship with her partner, she decides that they'll go out on a date every week. They'll go to a restaurant and leave their phones at home. That's all she decides to do differently.

All of this gives Lena so much extra energy that she starts making some extra sales calls every week. She has three more conversations a day than she did before. She goes from ten calls to thirteen calls. Not a huge change.

What do you think of Lena's plan? Does it feel insurmountable? Would you be able to eat a more nutritious breakfast, take your bike to work and climb the stairs, do just a little bit more at work, and devote a couple of hours of "quality time" to your partner every week? Perhaps you could listen to audiobooks while you eat breakfast.

We're not talking about gigantic leaps here. Just small, simple things that you and I could manage if we decided to do them.

Karin

Karin goes on exactly the same as usual after the seminar. She has a vague conversation with her husband about how they ought to take a trip somewhere together and work on their relationship (something one of the lecturers talked about), but they don't decide on anything. They talk about whether they should renew their gym memberships. Nothing else happens. But Karin feels quite satisfied. She doesn't see any real problems with her life.

Mari

Mari . . . hadn't really heard any of what was said that day at the seminar. But she, too, is going to change some of her behavior. We can speculate as to why, but she makes some unfortunate choices every day. She used to go to the gym fairly regularly, but now she's had a busy few weeks at work, so she misses a few workouts.

She takes a handful of toffees from the receptionist's bowl before lunch and another when she goes home. You need something sweet when your blood sugar gets low. Unfortunately, sugar makes you tired, and that affects her job. She starts to make *fewer* sales calls. Instead of an additional three calls, she now makes three fewer than before. She's now down to seven phone calls a day. She busies herself with other, more important activities at the office. She spends some time looking to update her fall wardrobe with a little online shopping. It works. Orders are still coming in at a fair rate, and nobody's fired.

With the sun setting earlier, it's nice to have a glass of wine now and then. Sometimes with dinner on Wednesday, Friday, and Saturday. Not to mention the bottle of wine that stays on the table all Saturday night. She doesn't really know how much wine she and her husband actually drink. But the neighbors haven't complained.

THE SIXTH MONTH

What's interesting is that if you check in on the three friends after six months, you won't notice much difference. Lena, Karin, and Mari are all doing fine.

Lena wonders sometimes. She started to try to improve her life, but she doesn't see any results. So what's the point? Why do all that work? She perseveres, however, and continues to read interesting and inspiring books to help her grow and develop. She sticks to her plan at work, and makes sure she keeps her bike ready to go.

Karin is hardly aware of what's going on. Everything just continues as usual.

Mari might not love her life, but nothing's really changed.

THE TWENTY-FOURTH MONTH

We move farther on in time.

After two years, quite a lot has happened. Let's start with Lena.

Lena

Lena is now very successful. As a result of her daily exercise and her changed diet, she lost ten pounds. That's given her more energy and she started going to work out at the gym. The fact is that Lena, now forty-three years old, has never felt stronger.

She reads at least thirty minutes every day. Which means that she's plowed through more than two hundred books about marketing, leadership, communication, and personal development. She's encountered lots of new ideas, many of which she's tried in her life.

Her more active work has made her Salesperson of the Year, and her performance-based salary has more than doubled. Thanks to the quality time she and her partner now spend together, their relationship has never been better. Life is wonderful. Her CEO mentioned the possibility that she might be able to take over the entire sales department next year when Sarah moves on to another job.

Karin

Karin has continued to go on doing what she's always done. She's generally slightly dissatisfied with life. She thinks it's stressful, she hardly has time to do everything she needs to, her children are dissatisfied, and her husband is his usual self. She's in exactly the same place she was two years earlier, just a bit more bitter than before. She feels uncommitted, frustrated, and blames the whole thing on the government.

Mari

Mari . . . has gone in another direction.

She eats too much at every meal. For a long time nothing happened. But now her clothes don't seem to fit. She can't understand it. She hasn't done anything different, has she?

What Mari doesn't notice is that those big meals make her rather drowsy in the evenings. She doesn't sleep so well either. And waking up in the morning feeling tired makes Mari grumpy.

After a few months, her grumpiness and her tiredness make themselves felt at work. The number of sales contacts she makes every day falls even lower. Her boss wonders what's wrong, which makes Mari completely furious. Now she has a bad relationship with her boss, too.

Mari is often grumpy, tired, and stressed. So when she comes home she treats herself to something tasty as a consolation. Her energy level goes down. When her husband wants her to join him and go out to walk the dog in the evening, she starts to say no. She's too tired. Her husband misses that time with his wife but hasn't really suspected that anything is wrong. But there are other things she doesn't feel like doing anymore. The less they do together, the worse things are between them. The less she does, the more tired, sluggish, and grumpy she becomes.

Mari doesn't like what she sees in the mirror. This hurts her self-confidence even more, and she starts to feel more and more unattractive. Her romantic side is put on hold.

What Mari doesn't realize is that her way of withdrawing makes her husband feel that there's something wrong with him. To avoid being intimate with her husband—she simply hasn't the energy right now—she stays up late and watches meaningless TV shows. Her husband becomes more and more worried. Doesn't she love him anymore?

He becomes more demanding, which makes Mari withdraw even

more. She isolates herself. Her husband starts to protect his own feelings. Instead of trying to get his wife to do things with him, he starts going out more often with the guys.

Mari sees that he gets dressed up on the weekends and disappears to the pub. She's never been jealous, but now she wonders if something is wrong. It's obvious that her husband has something going on. Mari stays at home and eats more, drinks more, and falls into self-pity.

She doesn't connect any of this to the small choices she started making two years earlier. Instead, she starts thinking about her husband. And soon her entire relationship is in danger.

SUMMARY

This is a modern version of the old fairy tale of the hare and the tortoise. Somewhere along the way, we as a society have forgotten the value of hard work—the work ethic—and staying power, and that rewards come to the person who has the patience to wait for them. A lot of people seem to think that the world owes them something. That they have a right to this or that. But it doesn't work like that. You do owe it to yourself to make the best of the life you have.

When a person makes some small positive choices, there will be results. It might take a while, but eventually the reward will come.

When the same person, however, makes some small negative choices, this will often lead to bad consequences. This, too, might take some time.

But, and this is just as important, if you don't make any choices at all and instead simply drift along in life, you'll actually be halting your own growth. This will eventually catch up with you, and you'll start slipping backward. This applies to most of us. We haven't even thought about the choices we've made. We just exist.

But by being a little observant, it's possible to change things completely. All you need to do is see your own power in the situation.

If you could choose, which of the following alternatives would you vote for?

1. You choose your own goals and decide how you'll get there.
2. Other people tell you where you should be, what you should do, and when it should happen.

The choice should be obvious. To see how little changes can have a big impact, we're going to follow Lena through the next four chapters of the book.

22

How *Not* to Achieve Success

So, how do you achieve success? There are many descriptions of what the path looks like. Successful people have some shared characteristics. This isn't about who they are or how they think or how they function. It's about what they do. Success comes from what you do, nothing else.

We've often been told that to get anywhere in life you need to do some combination of the following things:

Work hard.
Be passionate.
Focus on your own strengths.
Practice makes perfect.
Never give up.
Never be satisfied.
Be grateful.

Parents, bosses, performance gurus, and a whole crowd of other people say these kinds of things. Do all that, and joy and affluence will follow. And, sure, it's good advice. It's a hell of a lot better to follow such a plan than to just loll around and hope for a winning lottery ticket.

But we need to ask ourselves this question: Is it good advice, is it *useful* advice? Working hard, for example, sounds like obvious good advice, right? But what if you work really hard . . . at the wrong things? Then where do you end up? Sure, you might make it partway to meeting your goals. But I'm absolutely certain that you know lots of people who work hard, really hard, without getting anywhere at all.

You should be passionate. I think so, too. I like working on stuff that I feel passionate about. But sometimes, on mornings when I get out of bed at three o'clock to get a taxi to the airport to fly to God-knows-where, I feel a shockingly small amount of passion. Mainly irritation, to be honest. I am, however, obliged to do the job anyway.

How about focusing on your strengths? What sort of advice is that? Certain people in my type of work are of the opinion that the easiest way to achieve success is to build on your natural strengths. There are even tools that will measure what your greatest strengths are. And it does sound like a good idea. Why slave away at something that doesn't come at all naturally? Why make everything harder than it has to be?

But think about if for a moment: if you build your life on your innate strengths, it will be a tough battle. You've presumably had the same strengths since you were twelve years old. Which means that at age forty-three you should still be building on what you were good at when you were twelve. I'm not buying that. We need to develop new skills.

And "never be satisfied" is absolutely the worst piece of advice of all. I must have said it myself at least a thousand times. Nowadays, I bite my tongue when I'm about to mutter a similar cliché.

It is okay to be happy, but you should never be satisfied. Then you just end up fat and happy.

It wasn't so long ago that I told my wife over a cup of coffee that

I'd received the highest rating of any lecturer in the past ten years in a certain public forum. A big deal for sure. But, I said, and hid my face behind the cup, it doesn't feel like anything special. I should have been able to get an even better rating.

It's been so drilled into me that I should "never be satisfied" that it's become absurd. In my case, I've developed a kind of distorted perfectionism that probably irritates everyone around me. For the first fifty years of my life on this planet, I've basically never been satisfied with anything I've achieved at all.

Think about it. If you never get to be satisfied, happy, and genuinely pleased with what you have achieved—what the hell is the point of it all?

During my career as a management consultant and leadership coach, I have met many incredibly successful people. Some of them have been superb top performers. And they have been extremely satisfied, happy, and proud of their successes.

They still want to improve their results, work so that their clients are even more satisfied, or reach even further and create more success. But they are also satisfied with what they've achieved. That sort of peak performance gives many people positive energy, rather than terrible performance anxiety.

There's no doubt but that the attitude of never being satisfied has damaged me personally, and many others like me, and turned us into dissatisfied ghosts hunting for better, better, better and more, more, more.

So skip the whole idea of not being satisfied.

Success, performing, getting somewhere—however you want to define it—should be pleasurable. You should celebrate, be joyous and really satisfied.

Then you can create new goals and paint new visions and all of that. But we should never forget to celebrate what we've achieved.

MY OWN SEARCH FOR SUCCESS

Obviously I've been there, too—searching for the path to success. I've read loads of books (we're talking hundreds of books) about how to become successful. In addition, I've spent a small fortune on various types of lectures and seminars, and I've listened to I-don't-know-how-many hours of YouTube videos, inspiring audiocassettes, and (later on) CDs. Probably thousands of hours.

And I really did follow the recipe that everyone—with just a few exceptions—talked about. I worked hard. I searched for and indeed found my passion. Worked with visualizations and affirmations, took Neuro Linguistic Programming tests, and practiced, practiced, practiced. I focused on my strengths until I saw that they were not enough.

And you know what? It worked. A sort of career materialized. Bit by bit I built up a reputation as somebody who got things done. I earned a bit of money and led people forward. For many years, things went along very nicely, in fact. I thought that I had found my place in life.

But then . . . things stopped happening. Everything slowed down, and I suddenly found myself in some sort of mental quicksand. It was as if I'd landed on a plateau with no way off. For years, everything stood still, I was treading water and realized that, if anything, I was moving . . . backward. I was still working hard, sacrificing evenings and weekends—but not getting anywhere. And all of a sudden I found myself far from my own vision. It was painfully frustrating.

Of course, I realized that I'd achieved certain successes—mainly with regard to my career—but I didn't really know why that was. For some reason, I wasn't as disciplined as I should be. Really, I wasn't the best at anything. Nor did I think that I contributed enough to the business. My own values and my own work ethic meant that I was completely smothering myself.

It took me several years to discover that what had gotten me on track—working hard, being passionate, focusing on my strengths, practicing, not giving up, never, ever being satisfied but only grateful—wasn't enough in the longer term.

GETTING STUCK ON A PLATEAU AND NOT GETTING ANYWHERE

I'll be candid and admit that at that time, I simply felt dissatisfied. I slept poorly, nothing was fun, and I was stressed morning to night. *Despite the fact that I was still performing well!*

What I didn't understand until much later was that the old advice was about individual success and short-term results. It meant that I was in the game, absolutely. And it kept me in the game. But it didn't match the potential I knew I had.

I worried that I didn't have a clue how to achieve success and feel good at the same time. I realized that long-term success demanded that I also think in the long term.

When I actively shifted my focus to what we're going to talk about in the next chapter, a whole tangle of knotty problems began to unravel. I, of course, still have a ways to go, since I came to these realizations so late in life.

One of the biggest issues is that when you're not seeing the results you hope for, you tend to start to let go. And you start sliding backward. Which is exactly what ended up happening to me. It felt as if I were on my way back to the same point I'd started from.

The crazy insight was that I didn't even know the definition of "success." The only thing I knew was that I wanted to feel smart and that I wanted others to see me as somebody who mattered. But that was so vague that it didn't help in the slightest.

So I was obliged to start thinking about what we're going to talk about: What is success?

SUMMARY

Not every method works for everyone. What makes one individual successful is not necessarily the same as what makes his or her friend successful. Sometimes you need to sit down and think about what works best for you yourself. However, there are certain things that are universal. And one of the most important is to know how you personally define success. And why it is so important that you be successful.

You need to devote time to thinking through what you want. You can't just listen to what others say or want for themselves. This is a part of your own responsibility toward yourself. Think actively, try something, but if it doesn't work out, change your strategy. Try something else. Don't just keep on treading water. If you end up on a plateau and feel like you're stuck, then it is time to look up. And pick a new direction.

But first, decide what success means to you.

23

How Do I Know If I'm Successful?

Let's leave the difficult world of adversity behind us for a moment and look ahead. Let's talk about success instead. Because the more success you have, the better equipped you will be to meet obstacles when they arise.

There are endless ways to define success, and some of them are—to be honest—rather convoluted and over the top. If we use Microsoft Word's thesaurus to help us and look at a few synonyms for the word "success," we'll see: *achievement, accomplishment, victory, triumph, realization, attainment.*

That's not bad, is it? Except for the fact that we still have no idea what success really means.

WATCH OUT FOR SNOBBERY!

There are people who like to put others in a box. The best example of this is when you're at a dinner and are asked, *What do you do for work?* And depending on how you answer, it can go well—or really badly. And the result depends, of course, on the questioner's opinion of whether you've chosen the right career path.

Not long ago, I was at a wedding party. One man at my table must have been asked that question at least five times during the evening. *What do you work with?* He answered, *I work with something I really love.* None of the questioners reacted exactly positively, despite the man's fluent and appealing description of his profession. Upon hearing his answer, most people tried to get out of the conversation as quickly as they could. (He sold cars, which has never ranked particularly high on the "approved careers list." Which is strange, since most of us buy cars.)

As an example of the opposite behavior, we can take a mother who doesn't care the slightest about what her children achieve in life and loves them unconditionally no matter what. Unfortunately, most people aren't that mother. Instead, lots of people make a direct link between our jobs and how much of their time and attention we deserve. My theory is that this is why we care so much about our jobs and our careers. We need this social acceptance to actually feel successful.

Most likely, our obsession with material things comes from the same motivation. We don't really need the things we acquire, but we do sometimes need something to display to others. To put on a show. A fancy car, a luxurious house, the latest cell phone, the snazzy running shoes. It's no coincidence that the logo is on the outside of those shoes. It wouldn't be much use on the inside. So the next time you see somebody driving around in a Ferrari, don't assume that he's a greedy jerk. Think instead that there is somebody who needs a lot of confirmation and love from those around him.

But there is also an interesting connection to our current times. If you listen to prevailing wisdom, you'll often hear that you can become, and do, whatever you want. Anybody can be successful if they work hard enough. We look at successful people such as Bill

Gates and think that it would be really great to be as rich as him. He never even graduated from university. All you need is an idea, a lot of energy, and possibly a garage.

ENVY CAN BE A DRIVING FORCE

Let's be honest. Envy is an important driving force. Even if it doesn't look pretty, it should be quite clear to us that our presumably egalitarian society has cultivated quite a lot of envy. Think about it: If we can all be whatever we want to be and achieve massive success, then it becomes a problem when some of us do and others don't. So we start comparing ourselves with each other.

Strangely enough, we're not, however, envious of Bill Gates. Not really. He's a fabulously rich nerd with so many billions in the bank that the numbers are hard to fathom. You simply can't compare yourself with him. Or why not the king of Sweden? He is also fabulously rich and lives in a very large mansion, but he talks in a rather weird way and, on the whole, is impossible to relate to.

No, the people we compare ourselves with are those who are closer to us. Who are they? They're the people who remind us of ourselves in terms of background, education, sex, and age. And that's why you should never go to a high school reunion.

In today's society we tend to look similar. We wear the same type of clothes, most of us can afford the same gadgets and gizmos to fill our pockets. Most of the people you interact with do, despite everything, have a job. So we look alike on the surface, and yet we aren't really alike. Social equality often hides deep inequality below the surface.

"Self-help" books (even though I don't like that term) are probably partly to blame for this.

If you look at the bookshelves, there are lots of subcategories, but basically there are two kinds of books. Either they say, *You can do it! Everything is possible!* . . .

. . . or there are books about your poor self-esteem, i.e., how you see yourself. And if we're totally honest, the day we stop comparing ourselves to others, our self-esteem will shoot through the roof.

YOU ARE SUCCESSFUL FOR YOUR OWN SAKE

Do what is important to you, and do it for your own sake. Not just so you can show off to others and say, *Look what I did!* Because the moment you do it, you'll be judged and often found wanting. And the people who remind you of yourself will detest your success.

The closer they are to you, the more they are going to dislike you. If they have a similar job, education, and attitude, they are going to be even more irritated by your success. Think about that.

Your biggest fan is somebody you don't know. But your greatest hater is probably somebody you know. Sorry, but that's my experience.

MAKING YOUR WAY UNDER YOUR OWN STEAM

Today, we live in a society that values the right and possibility of achievement for everyone. Personally, I couldn't care less about your background, the color of your skin, or what your last name is. In theory, if you do the right things, then you'll make progress in life regardless of who you are. As we know, the reality of life is far more complex, and inequality and discrimination are undeniable aspects of our society. But it is also undeniable that we enjoy far more social mobility and opportunity than in previous centuries: if you key in the correct combination, the lock will open regardless of what sort of haircut you have or where you live.

And that, in broad terms, defines a meritocracy. You make your way in life on your own merits, not based on what your grandfather did or didn't accomplish. If you work hard, then you deserve to be at the top.

The problem with that picture, however, is that it implies the opposite: if you sit at home and laze about, then you can't blame anyone if you end up at the bottom.

In other words: we are all responsible for our own success.

At one time in the world, the responsibility for our lives rested with God or equivalent higher powers in the form of fate or the universe or the sun, or something else that you couldn't understand. Later on, in some cases, the state took care of us, but nowadays a great deal lies in our own hands.

You're responsible for your own success; it follows that you are also responsible for your own failure if you choose to squander your resources. That's tough. I find it hard to accept. But, nevertheless, it's hard to ignore.

A wise philosopher has said that a society is defined by its ability to take care of the weakest, and that is an important idea. We should never forget it. I believe that society, the state, the government, and other organizations are definitely necessary to ensure that nobody suffers unaided due to a rotten economy, unemployment, physical or mental unhealth, and so on. That is one of the reasons I don't have any objections to paying taxes.

Self-help books and inspirational lectures can be useful here. They can help us envision success, however each and every one of us chooses to define it. How do we define success? And who should have it?

Everybody, if you ask me. Since everyone has a different definition of success, resources will not run out.

WHEN WE CAN ONLY RELY ON OURSELVES

The psychologist Alfred Adler believed that winners and losers can only exist if we accept that life is just one long competition. If we stop competing, then in the end there will only be winners—or losers. The only person you need to compete against is yourself. The person I am today can compete against the person I was yesterday. The person I am tomorrow can compare himself with the person I am today.

With this perspective we can avoid so much stress, and our self-esteem will be strengthened. We can focus on our own development, our own success, our own place in society without having to keep track of what everyone else is doing. Does that sound appealing?

There are ample opportunities for success—if we choose to make use of them.

YOU DECIDE YOURSELF WHAT SUCCESS MEANS FOR YOU

Success is something that each and every one of us needs to define ourselves. We first have to be bold enough to distance ourselves from what everybody else says and create a personal definition of success.

For me, success is *achieving a goal that is worth achieving, while at the same time becoming something worth becoming.* But this is *my* definition. You don't need to agree with my definition, since success is more of a feeling than a result.

We've all heard of extremely successful people who suffer from the deepest inner despair imaginable. Enormous achievements, piles of money in the bank, respect and admiration the world over. But inside themselves, they may be deeply unhappy. A lot of this is because we can't stop comparing ourselves with each other. And there is always somebody who's done it even better. So forget that idea, and concentrate on your own success. That will get you a long way.

To get you started, I want to give you some ideas for your own thinking process. Here are some suggestions to think about. Could these be ways that you personally define success?

HAPPINESS = SUCCESS?

Does that sound good? People are happy when they have everything they want. What more can anyone possibly ask for? It must have been simpler to get what you wanted years ago when there wasn't so much to get. Nowadays—and now we're back to where we were a moment ago—everyone else has more than I have. That's why I'm unhappy.

Researchers exploring the concept of happiness have found three factors that seem to attract extra joy and happiness: money, marriage, and children. If we're well off in those three areas, then we're going to feel successful.

Many people—though not all—would say that happiness means having so much money that you can do whatever you want. Maybe even having so much money that you can afford to be honest with anyone you want. Or "fuck-off money," as it's colloquially termed.

MONEY = HAPPINESS?

Money is hardly the same thing as success or happiness. No, money can't buy you happiness. Poverty, on the other hand, can't buy you anything at all. So next winter try to explain to someone sleeping in the park that money really only creates problems.

But then what's the answer? Does money actually make you *un-happy*? I heard that endlessly when I was growing up. Money doesn't make anybody happy. There was, however, no concrete proof offered to support this statement. So it's probably something we just reiterate because we're used to hearing it. Previous generations often had very different ideas about money.

What's funny is that there's research that supports the idea that money actually does make us happy. If you don't have anything, then you become happier by gaining money. But that only applies to a certain degree. Having billions doesn't seem to be the happiness guarantee you might think it would be. Perhaps such wealth simply means that you have more to lose.

In a study carried out at Harvard University, researchers found that the happiest Americans earned about $75,000 a year. Above or below that amount people weren't anywhere near as happy. More money doesn't mean happier people. But neither does less.

GETTING MARRIED = HAPPINESS?

Marriage makes people happy. Otherwise they wouldn't get married. And married people are, statistically speaking, happier than unmarried ones. Even though married people are happier than unmarried ones, their level of happiness doesn't remain constant for the rest of their lives. The greatest happiness is enjoyed the years before and directly after the actual marriage ceremony. Then it evens out, and it's not until fifteen years later that the (un)happiness is back on the same level as before. But fifteen good years isn't bad at all.

Oddly, another thing that clocks in at the same level on the happiness-intensity index is . . . divorce. How can that be? Simple: some people have gone and married the wrong person, and they immediately become happier once they've ditched the partner in question.

According to several studies with similar findings, the happiest marriages are those in which you can say that your partner is your best friend. Those marriages seem to be the ones that last longest and make people feel their best. Not a bad definition of success. And then you probably have more than fifteen years to look forward to.

ARE CHILDREN THE KEY TO HAPPINESS?

So what about children? Don't we take it for granted that kids make you happy? There's nothing that can make a person happier than a child, right?

Regrettably, it's not that simple, not at all. Available studies reveal the unfortunate truth that couples *without* children are a great deal happier than couples *with* children. Especially when the children are still living at home. Not to mention couples with small children. They are rarely completely happy.

In a study of one thousand American housewives who reported on their levels of happiness and unhappiness over a long period of time, the following factors were compared: socializing with friends, eating, going shopping, keeping the house nice and clean, or being with their children. While socializing with friends ranked very high on the happiness scale, socializing with your children rated the same level of happiness as cleaning the toilet. It was more fun to go shopping. This particular research study was carried out by a Nobel laureate, so there must be something there.

Of course, this doesn't apply to your kids. Or to mine. And there are, naturally, lots of parameters to take into consideration. For instance, the happiness connected with raising kids varies in different parts of the world.

NOW IT'S YOUR TURN. WHAT IS HAPPINESS FOR YOU?

What would make you really satisfied? Peace of mind? Being able to work your absolute dream job? A house in the Maldives? A billion in the bank? Staying in good health? Married life? The courage to aim for higher goals? Achieving something you've always longed to do? Growing and developing? Daring to face your fears?

A lot of people who are asked what they would do if they were economically independent answer with different variations of . . . nothing. That is, they'd take an unlimited number of sabbaticals or just lie on the sofa at home and take it easy, play video games, or something else on the same theme. But we know that none of those things are going to make most people particularly happy.

Let's leave the happiness research for a while.

You need to have a long think about what happiness looks like for you.

SOME TIPS FOR DEFINING YOUR OWN SUCCESS

Let's be serious. Think about what you're doing and where you are when you *don't want to be somewhere else*. When you're in the right place and do exactly the things you'd like to be doing.

Where are you? What are you doing?

The answer could be, of course, that you're lying in bed and watching a Netflix marathon and that you've never felt better. Absolutely. The only problem is that it's slightly difficult to support yourself that way. (I don't want to ruin the party, but realism is a necessary element here.) Unless your job is to write about TV shows and you can work from home, of course. Then that might be the right thing for you.

But it's probably something else.

If success for you is having $5 million in a savings account, then I think you should go out and look for ways to get hold of such an amount. But if success for you is to put aside a little bit every month, that's just as good. You deserve success as long as you achieve it without hurting others.

WHAT KIND OF TIME FRAME?

Winning the next competition or clinching a big business deal is a short-term goal. That was one of the traps I set for myself many years ago: I didn't think in the long term.

Achieving economic independence for the rest of your life is, for most of us, probably a long-term goal.

But success basically demands continual work. You don't *own* success, but you do *rent* it. And the rent is due every day. Ask any successful person. The second you lean back and declare, *I've arrived,* then the decline will start. So make sure that doesn't affect you too soon in life.

SUMMARY

Define your own picture of success. Decide whether you are looking for a feeling or a visible result.

If it's a feeling, what is that feeling? Happiness? Security? Joy? Energy? Freedom? Influence? Responsibility? Calm? The feeling of doing good? Helping others? To feel you are important? To have power?

Is your vision of success linked to a specific result?

Is it about your physical health? About how you feel mentally? Is it an economic goal? A career goal? Something material? Do you want to work at a nonprofit? How?

I can't say how you should feel or what you should think about these things. All I can tell you is that my definition of success is not the same as yours. But that's okay. What is important is that you know what *you* would describe as success.

And in the end, this is about the simple, but so intangible *feeling good*.

So: *When* do you feel good? *Where* are you then? *What* are you doing? What are you doing when you *no longer wish you were somewhere else*? And *how* can you stay there for as long as possible?

24

Make Your Own List of Successes

In the first half of this book, you made a list of setbacks to help give you a sense of the obstacles you've already encountered in your life. We considered whether the things on this list were really setbacks and what you might have learned from those experiences.

I'm not one to spend a lot of time thinking about the past. It often just opens up old wounds. But there is one other thing we need to take a closer look at—all your previous successes. Because there are definitely a lot of them, even though it might not feel like that.

You have lots of successes in your track record. You might not think about them, but there's an important benefit to listing the things you've been successful at.

Here come those brain researchers again. They say that we're programmed to focus on the negative. We can't help it. But we can balance things out by reminding ourselves about the things that are worth celebrating.

Perhaps you're one of those people who celebrates every little success, but if you're like most people I know, then you'll tend to remember mistakes more clearly than victories. Strong feelings stay with you longer, and failure is associated with stronger emotions than winning is.

The truth is that the majority of us have a lot more successes than defeats in our lives, but if you ask around, it sounds like the opposite. That's a pity. But we're going to fix that.

You don't have to shout from the hilltops that you're a fantastically successful person. But you are going to put together your very own list of triumphs.

Many years ago, I attended a class where the consultant told us to write down—in no particular order—at least thirty successes.

Most of the participants could do this fairly easily, but I suffered a sort of mental block. I couldn't think of anything. Everything I could remember sounded boastful and arrogant. Who wants to look conceited? Then the woman leaned over toward me and said, *Thomas, how did you get here?*

By car, I answered miserably.

Well, then, you passed your driving test, she said, and pointed at the sheet of paper. She had a point. Passing your driving test is actually quite difficult. And that's where the idea for this activity was born. I found that I needed different types of inspiration depending on the situation, so I sorted the successes into slightly different subheadings.

As an example, you can write down small successes you might not even think of as successes. Things like the fact that you haven't been late to work or school a single time in two years.

THE AUTHOR'S OWN LIST

I've done this exercise myself. Years ago, I just jotted everything down on a piece of paper, but nowadays I've sorted the details a little.

My list of successes would look like this:

Successes	Personal	Work-Related
Small	I passed my driving test after only four lessons when I was eighteen.	After fourteen years working in one branch, I stepped out of my comfort zone and switched jobs completely.
Medium	I live in a lovely house in the countryside.	I control my own time 100 percent. I didn't give up my writing even after twenty years of refusals.
Big	I succeeded in persuading a wonderful woman to marry me.	Together with my wife, I run a successful business that shares my message of understanding and better communication.
Fantastic	These days, I care very little about what people think of me.	My books are available in more than 100 countries all over the world and in more than 40 languages.

I write down new things as soon as I think of them. But I also read through the list now and then. Especially when I'm working on something tricky or intimidating and I notice that my self-confidence is shaky.

If I'm going to pitch a big project with lots of zeros in the price tag, then I might pick up the list of work-related successes. Sometimes I look back at my entries over ten years to give myself a little boost. I just looked over that list. It has more than twelve hundred successes. They aren't all fantastic and life-changing, but some certainly are. And there are always more than I think there are.

I'm always surprised when I realize how quickly I forget the good things. Like everyone else, I find it easier to remember the bad things. I don't fight that tendency. I still haven't found a way to actively forget things, but I balance the negative things with my list of successes. And I can attest to the fact that it is incredibly helpful if you want to keep your focus on the future.

WHAT SHOULD YOUR LIST INCLUDE?

Anything at all! Include everything you can remember that was positive. Don't stop writing until you have one hundred things to include on it. Keep it nearby—in your desk drawer, perhaps. Add to it regularly. Every time you do something well, put it on the list.

Why not? Forget the excuses about feeling stupid or not having enough time. I'm not asking you to put the list on a billboard or plaster it on the side of a bus. You can, but you don't have to tell all your friends what you've written on the list. Write it for your own sake. It will make you more confident and remind you that you're actually fairly successful already.

So list all your classes, certificates, exams, driver's licenses, your children, having a good job, raises you've received, that you feel good, that you go to the gym every week. Perhaps you're a good boss, or you have a fantastic partner, or you can sing every line of "Bohemian Rhapsody," or you managed to fix your first car, or you renovated your kitchen all by yourself without using the curtains to hide any missing window trim.

One hundred things.

Do you accept the challenge?

Of course you do. Get to work. Just do it.

SUMMARY

Negative experiences linger in our memories. One way of balancing them is to keep track of the positive things. So start your own list of successes today!

Just like when you watch the news on TV and notice that most of it is terrible, you'll be negatively affected if you don't seek out the positives. I'm not encouraging you to be naïve and pretend that everything is perfect when a genuine crisis is at hand. But all of us need a measure of balance.

Now we're going to look at what you can do to have a lot more things to add to your list.

25

Harry, Part Two: The Solution

I'm sure you remember Harry from earlier in the book. The guy who wanted to get into better shape. He started going to the gym, running in the mornings, dieting, changed his daily routine, stopped drinking beer, and so on. But it didn't work. After six months, he gave up the project and felt worse than before. Despite all his good intentions, ambitious plans, and genuine desire to change, he didn't reach his goal. He looked for success but got lost on the way.

Why? Let's quite briefly recall what went wrong:

1. He didn't know *why* he was doing all of this.
2. His goal was far too *vague* and *fuzzy*.
3. He took on *far too much* at the same time.
4. The results were initially *invisible*.
5. He lacked *persistence*.
6. He underestimated the difficulty of *breaking old habits*.
7. He *surrounded* himself with the wrong people.
8. He drifted.

As I mentioned earlier, it's rarely any one thing that causes us to mess up. It's far too easy to point at only one thing as the villainous cause of failure, but that also means we risk missing the real problem. And there is almost always more than one.

It was the bad weather. Or there just wasn't enough time. Perhaps it was too boring? Or maybe it was everything, *plus* a few other things?

If you wanted to help coach Harry so that he learns something from this experience, what would you say? We'll simply look at the difficulties one at a time and see what solutions we can find.

1. HE DIDN'T KNOW WHY HE WAS DOING ALL OF THIS

Would Harry have felt successful if he'd managed to get in shape? If he had a conversation with his doctor, who explained he was shortening his life by at least twenty years through his unhealthy lifestyle, would that have been enough to get him to continue with his ambitious program? We can only speculate here. If his wife had said that she dreamed about the man he was twenty years earlier—appealing to his ego—would that have kept him on track? Well, maybe.

On several occasions in this book, we've touched on how important it is to know your own motivation. So how can you find your *why*?

Decide What Needs to Be Fixed

The simplest way to find a *why* is to identify the problem you want to solve. The challenge, however, is not to get stuck on the solution too quickly, because it might be a cul-de-sac. Sometimes you simply need to step back and see the bigger picture. Going to the gym—that's one

solution. But *what* exactly does it solve? Being overweight? Not having enough muscle? General stiffness in your body? Rheumatism?
Social isolation? Boredom?

Regardless of how boring it might seem, you can put together a
short list of things that aren't working in your life. Here are some
examples:

> *I don't get home in time to put my young children to bed.*
> *My mother is sad because I don't get in touch often enough.*
> *I feel stressed as soon as I arrive at work.*
> *My partner and I argue about money every week.*
> *The new car turned out to be way too expensive, and now I*
> *can't sell it without looking like an idiot.*
> *I find it hard to go up the stairs because I've put on so much*
> *weight.*
> *I have a good job, great kids, a good relationship with my part-*
> *ner, but I'm still not happy.*
> *I have a good job, but it feels as if I should do more for others.*
> *I'm envious of some of my acquaintances for their career suc-*
> *cess, and that makes me feel a bit ashamed.*
> *I don't have time to read, which is my favorite hobby.*
> *It is difficult to stop using my cell phone at night, and that*
> *makes me sleep badly. I scroll back and forth between dif-*
> *ferent social media pages, and when it's time to sleep I feel*
> *wired instead of relaxed.*

One of my clients recalled how her husband noticed that she was
happy whenever she went to take their dogs out on a walk, but usually irritated or almost angry when she came back. He tried to understand what was happening: if the dogs had misbehaved, if the
weather was bad, and so on. Until he realized that she got angry
when she walked past the house next door, which was the last house

she passed on her way home. His mother lived in that house, and for several decades they'd had a long, unresolved conflict. The man mentioned this to his wife, and she agreed that his mother's house reminded her of this unpleasant conflict.

Now he knew what the problem was. The conflict with his mother. Short-term solution: walk the dogs on a different route. Long-term solution: raise the problem with his mother and try to find a resolution.

What Problems Are You Struggling With?

What does your problem look like? When do you feel irritated, dissatisfied, exhausted, angry, or generally stressed?

If you know what the problem is, then you also know what you want to achieve. My best tip is to start with something that is feasible. Not because you're going to work miracles by fixing small things, but because it's hard to change yourself and your habits, so you shouldn't go for a total transformation right off the bat.

We can use Harry as a reference here. Let's say that you, too, want to make healthier choices in terms of nutrition, exercise, sleeping, and alcohol habits.

That sounds great, but *why*?

It isn't enough to say, *Well, it's a good idea to live healthily.* Everyone knows that. But we still don't do it. *Why* is it important? What's the *real reason*?

Why do *you* want to be healthier?

Do you not have the energy to play with your kids? Do you sleep badly because you have too much coffee or alcohol before bed? Does the thought of being on the beach in a swimsuit make you panic?

What exactly is the problem you want to solve? It needs to be specific, and the more honest you are with yourself, the stronger your motivation will be.

The Problem with Being out of Money

If we take one of the earlier examples and look for the all-important *why*, it might sound like this:

My partner and I argue about money every week.

What do those arguments lead to? Maybe they make you stressed, or you're in a bad mood, your partner is angry, the kids are frightened, and the whole house is seething with bad vibes. Is that a good enough reason to deal with your finances? Or would you rather bury your head in the sand?

Imagine that you've lived paycheck to paycheck all of your adult life. You haven't given much thought to all this talk about finances and saving. In fact, it's never been a problem. You have had a job, a decent salary, you have been able to support your family in a reasonable way; you and/or they have been able to travel and see the world. Your salary is enough to pay the mortgage for your house, and you're content. But somewhere in your forties you start thinking and look at how much you've set aside after all these years of working life.

The risk is that the balance in your savings account is . . . frighteningly small—if it has anything in it at all. In fact, you're in good company. A lot of people run into problems if a month's salary payment or a pension payment doesn't arrive. Two months' salary? Not at all good. Three? Panic in your wallet.

But why should you save? It's a good idea to connect the behavior to a specific problem you want to solve.

The stress every month when the bills have to be paid. Your partner's wish for vacations that are far too expensive. The size of your shared bank loan. Or maybe your neighbor's new, very expensive car. As I've said, envy is also a driving force.

But it isn't just about health or economy. It could easily be about your career.

Why Not Aim to Get That Fancy Corner Office?

You can take a big step forward in your career if you make an extraordinary effort and work extremely hard for three years. You'll have the chance to be promoted, get a higher salary, greater freedom, power, the possibility to have influence, and so on. But you notice that your boss looks rather worn out. Perhaps you ought to see her example as something of a warning? Better to stay under the radar and avoid too much responsibility. After all, a splashy career isn't right for everybody. And there is no rush, right? You're still young!

There are many misunderstandings here as well. It's not unusual for me to hear the comment, *If only I had a better position and a better salary, then I'd really show them what I'm capable of and put in a lot more effort at work.*

In the real world, unfortunately, it works exactly the opposite. First you do a really good job in your current position, then you might be considered for promotion. And what if this promotion is three years away? Why slave away for something that *might never happen*?

And here we are again: What is your *why*?

Why do you want to make a career?

What would this career give you when all is said and done? Not give to the people around you, but to you yourself. What would you gain from achieving a particular goal?

Some people might answer, *I need a higher salary so that I can take better care of my family.* That's a good and unselfish reason. But it's not enough. You need to dig down to what it would mean to *you* to be able to take care of your family. Your personal gain.

Would your life be magically stress free? Would you have immense personal satisfaction? Would you look like a hero to your immediate family and other relatives? It all boils down to figuring out what makes you feel good; there's your answer. Because in the end, that's what all of us want.

To feel good.

Lena Knew Exactly Why She Did It

At the beginning of this part of the book, we talked about Lena, who had gone to a conference and decided to make something of her life. Of the three friends, she was the one who managed to change her life, so let's look at how she went about it.

When Lena, at home with her partner, Catherine, raised the subject of changing her approach to health, education, and career, they jointly agreed that they had nothing to lose. They lived a good life with steady jobs (and salaries). But they realized that there was the potential for more. So why not try to make some changes based on what Lena just learned at the conference? Catherine saw it as a challenge and gave Lena all the encouragement she could.

What was Lena's *why*?

She had realized her potential was greater than the life she was living. So why not give it a try? She'd gotten the inspiration to push her limits in a way she hadn't done for many years. She discovered that she had become stranded on a sort of plateau in life without ever noticing that her life had stagnated. Her problem was simple. She was bored with her usual work. Everything was fine, but it gave her no energy. And she was frustrated with her health and weight.

Since she was a person who didn't like standing still, she decided to try something new. That became her *why*. And that motivated her.

2. HIS GOAL WAS FAR TOO VAGUE AND FUZZY

Let's say that Harry has figured out what his *why* is. He knows why he wants to start this new healthy lifestyle. So what should his goal be? He needs to have a direction.

Direction is far more important than speed. Many people are on their way nowhere . . . in a hurry. If they'd identified where they were going, then they might have actually gotten where they wanted to go instead of ending up in a ditch.

Just like before, there are different ways of thinking about and creating goals. Goals are a bit like diets: Not everything works for everyone. But every diet works for somebody.

You Shouldn't Have Too Many Goals at the Same Time

In order to avoid setbacks, and create success, you need to take the risk of setting a defined goal. And preferably a fairly tough one. Even though there's a risk that you won't manage to reach it and will be discouraged, you're going to be on the right path.

I've seen sales organizations that set ten, fifteen, or as many as twenty different goals for their salespeople. Activity goals in the form of the number of conversations, number of meetings, number of follow-up calls. But also pure sales goals. If you have twenty-five products and need to meet the goals for each of them . . . well . . .

Hopeless. Nobody can focus on so many things at the same time.

One goal at a time. That's the best method. You can have several goals, but if you aren't used to setting concrete goals and achieving them, I still recommend one at a time.

Financial goals. *That means money.*

Relationship goals. *Family and everyone else.*

Health goals. *Eat nourishing food or meditate.*

Training goals. *Build up your strength.*

Material goals. *Things, cars, houses.*

Career goals. *Be the best in your field, or start your own business.*

Experience goals. *Travel. See new places.*

Ego goals. *Your own personal development.*

Competence goals. *Learn new things.*

Spiritual goals. *Could be anything.*

Does all that make you have a heart attack? It can be hard enough to start drinking water with your meals instead of diet soda. Take all of this with a bit of positive thinking—*you can do it*—and *hallelujah*.

Write this down: Decide what is your most important goal—singular. Write it down on a piece of paper. But just one thing to start with. One.

It doesn't need to be a work-related goal. It doesn't have to be terribly ambitious. But you need to understand the goal and you need to be able to measure it.

Let's say that you aren't satisfied with your weight. You think that you weigh fifteen pounds too much. A reasonable goal would be to lose fifteen pounds.

But that isn't the best option. It's going to make you focus on losing weight, not on maintaining a certain goal, and you will end up creating problems for yourself that you don't need. Instead try setting a goal such as: by _____ month this year, I am going to weigh _____. You want a goal weight, not just weight loss. Just focusing on the weight loss instead of your goal weight can create a block in your thinking. It's easy to start chasing the weight loss itself, instead of focusing on the goal.

This is the only goal you set.

Avoid *simultaneously* starting a German course and learning at least a thousand words in three months. Nor should you renovate your house or have the goal of finishing the new veranda *before* the Fourth of July.

If you also have an economic goal, I would recommend that you wait on that, too. You can start working toward your first million when you've hit your goal weight. Otherwise, there will be too much to keep track of.

If you concentrate on making your goal weight, then you can keep your mental focus there, which increases the likelihood of reaching your goal. And it's important that you *do* reach the goal, because you need that success. It gives you the energy and self-confidence to take you to the next item on your list.

One thing at a time. That's the solution.

Be Specific When You Set Your Goals

Harry wasn't specific. He just wanted to get into better shape. That's why he didn't get anywhere. I'm sure that after two months of training and dieting, he was in better shape than before he started. But was it good-enough shape?

Say that you want a higher salary. Your annual salary discussion is coming up, and you hope to get a bigger slice of the pie this year. You go into your boss's office and tell her you want a higher salary.

Sure, says your boss. *You can have ten dollars more a month.*

Are you satisfied now? No.

So you try again.

Okay, we can talk about it, she says. *How much more?*

If you start stammering and can't answer, then nothing is going to come of it. And you shouldn't ask her how much she's prepared to give you. She might answer: *Nothing.*

What you need to say is: *I want another $250 a month.*

Then the negotiation can go from there, but that's a whole different topic.

If we apply all this to Harry's situation, we could say that what he should have decided was that by the last day of the year, he would weigh _____ pounds and have a body-fat ratio of 15 percent. That concrete goal would have had a much better chance of working.

How Did Lena Create Her Goal?

For Lena, it started as something fun. But as she began to see results—weight loss, insights after reading interesting books, and objectively better sales—the entire process became more exciting. It wasn't until she had experienced the changes that Lena actually set her own goals for what she wanted to achieve. I personally would have done it differently, but as I've pointed out many times—the process is not identical for everyone. Once she and her partner formulated clear goals, things really started to change.

The goals she set up were very concrete:

- Read for 30 minutes every day.
- Cycle to work every day unless it is raining or snowing.
- Take the stairs 100 percent of the time.
- Make three extra sales calls every day.

You can't be more concrete than that. Yes, it's more than one goal, but it worked for her. You need to find your own way.

3. HE TOOK ON FAR TOO MUCH AT THE SAME TIME

Harry did everything at once. This is another problem that is more likely to lead to setbacks rather than success. He changed his diet and drinking habits, added a lot of gym time and intensive training, and changed his daily routine. It was a total makeover. Great ambitions. But it didn't last. That's an important lesson to learn. You need to limit yourself so you can go the distance.

This isn't a book about fitness and health, but Lena had a completely different tactic. Let's compare what she did on the health front.

She Took Completely Manageable Steps

Lena didn't ask the impossible of herself. Even though she'd gone to the gym now and then, after a crazy time at work, she had gotten out of shape. She had gained about fifteen pounds over several years.

However, she only did three things to solve the problem:

- She changed her breakfast from rather unhealthy to healthy.
- She biked to work whenever possible and took the stairs up to the fifth floor year-round.
- She also drank more water throughout the day.

And that was it. No super program with nineteen steps. No weird diets. No gluten-free or juice-only or put-butter-in-your-coffee strangeness. No kick-start, no Weight Watchers or *Biggest Loser*. No gym routines with five hundred exotic exercises for a flatter stomach. Just simple things she knew she could manage.

The solution was very simple: since Lena's partner did the grocery shopping ninety-eight out of ninety-nine times, she was instructed to buy the healthier breakfast foods Lena had committed to.

Step 2 was about biking to work when it didn't rain or snow.

Since Lena already had a bicycle and knew how to ride, all she had to do was pump up the tires and get the bike ready to go in the evening. She had to get some sensible clothes, but since Lena was an adult, she didn't fuss a lot about having to buy the absolutely best (most expensive) windbreaker or a pair of multifunctional bike shoes.

The third step she took was to drink more water. She used to drink a lot of coffee and some fizzy drinks now and then. But now it was going to be just water. She did find that it was difficult to remember to drink enough water, so she set an alarm on her phone to ring once an hour between eight in the morning and eight in the evening. Each time it buzzed, she drank a glass of water.

The Result?

What happened when she made these small changes? Answer: Lena lost a little weight, just over fifteen pounds. Her health improved. She built stronger muscles. Slept better. Had more energy. She was happier, which affected her work and home life. She could do more in a day.

Would it work as well for you or me? We don't know until we try.

Those little activities gave her the energy to do other things, too. She started reading for half an hour every day.

Every week, she and Catherine went to a restaurant and left their cell phones at home.

Anybody could do these things. According to Lena herself, setting these goals was one of the most important decisions she made. She was pleased that she hadn't tried to also add three days at the gym, enroll in two online courses, and cut out television at the same time.

Don't Start Doing Too Much at Once

Start with a few things. Not everything at once. You can't imagine what this will mean for your motivation and self-confidence. Every time you succeed at something, you'll get new motivation to tackle the next thing, and then the next after that. And the next.

Lena's attitude to her work was the same as with her health.

She decided to make three extra sales calls every day. She went from ten calls to thirteen calls. A 30 percent increase might sound like quite a lot, but we're still only talking about *three* calls. Total time for this—less than thirty minutes a day. After two years, her sales increased by more than 200 percent.

To keep her motivation up, she read inspiring books about subjects like marketing, social competence, and communication. Even though she certainly didn't follow all the advice in all the books, she did learn something from every book. That's how it works.

Getting the Job Done

This is how you start: Look at your most important goal, the one you decided to focus on in the previous chapter. Write down this clear, specific goal at the top of a sheet of paper. Then make a list with twenty to-do points, activities that will bring you closer to that particular goal.

Your list might look something like this:

My overall goal in area X (Perhaps: To get my first management position in the next two years)	
Task 1—to achieve my goal	Let the HR department know about my interest in management opportunities.
Task 2	Read ten books about leadership.
Task 3	List my greatest models as leaders.
Task 4	Start acting like a leader now.
Task 5	Go to at least four lectures on leadership.
Task 6	Schedule time to attend a leadership training course.
Task 7	Find a mentor who can show me how management works in real life.
Etc.	Etc.

The first five things will be easy to come up with.

The next five will take a little longer and a bit more thought.

The last ten might be a problem. When you get to number fifteen, you might have a headache. But don't give up until you've come up with twenty steps. Make yourself do it. Then take a little break.

When you're ready—look at your list again. And ask yourself:

Which of all these points will get you to your goal the fastest? If you could only do *one single thing,* which would it be?

When you look at the list, this item will jump out at you. It's going to be obvious what it is. Underline it. Red pen. Three lines.

Now, if you could do one more thing to reach your goal, what would the *second* most important activity be? It's just as likely that this will also be completely obvious.

A final time: What is the *third* most important thing that would help you achieve your goal?

That's it! Now you've got it.

Now you have your *three most important priorities* clearly listed.

Your list might look like this:

My overall career goal: To get my first management position in the next two years	
Task 1	Explain to my boss that this is my new ambition.
Task 2	Attend an in-house leadership course.
Task 3	Identify my strengths and weaknesses in that area.

Write down the goal plus these three activities on a new sheet of paper. Throw the old piece of paper in the trash. Forget all the other steps for the time being. You're never going to do an additional seventeen things. I mean that. Throw it away. This is one of the most important things to do to achieve success. Remember Harry. Don't bite off too much at once.

Your Final List

Now start working on the three most important activities. But only those. These three activities are what you need to really concentrate on. Everything else is unimportant by comparison.

When those three things have been accomplished—add three new activities to a new list. You're going to realize that the first list wasn't quite the solution you thought it was. With your new knowledge and more experience, you now realize that you need to try some other methods. This is also a good example of adaptation.

4. THE RESULTS WERE INITIALLY INVISIBLE

Even very small decisions can, over time, lead to incredible consequences. Both good decisions and bad decisions lead to results in some form. But those results won't always be apparent right away. Time makes everything clearer, whether it be positive or negative.

If you make a bad choice, it will be noticeable in the end. The good news is that if you make a good choice, that will also be noticeable—in the end.

On top of all the other setbacks, Harry saw no results from all his efforts. He could have accepted that results take time and stuck to his plan nevertheless. He started a diet, he did his workouts, he denied himself every imaginable form of pleasure and fleeting happiness, but he still thought that nothing happened. After six months, he was still overweight. In fact, he *put on* weight at first, as often happens. He was sore from all his effort at the gym, he was bored, and he missed the little pleasures he was denying himself.

He needed to accept that you can't lose more than a pound or two a week. Besides, when you go to the gym, you build muscle, which weighs more than fat. We know that. It means that losing weight goes even slower.

But we can look at other examples besides health and fitness. It works in the same way with your finances. It can take a really long time to see results.

What Was the Difference Between Harry and Lena?

This is what's so interesting. The small actions that Lena took gave her fantastic results—in the long term. There wasn't much to see at first. She wrote down her initial (minimal!) progress in a journal. But since she had nothing to lose, she carried on. In two years, she hardly recognized herself anymore. When she bumped into old friends, they were astonished at the change. She was told she looked five years younger than she did two years earlier. If nothing else, that was good for her ego.

How Did Lena Stick to It?

When I told Lena's story earlier, I took a couple of shortcuts. The big difference is that in real life she had serious doubts about herself in the beginning. She knew she was good at her job, and she knew that she was appreciated both as a colleague and as a good mother and wife. But she didn't believe in her own ability to change herself. She thought that the ability to change was out of her reach.

Lena had heard all those inspiring stories about the dyslexic who had written ten books; about the orphan who'd started the world's biggest company in the X area; about the entrepreneur who'd gone into bankruptcy time after time but never given up; about the boy with no arms who now competes in the Olympics. She'd read books full of such glowing stories and she heard even more when she attended that first conference with her friends.

Successes That Irritate

In all honesty, these examples tended to irritate her more than anything else. How could those damned motivational speakers compare her with these superstars? She was just a completely ordinary woman and employee; what possibility was there for her? She couldn't see that these people had once also been just as ordinary as her.

Lena was certain that she wasn't well educated enough to get anywhere. And more school wouldn't help her, anyway, because she probably wasn't smart enough. Besides, with two children and a partner who demanded a lot of her when she was home, she didn't have time. And as if that wasn't enough, she thought she was too old to change anything. She had, after all, just celebrated her birthday— forty years old. In her mind, she was already past her prime.

It was not until Lena bumped into an old friend, a woman from her high school, that the scales started to fall from her eyes. Her friend had taken some courses in programming without really knowing where it might lead. Then she'd practiced her skills. When a better, and better-paid, job turned up, she applied—and got it. Two years later, she started her own business and now had fifty employees. She'd just received an award for Woman Entrepreneur of the Year.

This friend was, to be honest, not especially smart. How was she so successful? Lena wasn't envious. She realized that her friend had worked hard to get where she was. But she couldn't understand how it had even been possible.

And then she realized the truth: it's about choosing to believe that you can do it, and then starting.

And that was exactly what she did.

She changed her diet, her exercise routines, and her client marketing strategy at work.

Lena doesn't have her own business, but she is the boss of her former boss. She runs the most profitable division in her international group, and she already has the highest rating from her staff of all the divisions across the world.

How long did it take for her to go from a good but rather disillusioned salesperson to her current success?

Seven years.

Be patient, which isn't always easy.

5. HE LACKED PERSISTENCE

A lack of "staying power" is often the difference between those who stick to something even when results are slow to appear and those who give up. Our warrior gentleman Harry had the best intentions but met with so many difficulties that he finally gave up.

But others manage to do what Harry failed at. Why is that? It might mean that there wasn't really anything wrong with the plan. Was there something wrong with Harry? History is full of examples of people who climbed up out of ditches so deep they seemed bottomless. Edison and his ten-thousand-light-bulb experiment, and J. K. Rowling, who hardly had food on the table and was met with rejection after rejection before a publisher accepted *Harry Potter*—to name just two.

What did they have that Harry lacked?

Answer: endurance. Lots of it.

Do you have limited endurance? Then don't write a book. Or: write a book. Perhaps you'll surprise yourself and show more endurance than you ever thought you had.

Earlier, I listed some things to keep in mind if you, for example, want to write a book. All (published) authors presumably have a lot of persistence. How do I know? Because it seems to take half an eternity to get from idea to finished product.

It doesn't matter how good the book is in the end, or if you like it. You need determination and persistence to write even a bad book. The simple fact that a book is published by one of the large publishing houses is enough to affirm that a great deal of effort has gone into it.

We authors remind ourselves all the time why we write. And if this *why* is sufficiently strong, it's a bit easier to keep on going. But even with a strong *why*, you need a sort of stubbornness that is sometimes hard to describe in words.

Allow me to use myself as an example.

My File of Fuck-Off Letters

That's right. A whole file full of letters from various publishers who politely, but with upsetting clarity, said no thank you to my manuscripts.

It's over there on the bookshelf by the window. Filled to the rim.

Year after year, sitting and working away, putting in a thousand hours a year on this weird hobby without having the slightest indication that it would ever lead to anything—that's what some people would call madness. I call it determination, perseverance, an immunity to setbacks that is somewhat hard to explain. A degree of defiance and perhaps a measure of pigheadedness.

For me, it did work out in the end. After pestering the publishing industry for twenty years or so, I finally made it through the eye of the needle.

But How Do You Develop Perseverance?

My experience is that perseverance lies in accepting the situation as you encounter it. Understand the fact that you're going to meet with setbacks on the way to success.

For me, it's been helpful to break things down into small parts. Then they aren't such a pain to deal with.

Let's say that you want to do some push-ups. You start with five at a time.

Five? you might be thinking now. *That is not many!*

No, but after a while you can do another five. After a while you can do ten more. After a while you can do another ten.

Now you've done thirty push-ups.

How did you go from five to thirty? It's a miracle.

Breaking down what needs to be done into manageable parts is the key to developing perseverance and not giving up too early. Even if you have an outstanding vision and a detailed plan, you still have to look at the next step and start there.

When it came to writing, I accepted that I could only influence one thing—the quality of the manuscripts I wrote. Everything else was beyond my control. How a manuscript was received, whether the timing was right for the idea I was working on, whether the market needed a male detective-story writer just then—I put all of that to the side.

For me, staying power implies continually reminding yourself of your *why*. It's about keeping your final goal in mind while accepting that you check off partial goal after partial goal on the way there.

Look back at what you've done. Look at everything you've survived in life up to today. Go back to your list of setbacks and your list of successes. You've gone through so much. Praise yourself for it. If you've managed all of that, then you're going to handle a whole lot more. Believe me. You've got it in you, if only you trust yourself.

You simply have to take one more step. And one more. And one more.

Did Lena Have Staying Power?

As we touched on in the previous chapter, Lena had a certain degree of staying power. On the other hand, why didn't she use it until she was in her forties?

This is where Laterville comes into play. Life simply chugged along. The idea of doing something more simply hadn't occurred to her before. She had no *why*. She hadn't made any goals. There was no plan. But once she had these things, it was easy for her to start and to continue along the path she'd plotted out for herself—even though the results were slow in coming. And then a fortunate personality feature appeared: perseverance. Her desire to succeed was apparent in the way she endured even when the results didn't come quickly.

She Made Sure She Had Staying Power

The real boost came when she bumped into that old school friend who'd enjoyed so much success, despite Lena's assumption that the woman wasn't particularly smart. However sad it may sound, a bit of envy isn't bad as a driving force. And that is what made Lena kick into gear. She added more things to her schedule at work, for example. She took on more work tasks, offered her time to her bosses, and did everything she could so that everybody would see that she was ready for more responsibility. The old school friend gave her the motivation to stick with it. Lena wanted to prove that she could be just as successful, which helped her to persevere.

6. HE UNDERESTIMATED THE DIFFICULTY OF BREAKING OLD HABITS

Harry wasn't aware of his own habits. Habits are one of the most important keys to change. You can easily become more aware of your own habits by being observant of your daily behavior. Take time to consider what's a habit and what's an active decision. There's a great deal of research on this, and I strongly recommend that you look at the Further Reading list at the end of this book to find out more.

Depending on which researcher you ask, between 45 percent and 50 percent of everything you do is a habit, be it good or bad. What clothes you put on in the morning, how you drink your coffee, how you drive your car to work, how you start your workday, how you choose which lunch restaurant to go to, how you behave when you see a pile of oven-warm cinnamon buns, how you start your workout at the gym, which TV shows you watch.

But regardless of the exact percentage, an awful lot of what we do is simply because we are on autopilot.

What Is a Bad Habit?

As we said in the first part of the book, a bad habit is anything you do that works against your goals.

If, like Harry, you want to get in shape, then desserts are bad habits. Drinking beer with your meals is a bad habit. Slouching in front of the TV on the couch for hours, instead of pedaling on your exercise bike, is a bad habit.

Always taking your work home with you in the evenings is a bad habit if your family is the priority. It doesn't make any difference if you think you need to finish up some work; if your family is the focus, then overtime is a bad habit. Full stop.

Buying things you don't need, without even thinking about it, is a bad habit. Especially if you have a specific savings target.

How Is a Bad Habit Created?

The solution to bad habits is in fact relatively simple, but it isn't easy. The first thing you need to do to break a bad habit is to realize and accept that that's what it is—a bad habit. Exactly like when you drive home in the evening and really should do an errand on your way back, but before you know it you're already home. Your subconscious steers you home while you're thinking about something else.

If we look at Charles Duhigg's method in his book *The Power of Habit*, we'll find some interesting things. For a habit to become established, three things need to happen—regardless of whether the habit is good or bad:

1. The habit needs a *cue* of some sort. A trigger. Something that sets off the impulse to act in a particular way.
2. Then it needs a *routine* type of action. Something that you do similarly every time. A habit is the repetition of a particular action.
3. And finally comes the *reward*. Something that stimulates you to perform that action again.
4. But, and this is where the danger lies: once this pattern has been repeated a number of times, the habit is established. Then the whole thing gets flipped. You're going to feel a craving for that reward, and go straight to the second point without needing any cue. That is how habits are created.

So how does this work in real life? If you're in the habit of stopping at Starbucks on your way to the office and buying a triple latte with extra everything—for six dollars and 350 calories—but would like to break the habit: Recognize that it is a bad habit. And then choose another route to the office.

When you see the coffee shop—that's the *cue*—where you usually buy this coffee derivative, your autopilot clicks on and you go in and buy your coffee; that's the *routine* type of action. The *reward*, the third step, is when you drink the coffee. It's extremely tasty. You get a dopamine boost and experience short-term satisfaction and happiness.

But after a while, you'll start thinking about that delicious latte with all the toppings, even when you're not driving to work. Now you have a craving, a strong desire for that particular coffee. This is when you leave your desk and nip down to the shop of your own free will. The coffee will still be very tasty. But perhaps not what you need to be guzzling if your goal is to reduce your calorie intake. Or save money, for that matter. A latte every day during a whole year is—$2,190. Or 127,750 calories.

How Do You Break a Bad Habit?

If you look over the three-point activity list you made to help you lose weight, and you don't find any triple lattes with extra everything on them mentioned, then you already know this will not help you meet your goal. If you're sufficiently self-aware, you'll notice that this is an unhelpful routine even before you create a habit.

But you can also use the same approach if you've already established this bad habit. The best thing to do is simply to avoid that particular shop. Before you think, *But there are other coffee shops on my route,* remember that it's going to take a while to establish the same habit in a new place. And now you're aware of it. You won't fall into the trap again.

What About Harry? What Should He Have Done?

If Harry, for example, had always had a beer with his dinner at home, then the first thing he needed to do was to recognize that habit. Then he would have had to work out a solution. It would, of course, have been simplest to stop buying beer to have at the house. That sounds so simple that it's almost silly, but it does make it more difficult to drink beer. Or he could put a note on the fridge door with the message: NO BEER TODAY! He might have realized that what he really craved was a cold drink with bubbles in it. Perhaps some seltzer would have done the trick.

What Lena Did About Her Habits

Lena, too, had trouble establishing her exercise routines since she hadn't exercised that much in recent years. She noticed that it was a problem if she didn't have her gym bag ready and in the right place. She needed a change of clothes and toiletries so she could shower once she arrived at work. It was easy to think of excuses and skip the bike ride. Instead, she started packing her bag the night before and putting it by the front door. When she got into that routine, she created a new habit, which meant that she didn't have to make any active decisions in the morning. If the socks and towels weren't already packed, there was a risk that she'd actively make the wrong decisions during that stressful half hour early in the morning. It's better to establish the habit of packing everything the previous evening. (I know people who even take their gym bag out to their car the night before, since they know that they otherwise might "forget" the bag in the morning. That's insightful.)

Bad Habits Exist in All Areas

Habits can also appear in your relationships with other people. Every time Göran opens his mouth, you prepare to start contradicting him, regardless of what he says. You do it automatically. Or when Sara says something, you're going to agree. Of course, this can be about prejudices concerning different individuals, but a habit is a habit, and your autopilot kicks in faster than you can even get a sentence out.

Observe your habits and write them down. For the ones that you're not satisfied with, also write down an alternative behavior.

For example, it's your custom that every day at 3:00 P.M. you go down to the cafeteria and have a coffee and cake. While you do this, you exchange a bit of gossip with your colleagues. No problem; that might be something you enjoy. If you want to avoid having all that extra sugar, though, set your alarm to 2:55 P.M. and go across to your coworker's desk and start gossiping a bit with him or her.

A Concrete Plan to Break Your Bad Habits

This is what you can do:

To help you achieve your goal, write down the negative effect of the habit, for example: it prevents you from keeping your food budget in check and saving money every month.

If you tend to waste money at restaurants and bars with your friends, next time take your car. You'll save lots of money because you'll have to drink less (and save the cab fare) and you'll wake up well rested the next morning.

To break a bad habit, you need to accept it. Then you need to write it down and clearly write down an alternative behavior or habit you'd like to replace it with. Like I said, simple, but not easy.

My bad habit is . . . (Write down anything that prevents you from reaching your goal, whatever it might be.)	An alternative behavior would be . . . (Write down what you can do instead.)
I always do the grocery shopping spontaneously without knowing what I really need.	I have a list in a prominent position in the kitchen, on which I regularly write down what I need to get at the store. I never put anything in the grocery cart that isn't on my list, no matter what the kids might be begging for that day.

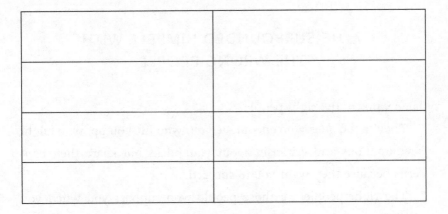

Good Habits—and Bad Ones

When considering a habit, which ones should be considered bad?

Sitting with your cell phone in your hand while you're having dinner might not be a good habit, but if it doesn't affect much, then perhaps it isn't really a bad habit, either. It depends on whether you should be doing something else instead.

If, before every marathon study session you usually play video games for exactly thirty minutes, that's probably not a problem. It could be your way of getting ready. But if, on the other hand, that half an hour becomes three hours every time, then it's a bad habit that could poorly affect your test scores and stop you from starting a promising career.

Just like with everything else, everything does not work for everybody. That's why you need to take a good look at yourself and decide: What is an honest evaluation of your particular case?

To break a bad habit you need to make an active decision. It takes time to establish a new habit. You just have to accept that.

Make it a habit (ha ha) to observe your own behavior. Spend a few minutes every day thinking back over everything you've done. How much did you do as part of your routine, which means habits, and how much did you actively decide to do?

7. HE SURROUNDED HIMSELF WITH THE WRONG PEOPLE

Then who are the right people?

They're the ones who encourage you, who lift you up, who might have opinions and criticism about your ideas but share their concerns because they want you to succeed.

The right people are those people who support you when you have a goal, who understand that you want to grow as a person. They're the ones who don't feel threatened by the fact that you are fully engaged in growing and developing.

The right people are the ones who make you smile when you think about them.

The right people are the ones who accept and embrace change—even when it feels uncomfortable.

The right people are the ones who can admit that they were wrong.

The right people are the ones who have the mental flexibility to change their opinion when they hear a persuasive argument.

Harry didn't really have any support when he started on his health journey. His wife wanted him to watch TV and drink wine. His co-workers thought that he should have a few beers and be one of the guys. Nobody encouraged him. Even if nobody directly persuaded him to continue to live in an unhealthy way, he didn't have any real supporters.

It would have been so helpful if his wife had simply said she was pleased he was getting in better shape because she wanted them to have many more years together. She might even have considered her own less-healthy habits. I don't mean that she needed to suddenly follow Harry's exact health plan, but sometimes it's easier to create change if we help one another.

A gym buddy would have helped as well. Perhaps a coworker who was also looking to lose a few pounds. If there are two of you, your friend can encourage you when you get discouraged.

Everything Is Impossible

For certain people, just about everything is impossible. The first thing they do when they hear an idea is to start looking for faults. Soon enough, they'll have found no fewer than five reasons why it isn't going to work (which is a bit of overkill because one would be enough).

These are the kind of people who would criticize you if you walked on water: they'd just claim that you only did it because you can't swim.

Stop listening to that kind of talk. When people say something is impossible, it means that it's impossible for *them*. Not for you.

If you want to start a business, then you shouldn't listen to your brother who works as a nurse. Or to your friend who has never run a business. The person you should listen to is somebody who has already started several enterprises of his or her own. And preferably has hit a few roadblocks along the way. That's the person with the right experience.

You shouldn't take advice about the world from college professors. They have no idea how the world really works. They can explain theories, not practical reality. And you shouldn't take exercise advice from a couch potato.

Negative people can be exhausting in the long term. Especially the pessimists who claim that they aren't negative, just realistic. But most of what you worry about is never going to happen. That means the optimists are the true realists. Being surrounded by negative people is like breathing poisoned air. You can only inhale so much before it starts affecting you. Negative people affect you mentally. They break your spirit, your desire to move ahead. They point out faults and shortcomings in everything, and when you ask them to stop, they tell you that they're only telling it like it is.

Surround yourself with the right people. Full stop.

What Should You Do with Your Relationships?

Let's say that you have the fantastic goal of starting your own business. Your friends are going to helpfully explain that you don't know anything about the field. Your brothers and sisters are going to call you a reckless risk-taker who doesn't understand that the well-paid, secure job you currently have is much better. Even your own mother is going to tell you to sit down and take it easy instead of working on a Sunday.

I understand that you love your mother, and she certainly loves you, too. She believes in what she is saying and she wishes you well. But her advice won't help you reach your goal.

This is why close relationships are so hard. If you don't have the same vision for the future, you'll end up getting in each other's way.

So What Do You Do?

The short answer is that you thoroughly consider the relationships that don't work.

The first time I heard about a man who cut off contact with his parents, I was shocked. I'd never heard anything so extreme. But when he explained why, I was less judgmental.

His parents were critical of everything he did. They were negative about his education. They questioned his choice of profession. They talked disparagingly of his wife. They didn't like the area where he lived. His mother complained about the way he dressed; his father complained that he drove the wrong type of car. At family dinners, all he heard was that the food wasn't perfect, that there was a base-board missing in the kitchen, and that the children weren't polite enough.

After every encounter with either of them, he had a stomachache for a week. The anxiety, worry, and endless criticism were just too much. Finally, he informed them that he didn't want to have contact with them because all they did was criticize.

That's a really hard choice, and I'm not telling you to break off your relationships. But if a person in your life does nothing but in-troduce negativity and create problems . . . something needs to be done. Act. Discuss the problem with the person concerned. Reduce the amount of time you spend with him or her. Set clearer boundar-ies. But do *something*.

Lena Surrounded Herself with the Right People

Just like having a dedicated gym buddy, it helps if your partner is on board. Lena avoided that potential pitfall. Lena's partner was with her all the way. In terms of other supportive voices, Lena faced dif-ferent challenges. Her own mother was the greatest problem. When she saw that Lena had lost more than fifteen pounds and had actually started running again like she had in school, her mother said in her own way that Lena didn't look healthy. She was looking too thin and pale. Lena said that she'd never felt better in her adult life, but that didn't make any difference. Her mother suggested time after time that she should go to the doctor because of this "sudden" weight loss.

Lena Got Rid of People Who Were Holding Her Back

It wasn't just verbal criticism, Lena's mother brought cakes and sweets every time she visited. She literally filled Lena and Catherine's pantry with unhealthy things. At first, Lena didn't say anything, but after a few months of the silent battle, they finally confronted the issue. Her mother had come by and made dinner for Lena's teenage daughters. The girls had embraced Lena and Catherine's new healthy lifestyle. And what their granny served them, and also expected Lena to eat, was a total catastrophe from a nutritional point of view. Lena and her mother had a terrible fight, and, to be honest, their relationship hasn't been too good since that.

When I met Lena, I asked her how overweight her own mother really was. She thought it was somewhere between forty and sixty pounds. That, of course, was the problem. Lena's mother compared herself to her daughter and didn't like what she saw.

This was Lena's greatest challenge. To be able to live the way she wanted, she was forced to become more distant from her own mother. Lena made her choice and stood by it. They're still in contact today, but it isn't as warm as before. Her mother still can't accept seeing her daughter in good shape and enjoying a brilliant career. She herself had no education and worked in an administrative position her whole life. On the few occasions she still drops by at Lena and Catherine's new, very nice house, she often complains about something. She comments on the fact that Lena sometimes works from home, that she takes classes in the evenings when she should be at home with her daughters. *Can't you just sit down for once?* is one of her mother's favorite comments.

Lena told me that this was her greatest sadness. Her mother couldn't accept that she had grown as a person and had a new perspective on life. But Lena doesn't regret anything. *It's my life and I need to live it the way I want,* she reminds herself.

When I listened to Lena, I realized that this exhausting process also helped motivate her to keep working toward her goals. It helped keep her on track.

8. HE DRIFTED . . .

The last point is perhaps the hardest to see. Harry didn't keep his eyes on the ball. When the results are slow in coming or there are simply no results for a long time, you may not be able put your finger on what's wrong. When other things come into your life and steal your focus, then you begin to drift away from your goal.

Incidentally, often to Laterville.

One Degree Off Course Creates Big Problems

If you don't clearly see the effects of your actions, then the goal you imagined becomes a little hazier every day that passes. It takes so little for everything to go wrong.

If you are going to fly from Miami in the south to New York in the north, and the pilot sets his instruments slightly wrong, let's say just one degree, then you won't end up in New York, but somewhere in the North Atlantic Ocean. Just one degree wrong. That's not much, is it? But the result? Plonk.

In Laterville, things are comfortable. Everything just goes along smoothly. And you don't even notice that all ambitions and goals have simply . . . vanished from the radar. That's when self-awareness and introspection come into the picture.

How did I end up in such bad shape? How could I be totally broke? Why am I facing a divorce? How could Elin get the job instead of me?

You haven't done anything terribly wrong. You simply haven't paid enough attention. It might just have been one tiny degree wrong, and after twenty years you end up in the sea. That's how it happens.

An airplane that is flown manually is actually off course more than it's on course, but it nevertheless usually lands where it should because the pilot is correcting the course all the time. If the plane slips off course by a single degree, the pilot needs to steer back one degree. If the plane goes three degrees off course, the pilot needs to correct the course by three degrees. The pilot has a system for keeping the plane on course.

Your path to long-term success is to acquire a similar system. You need a system to warn you when you're off course and help you with a plan to get you back on track again.

The Magic of the Red X—How to Keep Track of the Tiny Details

Many years ago, I worked at a place where we had a couple of smokers. One day, one of these colleagues—we can call her Lisa—went in to see the boss and said that she wanted to stop smoking and that she wanted to let him know that her mood might be a bit up and down in the next few weeks.

Her boss, of the more hands-on type and always eager to help, immediately took things into his own hands. He gathered all the staff together and announced that Lisa was now going to be much healthier. To really show his support, he hung up a monthly calendar outside her office door where he marked the date with a big, red X.

This X, he solemnly proclaimed to us, *is Lisa's first day as a nonsmoker.*

Then, in front of the group, he got her to promise to put a new X on the calendar outside her door for every day she hadn't smoked.

This approach turned out to be smarter that anyone involved first realized.

Lisa struggled with her nicotine addiction just like anybody else who has tried to quit smoking. But adding a new X to that calendar every day gave her motivation to keep going. The other smoker in the firm did everything he could to get back his smoking buddy, but she persisted. Week after week, month after month, X after X—until going back to her old habit would have been a terrible defeat.

She simply didn't want to break the chain.

We Would Rather Keep What We Have Than Gain Something New

The psychological effect of this is twofold. On one side, it feels good to put an X on a list. It's the same feeling as when you cross out an item on your to-do list after you've done it. It feels good, and that's because of the dopamine kick you get when you give yourself this feedback.

The second effect is described in Nobel laureate Daniel Kahneman's research. He calls it "loss aversion," which refers to the unwillingness to lose something. Changes that make things worse—losing something—have more mental impact that improvements or gains. It's worse to lose than not to win.

The practical effect is interesting. We dislike losing twenty dollars more than we love winning twenty dollars.

If Lisa had gone back to her smoking, she would have lost her struggle and would have wasted months of red Xs. I remember in the break room she said things like, *I've done this for sixty days, so I can't give up now!*

None of us really understood what was happening, but she didn't want to lose the effort she had invested. And she hasn't smoked since that day.

We simply hate losing things, and apparently we've always felt that way. Once upon a time, when we lived on the savanna, loss could mean a direct threat to your life. Not having anything to eat led to death, while having a surfeit of food really made life only a bit more comfortable.

The same applies to marking an X on a calendar. If you've filled a whole month with red X after red X, then you want to keep them. You've worked hard for them, you've earned them. You're going to keep them, goddammit!

How You Can Use the Magic of the Red X

How can you make use of this extremely simple method to keep yourself on course, and not end up in a nice house in Laterville?

Hang up a calendar of your own on the wall. An old-fashioned paper one. Hang it up with the month fully visible so the whole house can see it.

Every time you do the right thing—take a step toward your goal, keep up a good habit, or take steps to break a bad one—put a big red X on that day. Every day you stick to your plan, check it off.

If you're working on breaking a bad habit, then put an X on the calendar when you didn't smoke / drink beer / buy chips / lounge in front of the TV instead of reading a book / put off making that important phone call / or talk over your partner. Or put an X for every positive choice you make—every time you tell your partner you love him or her / stay focused at work / go for a run / get home early enough to tuck the kids into bed.

Because it works both ways.

How long do you need to keep it up? Until the temptation to stop has gone away.

This differs from individual to individual, and naturally it varies depending on what habits you want to create or break. The median is normally around 66 days, so you should stick it out at least that long. But the fact is it can be anywhere between 18 and 254 days . . . so don't be discouraged if it takes a bit of time.

This very simple approach is equivalent to how pilots use a gyroscope to keep a plane on the right course.

Perhaps you have a vague feeling that *it can't be that simple*. That's okay. Sometimes the simple can be difficult. And how do you know that it won't work before you've even tried it?

Regardless of whether your focus is health, relationships, finances, career, education, or something else—tracking your progress will help you stay on course.

What Activities Do You Need to Track?

What habits do you want to establish? This can be just about anything. Go back to the section about breaking bad habits and consider what prevents you from following through on your good intentions.

I'd even go so far as to suggest that you tell your family / friends / work colleagues / boss / neighbors what you're doing. And ask them for active support. Hang up the calendar. Show it to everybody who wants to have a look.

No, it isn't embarrassing. Yes, it's going to be a bit weird at first. But how eager are you to really change? If your family sees that you've put a red X on the calendar every day for two months, they'll help you get back on track if you miss a day. The right people are going to say, *Hang on—shouldn't you be crossing off another day?*

Think of it like a sort of savings. If you set aside $5 a day for sixty-five days, then you won't want to throw $325 into the trash just because you don't want to put in another $5. No, no. You want to keep going. And *you are going to keep going* once you have started this simple system.

When you succeed—give yourself a reward. An appropriate reward—*not* something that is the exact opposite of what you're trying to achieve. For example, if you are trying a six-month period without any alcohol and made it through the first three months, then you should *not* celebrate with a night on the town. But you could buy yourself something really nice.

Lena Didn't Allow Herself to Drift

In Lena's case, her mother (without realizing it) inspired her to continue. The more her mother told her to take things easy, the more
committed Lena became. And this worked for Lena. But she also kept
a record of what she was doing. She had a notebook, and in it she
wrote down:

- the number of sales calls she made every day (thirteen);
- how many stairs she'd climbed every day (the minimum
  requirement was one thousand);
- how many calories she saved every breakfast (the sandwich
  and coffee had 265 more calories than the morning egg, so
  she added 265 calories every day in her notebook);
- how many pages she read every day (the minimum requirement was ten).

It wasn't any harder than that.

And What Were the Results of All of Lena's Activities?

Did Lena's efforts bear fruit? Was it worth all the effort? We only
need to look at her results. Because the results never lie.

Last year she was named Leader of the Year at her company. She
has twelve colleagues who report directly to her, and she's responsible
for a division that consists of more than three hundred people.

Her salary has increased by 600 percent since the day of that seminar.

She's been able to set aside enough savings that her daughters
won't need to take out student loans for college.

She and Catherine don't have a mortgage despite the fact that they
live at an address many would kill for.

Lena lectures a few times a year (that's how I got to know her) about her transformation from being a member of a team to becoming a respected and successful leader. She inspires thousands of men and women every year.

She and Catherine celebrated their tenth anniversary the same day that Lena had her fiftieth birthday.

She can still wear the same dresses she wore in grad school, which amuses her daughters (but not her mother).

However, the father of her daughters has harassed her family, forcing them to move out of Sweden. So, despite all this success, she still struggles with her own setbacks. As I said in the beginning of this book, nobody is immune to difficulties and adversity (which is why Lena is not her real name).

Lena's Advice to Others

Lena's parents taught her to work hard and not boast. That made her modest and means that she might not be the first person you notice when you walk into a room. Her self-confidence is so strong that she rarely opens her mouth to assert herself.

When I asked her what advice she gives to people who want to change their lives, she had two things to say:

The first is that if she can do it, then anyone can. If she can drink water throughout the day, then anyone can. If she can make time to read a book, then everyone can find time to read a book. If she can make three extra sales calls, then so can you. She's not the slightest bit unique.

She quickly learned that she was just as capable as the majority of the people she met. It took her a while to get over her inferiority complex about people who were in higher positions and had fancier educations. Once she had succeeded in liberating herself from her mother's negativity, she experienced new freedom in every part of her life, including her career. Of course, she wishes that her mother had been able to see how good all these changes were, but since her mother refused to see it, Lena made an active choice and created distance between them. She hopes that in the future their relationship will return to what it used to be.

Her second piece of advice is to always *adapt to the circumstances*. For example, she started reading books about marketing, but as her own sales went through the roof, she aimed higher and started to think about the alternatives. She began to think about leadership. When she was offered her first management position, she was already well equipped to lead a team.

When the company offered her a top position in another country, she didn't say, *But I live in Sweden*. She discussed the matter with her family and decided to take the chance and move abroad. She knows that it isn't forever. She can come back. But since her daughters are studying abroad and Catherine works internationally, it really doesn't make any difference.

Lena's final words during our last conversation were as follows:

My greatest asset was that I found it easy to step outside my comfort zone. It was never really a problem once I had realized that life could be so very much more. Nowadays, I actively search for things that I've never done before. And I'm excited about what I'll find. I'm never going to stop. I'm never going to go back to the person I was ten years ago.

SUMMARY

The eight points we've just gone through are crucial in determining whether you will meet your goals. Following them is not a 100 percent guarantee of success or security, though. They don't promise that you'll end up king of the castle if you follow them to the letter.

But if you follow them long enough, your chances of success will be far, far higher.

You won't know for sure until you have tried them, right?

Now it's time for more good news.

26

Attitude

A transformational journey like this will not happen by itself. It requires long-term effort to create lasting change. And your attitude to that change can be what decides whether or not you will succeed.

Your view of yourself and your own potential has a huge impact on the outcome of your efforts. Attitude, it's often said, is the key factor. Your attitude toward everything you see and experience. Your attitude toward what you do, your attitude toward others, your attitude toward yourself, your attitude toward the world around you.

If your attitude toward reading this book is open and you're willing to take in the content, you'll have a good tool to help you move forward in your life. Your chance of achieving true change increases.

But if your attitude is just to look for things to criticize, then you won't learn anything at all. You'll stay exactly where you were.

If your attitude toward your coworkers is that they're lazy idiots, they're not going to be keen to help you when you need them. But if your attitude is that they're brilliant and helpful, there's a much higher likelihood that you'll work well together.

If your attitude toward your partner is that he or she is the person you want to live with until you die, then you're going to find energy to stick with him or her even when things are rough. But if your attitude is that your partner doesn't have a clue, then you're not going to make it very long.

CHANGING YOUR ATTITUDE CAN BE COMPLICATED AND TRICKY

Attitudes are often based on things we've heard, seen, or experienced. We often embrace our parents' attitudes. Sometimes that's good; sometimes it's bad.

A close relative of mine, for example, is a person who casually states that everyone living on a particular street is a villain and a thief. Why? Because the houses in that part of town are so expensive that the owners must be involved in all sorts of shady dealings. When another relative, neither a villain nor a thief, moved to that neighborhood, the relationship essentially ended. The first relative stuck firmly to his attitude that if you lived on that street, you were an underhanded Scrooge. For years the unfortunate relative who had simply bought a nice house dealt with lies and idiotic comments.

If you're going to reach your most important goal and live the life you want to live, then you need to be aware of your attitude. It isn't about standing on a stage and shouting *Yes, I can!* Sure, do that if you want to. Maybe you'll make some new friends that way.

No. What I mean is that you need to listen to what you say to *yourself.*

You need to make the active choice to believe that you absolutely can follow Harry and Lena's eight points and reach your goals. You need to choose to believe that you have what it takes. You simply need to trust in yourself and your own ability.

As I've shown, there are no secret magic formulas to achieve success. There's no magic here at all. You don't need to meditate or visualize. You don't have to have a personal coach who costs the world. You don't need to write down your goals in a book every night and put them under your pillow. The methods I've described here are extremely simple. They're well tested and they are available for anyone to use.

Anyone who puts in the right combination will be able to open the lock. Even you. If you use the code, that is. You don't need a coach, a special education, or a ton of money. What you need is the right attitude and the conviction that you can manage it just as well as anyone else.

Regardless of whether you choose to call it self-awareness, self-confidence, self-assurance, or whatever, it means a deeply anchored belief that you have what is necessary.

CHANGING YOUR ATTITUDE IS A CHOICE

Believing in yourself is a choice you make. It's an attitude you develop over time. You need to choose to ignore what your past looks like. Forget how it was before. That's just history at this point. What's done is done, and there's no point crying over spilled milk.

Blaming a sad childhood—or a low salary or not having any money or not knowing the right people or a lack of time—is a choice to have a particular attitude. You're the one who chooses your own attitude. But that attitude has nothing to do with reality.

An old classmate from school, a pleasant and clever boy, got good grades and went off to college. He studied two years at Stockholm's prestigious business school, and then spent two years studying law simultaneously at Stockholm University. He completed the last two years of his legal studies in just one year. Five years later he had two very good degrees. Absolutely brilliant. You'd think that a guy like that would end up at the top of any organization, wouldn't you?

The truth is sadly different. He finds it hard to keep a job, regardless of how good it is. And the reason is his attitude. He believes that he isn't good at anything at all. He persuades himself that he's about to be exposed as totally incompetent. He thinks he was lucky to get through those five years as a student and that he lacks ambition, that his health isn't going to hold up, plus a whole lot of other completely irrelevant excuses.

The last time I bumped into him, we were both past fifty. He didn't feel well, didn't like his job as an administrator in a small firm that didn't pay what it should. He was waiting to be fired.

This guy's IQ is probably higher than that of 99 percent of the whole world. And I really do like him. There's nothing wrong with him. But there is something wrong with his attitude.

WHAT ABOUT YOUR OWN ATTITUDE?

When you look at the eight points I listed earlier in the book, do you genuinely feel that you can handle each and every one of them? Or do you think that it's fine for everyone else but that it won't work for you? If you don't know for sure that something is going to work, then you aren't going to do anything. You wouldn't be alone in thinking that. But it is a problematic attitude. The only way to know if something works for you is to try it yourself. Nobody else can do it for you.

Give it a fair try!

You can go from the top of the list right down to the bottom. Take the points one at a time. Can you find a *why* of your own? Do you know what your goal in life is? And so on. You can think whatever you like.

It makes no difference to me. But the attitude you choose is your own responsibility. And the very same moment you choose to believe that these steps aren't going to work for you, you've also accepted 100 percent of the responsibility for where you're going to be in the future.

Your attitude toward yourself is your own responsibility.

I'm not fond of jumping up and down and cheering that *everything is possible*. No, no. Not everything is possible. But a great deal more than we think is possible. We just need to believe.

UGH, I'M TOO OLD!

Before I started my own business, I was an employee for sixteen years. For a long time it was a secure job, and then it suddenly wasn't. As a former bank employee, I've seen firsthand how a team shrinks when cuts have to be made. So eventually I got out. For a period I ran a company with some business partners, before (after another seven or eight years) starting a business of my own.

We can discuss the pros and cons of all those stages, but sometimes I'm bothered by the feeling of having wasted parts of my life on the wrong things. But even though in retrospect I think the years were wasted, I gained important knowledge and insights that I still carry with me.

Many people have started new enterprises late in life. There are many examples.

Have you heard of Dagny Carlsson? At the age of 99 she took a computer course, and when she was 100 she started a blog that received a lot of attention in the Swedish media. She was immediately designated the oldest blogger in the world. After that, she wrote books, hosted a radio program, and at the age of 104 made her film debut. So don't say that it's too late. As I write this, she's 107 years old and is evidently thinking about getting a boyfriend.

BUT I DON'T HAVE A PROPER EDUCATION!

That's just an excuse. Educational qualifications can be of great help, but only if what you study gives you the tools to reach your goal. You don't need a four-year degree from a university to start your own business. You don't need five years studying psychology to work with people. You don't need to learn five languages to travel all over the world. You don't need a university degree in nutritional physiology to eat sensibly.

Besides, the statistics are clear: lots of the world's most successful people have hardly any education at all. It doesn't seem to have prevented them from being successful.

And if you do lack important knowledge—then go out and acquire it! Take an evening class, search the internet. Realize that it isn't the *diploma* you need. It's the *knowledge*. If you want to take a class just to have something to hang on your wall, then you've got it completely wrong. The classes are so that you can do a better job—nothing else.

BUT I'M AFRAID THAT I'M GOING TO FAIL!

We all are. All of us have fears of various types within us. It doesn't help to hide away. Fear only disappears when you act *despite* it.

I don't know how many salespeople I've met who have been afraid of being turned down by clients they need to call. And even though I understand that fear, the problem is not going to be solved by avoiding your job. On the contrary, it only gets worse by delaying the inevitable. A salesperson has no order before he calls. If he calls and is told no, he still has no order. What has he lost? Nothing!

Not long ago, my son found himself in a situation people call "between jobs." But he didn't apply for new jobs because he was afraid of being turned down, or that he would be laughed at, or that somebody would criticize his experience.

In the end, he plucked up his courage and went around to nine different employers in one afternoon. One of them got in touch seven minutes after he left and offered him a job for a trial period. What do you think happened to his mood? His attitude toward looking for a job was suddenly totally different. Not that it mattered, because after the trial period he was offered a permanent job.

I'M JUST NEGATIVE, OKAY?

There's a funny story about a guy who thinks he has won millions in the lottery. He seems to be the only winner, and the future looks bright. He jumps in the air, shouting with joy. When his girlfriend comes home and points out that he had some numbers in the wrong order, he deflates like a popped balloon. But, she says, *Wasn't it nice that you felt so wonderful, even for a little while?* He had the capability to be happy. Now it was a question of doing something with it.

It's the same with anger, being grumpy, or just looking for faults everywhere. They are all attitudes you choose yourself.

If you want to, you can choose to look at your options with positivity. I'm not suggesting you lose your foothold on reality and jump into the void in the hope that somebody will throw out a net in time. But my proposed plan doesn't involve leaping over tigers, or ideas for world domination. It's just based on ordinary common sense, one step at a time. I would even claim that it is fundamentally without risk.

BUT EVERYONE ELSE SAYS THAT . . . !

No, no. You're listening to the wrong people again.

You've heard the following saying: When you're twenty, you worry about what others think of you. When you are forty, you stop caring about what others think about you. But at sixty, you realize that they didn't think about you at all. They, like everybody else, were focused on themselves.

Most of the time, people are far too busy worrying about themselves and their own lives to notice yours. And the ones who do actually think about you are probably wondering what you think about them. So forget about all of that.

Let that insight be your guiding start. You don't need to wait until you're sixty to use it. You can start today. Leave Laterville and start living life.

SUMMARY

Work on your attitude. If your attitude doesn't fit with your plan, then it's going to be an obstacle. You need to take a good look at what your attitude is toward the things that matter.

First, write down your complete plan for success in a list like the following:

- Reexamine your *why* very carefully and write it down clearly.
- Write down your chosen goals, again using as few words as possible.
- Have another look at your list of the three most important activities that will help you reach your goals. If anything is vague, make it more concrete.

- Look at your bad habits and write those down, too. Remember that bad habits include any habit that hinders your progress toward your goal.
- Decide how much time every day, week, or month you'll devote toward your goal. And remember that changes take time.
- If possible, set up a schedule for when you'll do what.
- Make sure you have at least two people close to you who will support you and help you to make progress. Write down the names of the unsupportive people you don't want to talk to about the project.
- Decide on a method of tracking your progress.

Now look at this simple plan. Take a pen and paper and write down all the reasons you can think of for why you should *not* follow the plan you've created to reach your goals and feel successful.

Can you honestly find any problems with it? Are there any obstacles you haven't addressed? Which ones? What can you do to clear them away? Good; go do it.

But how do you feel? Do you feel genuinely positive about starting, or are you still thinking up excuses and waffling, so that nothing will get done? If that's the case . . . then you still don't have the right attitude. Until you have the right attitude you won't be able to make this plan work.

27

So How Do You Work Smarter?

In the first part of this book, we talked about how easy it is to waste your time on silly things. So how should we use our time? Are there ways to be smarter in how we use our time? Yes, actually there are. And most of them are about your own attitude to the concept of time.

The most common rationalization I hear, both from myself and from others, is: I am absolutely going to do all of that—when I have time.

And one of the big problems we have today is that there is never enough time.

On the other hand . . . there's never been more time than there is now. The question is only what you choose to do with it.

PANIC AS A SYSTEM

One of my former colleagues had a rather entertaining homemade priority system. Carina had seven letter baskets on her desk neatly stacked on top of one another with a handwritten label on each one.

Starting from the bottom they read: UNIMPORTANT, NOT VERY IM-
PORTANT, FAIRLY IMPORTANT, IMPORTANT, URGENT, ACUTE, and *PANIC*.
The interesting thing was that the exact moment she put a piece of
paper in one of the baskets—she forgot about it. Most likely, not even
she understood the system.

We called her the Bermuda Triangle. Everything that came within
her orbit disappeared without a trace.

THE RIGHT TASK, RIGHT MATRIX

Willpower isn't enough. I'm sure you want to use your time in some
sort of orderly fashion. Even if you're reasonably effective with your
time, you'll want to become even more efficient if you can. The problem with all models on the theme of time management is that they're
based on logical thinking. Give priority to this, delegate that. Sure.
That's all great. But we're not logical and rational creatures. We're
emotional. If you had set aside a Tuesday evening so that you could
catch up on some work at home, but your two-year-old toddles in
and wants to play, then your entire system breaks down, because
you're an emotional being and want to spend time with your child instead of your work. I'm not going to say anything about that, except
that the work won't get done.

The most common way of handling time is based on making priorities. People talk about ranking various tasks based on how urgent they are and how important they are. But while there's nothing
wrong with prioritizing, there is an obvious limitation to that approach: priorities don't *create* more time.

All they do is push the tasks around on your to-do list, so that
number 7 becomes number 1. Priority methods borrow time from one
task and give it to another. You still have the same amount of work.

Apart from the fact that you've wasted some of your time on—yes, exactly—setting priorities.

If you rank how *important* something is, then you know how *much* the task is worth.

If you rank how *urgent* it is, then you know how *soon* it needs to be done.

What is lacking is the more long-term viewpoint of considering how *important* the task is to achieve a certain goal. Because it does take time. So the question is: *Is the task valuable enough to merit that time?*

The question you want to ask yourself isn't: *What is the best and most important thing I can do today?*

The right question is: *What is the best thing I can do today that will make things better tomorrow?*

The whole term "time management" is a little suspect. Time passes, as I've said, regardless of what we do. What we need is perhaps a bit of *self-management*.

Now I'll give you a simplified model that is designed to help you establish priorities without actually taking things off your radar. Get rid of anything that doesn't belong on the list at all.

On the left side, we have wrong tasks. The activities you really

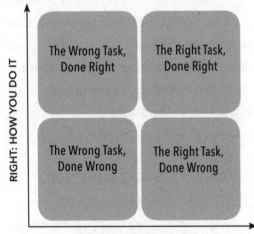

never need to do. Never ever. These aren't just given a *lower* priority. They should simply be *deleted forever.* That is why they're called the "wrong" tasks. But if you do choose to do wrong tasks, you can (as you can see in the matrix) also carry them out either the right way or the wrong way.

On the right-hand side, we have right tasks. These are tasks you should do. You can either do them in the right way or in the wrong way. Four fields, and everything is clear for you. It's really quite simple, isn't it? It doesn't need to be any more complicated than this.

Naturally this is a simplification. To all the management consultants I'd also add: there are other models, many of them very complex with various levels of priorities, but this one is perfectly adequate to illustrate the problem. We tend to complicate things unnecessarily, and often it's the consultants who get everything in a tangle. We invent systems that are so complex that we will be needed forever to interpret them.

THE RIGHT TASK RIGHT

Always do the right task in the right way. (You don't need to be Einstein to understand that.) If you do the right thing in the right way, you'll find yourself among the top 3 percent of salespersons, healthcare assistants, bosses, consultants, plumbers, self-employed people, driving-school instructors, authors, psychologists, brain researchers, or whatever you want. It works like magic.

THE RIGHT TASK WRONG

The second best thing is to do the right task but in the wrong way. Why? Well, the *right* task done *wrong* is still the right *task*. Since it's not particularly likely that you'll be the world champion at everything right away, it's a good idea to perform the right task as often as you can so that you start to get better at it. If you don't know how to do it the best way, ask somebody who has mastered it. Then do the same.

THE WRONG TASK WRONG

Spending time on tasks that don't lead anywhere, and doing them sloppily, too—no thank you. Throwing yourself into something you don't have the slightest knowledge about, and then doing it badly on top of that? Undeniably millions of hours are spent doing exactly that in the corporate world.

Wasting time on the wrong tasks that might create more problems than if you'd never done them in the first place? Drop those things in somebody else's lap. There's always somebody who likes to do, and who can do, stuff that you neither like nor are good at.

THE WRONG TASK . . . RIGHT

This is potentially the greatest problem. This is a really insidious trap and the greatest time thief: doing the *wrong* task *right*.

One out of two might not sound too bad. But the wrong task done right is undoubtedly the worst of all four categories since it makes the situation look deceitfully good. It's extremely easy to be tempted to do something you feel you're very good at. This is where you feel safe, doing things you know how to do.

But think again. Being clever at something that doesn't even make any difference? Can you imagine a worse waste of time and resources? Becoming really excellent at something that doesn't have the slightest connection with the job needing to be done is pure madness. What could be more inefficient than doing something perfectly that didn't need to be done at all?

TIME THIEVES

The two fields on the left in the figure in this section are time thieves.

Sometimes you can't avoid time thieves. If you work in an office and the printer gets jammed, you have to pull out all the different drawers and push them back in again searching for that one irritating sheet of paper. But does that mean you should study to become a printer technician when you have the time? Hardly. You ask somebody who knows. You do not, I repeat, *do not* become an expert on repairing printers. That's the kind of thing you should actively prioritize away. Delete those things from your consciousness and your to-do list.

But how do you know what's a time thief? What if there was a way to know what the wrong way to spend your time would be . . . in advance?

In fact, there is!

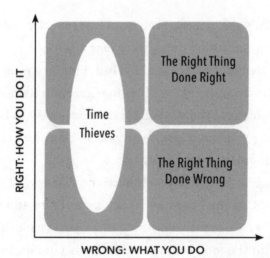

WHAT DETERMINES HOW YOU SHOULD SPEND YOUR TIME?

A good question that doesn't have a single answer, but the right thing to spend your time on is usually *What takes you toward your goal?*

If you want to visit Kiruna in the far north of Sweden, you take the train going north. The right thing, done right. If you take the train going south, you won't get to Kiruna. But the train is the right method, so the southbound train would be the wrong thing right.

What would be the wrong thing wrong in this case? A bicycle going south might be your answer, but this isn't completely black and white. Theoretically, you might make your way to Kiruna by cycling southward. After many miles and a lot of swallowing of cold water you might arrive at Kiruna's impressive gates.

THE MISSING LINK

To be really certain about the right thing to do, we need to add the tricky factor of time. If, for example, you need to be in Kiruna tomorrow morning, then your possible choices are suddenly limited. In that case, you can't even answer "by train," because you might not get there in time. You might have to fly there.

The correct definition of the right thing to do would be: whatever helps you reach your goal at the time *you need to arrive there.*

So the correct diagram should look like this:

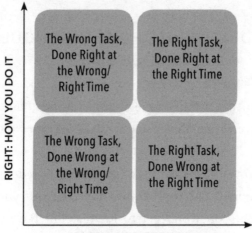

THE RIGHT THING AT THE RIGHT TIME IS DETERMINED BY YOUR GOAL

Your goal determines what you should do with any free time you have.

What's the right thing to do right now?

What's sometimes wrong is also sometimes right. What's wrong for you might be right for somebody else. What's wrong for you right now might be right for you some other time. Confusing—I know. That's precisely why the timing is important.

This is not an exact science, either. And you can do whatever you want whenever you want to. You don't need to follow this approach at all. But if you want to accomplish what you've made up your mind to do, then it might be a good idea to consider:

What is the right thing to do just now?

Put a yellow sticky note on your computer screen. On the bathroom mirror. On the kitchen fan. On the steering wheel. On the inside of your sunglasses.

Set the alarm on your mobile phone so that it vibrates once an hour during work hours, and whenever it rings ask, *What is the right thing to do in this moment?*

But stop wasting time as if you have unlimited amounts of it. Regardless of how old you are, you don't. It's time to take time—your time—seriously.

Besides, you already know what the right steps are. They're the three tasks that you gave the highest priority to on your list of activities that will help you reach your goal. Do them. If you can manage to do other things, too—go for it! But not otherwise.

SUMMARY

Time is your most important resource. Nothing is as valuable as your time. It's a resource that you'll never get any more of and that can't be re-created once it's past. You can't store it, and you can't get any more by swapping with somebody else or buying it.

Twenty-four hours a day. That's what you get.

You can get more of everything else, but time is limited.

How good you are at handling your time depends a lot on how you choose to look at it. Your attitude is key here as well. When you're young, it's easy to think that there is so much time that there's nothing to worry about. But the older you get, the more often you'll find yourself reflecting on the fact that time is far from endless.

Sit down and seriously consider how you think about the time you have. Does it feel like you use it for important things? Do you feel that you use it on worthwhile activities? Do you do anything positive with the time you have?

If the answer is yes, then congratulations! If the answer is uhmm . . . then you simply need to reconsider.

But, again, everything begins with you knowing where you are going—and why. It's not until you have both a goal and a reason that you'll know the right things to do and when to do them.

There is, perhaps, no right or wrong way to look at this issue of time. Per usual, people work differently. Which leads us to the finale.

28

Self-Awareness Will Lead You Down the Right Path

Before we summarize everything, we need to look at what's perhaps one of the most important insights you can have about yourself. By now, you know exactly what your colors are according to the DISC model. But let's take a quick look at what you could face in the form of risks and more specific pitfalls. Naturally, not all of this is connected to your communication profile, but there are definitely clues as to how you could avoid unnecessarily sleepless nights.

A central theme is that few people succeed entirely on their own. Often they need the support of others.

HOW RED BEHAVIOR CREATES PROBLEMS

You Reds have never found it hard to set goals. It's in your nature to be goal-oriented and focused on results. That's definitely a strength. The challenge is your tendency to set goals that are so demanding and seemingly so unachievable that it can be hard to get others to go along with you. Some people aren't even going to see the point of trying.

There's something you need to realize. I know that you understand, intellectually, that nobody can manage everything entirely by themselves. But the Red temperament also involves a permanent feeling of "I can do this myself." You're likely to rush ahead and then see who follows along.

This is a mistake. Without a team around you—coworkers, employees, colleagues, neighbors, relatives, friends, and not least, your partner—you'll probably never reach your goal. You might explain this away by saying it was the wrong goal, but no people, not even you Reds, manage on their own without support from those around them. The world has become more and more dependent on our ability to cooperate.

If you are primarily Red, then you're facing a challenge here.

Everyone else.

But have you ever heard of a successful hermit?

You need to train yourself to handle and work with the people around you. If your self-awareness is good, you'll already have learned this. But be aware that nobody is an island.

Your Path to Success

Your method of meeting others can be the key to how you reach your goals and become ridiculously successful. Memorize the following:

Most people take more time to come to a decision or give an answer than you do. You'll often be the fastest in the room. Sometimes you won't have any choice but to calm down and adapt your pace. If they can't keep up, then you don't need a team. . . .

Besides, people around you can misunderstand your very direct approach. Getting straight to the point at a meeting is effective, but the majority of the people you meet prefer a somewhat less direct method. They like to have a cup of coffee and mention something about the weather, about the economy, about the reason that you're having this meeting at all.

Yes, yes, you're right and they're wrong. But we're talking about simple solutions.

You can start by asking how people feel. And then listen to the answers. You won't believe how much valuable information you can obtain that will affect the project.

Don't just talk about how something will benefit you. Emphasize that you are not the only one who will gain from what you're doing.

Your way of looking directly at people and maybe raising your voice a little when you're feeling passionate can make people think that you're angry. I know, you haven't been angry in God-knows-how-long, but not everyone is like you, that's for sure. If people are afraid of you, then you're already heading toward trouble. If that's your goal, fine. If not—take it easy. If you're concerned or actually irritated, say, *Don't take this personally, but I'm starting to get worried about our deadline.* Try it. It's going to work a lot better.

Another thing: once we finally reach harbor, realize that a little break might be necessary. We know that you aren't satisfied even when you've reached your goal. That's okay, but let people relax a little. Then you can get back to work again.

And that's your strength. Setting new goals, always striving to move onward and up. Just use it in the right way.

You don't have to be satisfied. But it's good if you can stop for a moment and congratulate yourself on your victory. Then . . . back to the battle.

WHO SUFFERS AS A RESULT OF YOUR YELLOW BEHAVIOR?

You're a really nice chap, you know that? If you're mainly Yellow, then you have lots of fans. In fact, you're one of those popular people everyone else would like to be. Which means that you find it easy to attract people to your vision and your ideas. Or to you. With your excellent vocabulary and your natural talent for communicating effectively, you don't have any problems drawing others in to your projects, regardless of what they are.

But . . . that brings with it a variety of challenges.

People are going to want to join in, which is good. The risk is that they're going to say exactly what you want to hear. They know that you can be easily offended. You take things personally. Which means that your gang might try to protect you from bad news.

Besides, you aren't one of the world's best listeners. And people know that. They are actually very aware of the fact that you don't listen to what others say. And even if you hear the words, inside your head you're going to rewrite the conversation so that you hear what you want. It's only your ideas that count.

This is something you share with the red profile. If you have both red and yellow in your profile, you're definitely in trouble in this area. Both colors have no problem convincing or persuading others about ideas. But even though you're a creative person, you don't know everything. And when you share your best ideas, some people are going to think that your feet have floated off the ground—again.

How to Retain Your Popularity

One way of avoiding this pitfall is to make a few plans on paper. Take a step back and consider things. *Would this actually work?*

And now we come to perhaps the most important topic I want to talk to you about: your ability to follow plans. Many of you Yellows are excellent when it comes to creating plans for others, but you can't manage to follow the plan yourselves. If you even manage to get something down on paper—you aren't a world champion at documentation, either—then the question becomes whether you'll be able to find the paper an hour later.

I don't mean to be a naysayer, but you're not extremely structured. I'm rather convinced that if you've gotten this far in the book, then you've got lots of wonderful ideas based on what you've read. You'll certainly think that some of these exercises are great.

But have you stopped a single time and actually done any of them? Or have you thought, *That is so obvious that I'm just going to remember it?* Nope, that isn't good enough.

You need to surround yourself with the right people. And who are they? Perhaps folks with some blue in their profiles. Don't freak out, but some blue is a good complement to your visionary, creative, and inspiring self. Together, you could accomplish great things. All you need to do is talk through how you both like to work and how you could cooperate on area X.

In general, you need to pay a little less attention to your gut feeling, and focus a bit more on what the facts say. Do some strategic thinking about your amazing new project—whether it be personal or professional. There's nothing wrong with being fairly concrete now and then.

You might run into some speed bumps on your way. That's okay. You are a realist, aren't you? You know that you'll meet with setbacks, but don't let that intimidate you. You keep going on, since you have your plan. The advantage of your plan is that you don't need to have it in your head. You only need to write it down and then read what it says. It couldn't be simpler.

So mark off some time in your calendar today and make your plan. Follow the eight points in the book; that's enough to get you started.

HOW GREENS CAN GET WHAT THEY WANT WITHOUT WORKING UNTIL THEY DROP

As a Green, you're essentially a relationship person. You like people, but not too many at once, and preferably ones whom you already know.

Also, you don't like dealing with change. Sure, you realize that it's not ideal to just tread water all your life. Even if you're a secure, stable person, you still need a few new things in your life.

I'm not sure how you would personally describe success. It depends a lot on what your driving forces are. But your behavior doesn't often illustrate a desire to break old patterns and establish new ones. Even though there are some Green people who accept change, there are not many who actively search for ways to create these changes.

And this is one of your major problems. You might have read lots of good ideas in this book, but there is a risk that you'll put them aside and just "think it over."

Of course, it's good to change one's attitude, and there are positives to establishing new habits. But those old habits just feel so good! Or, they might not necessarily feel good, but at least they feel secure. And should you really go around trying to change everything?

The good news for you, my friend, is that there isn't very much you need to do differently. You only need to take on one little thing at a time, work at it, and then move on. No giant leaps necessary. Just ordinary, simple things.

Working with others is what you do best, but you should be aware of the fact that others might think that you're a bit slow at the start. Even when you have the facts and evidence laid out in front of you, you do tend to . . . wait and see. Only you know what you're actually waiting for.

How to Move at a Reasonable Pace

Regardless of what you would like to change and regardless of how you define success, you need to surround yourself with the right people. You're good at handling relationships, but sometimes you're a bit too kind. You need to dare to be more direct with others.

The people around you are going to think that you are nice and kind, but it's possible that they're also going to think that you don't really ever kick into gear. They might see your hesitation as a negative. Even if they want to help you, you might not have the same kind of drive as the Reds and the Yellows. On the other hand . . .

The Reds would really complement you. I know, that feels far-fetched, but think about it. Somebody who's good at getting things to happen would combine well with your slightly milder approach. That could be a really excellent combination.

Working together and cooperating well could lead to some great successes for you. You could share the work between you. The Red can help push you a little, and stretch your goal, while you have the patience necessary to wait for the result.

And a Red partner, when it comes to exercise, or marketing, or doing DIY projects at home, or anything at all, will make you be specific about what you really want. Sometimes you're a bit too vague, even for yourself. A Red person could, with your approval, of course, really get you to reflect and become aware of what you'd like to change. When everything feels right. And they're good at grabbing your hand and simply pulling you along. They don't listen too much to objections. If you have a good relationship, this person can just nudge you along in front of them at an acceptable pace.

And you'll thank him or her afterward.

THE REASON WHY YOUR BLUE BEHAVIOR IS NOT THE PERFECT SOLUTION

So you have mainly blue in your profile.

You are good at drawing up plans, and I'd be surprised if you haven't taken sheets of notes already. You probably haven't written directly on the book, though.

You've listened, absorbed, and can see a lot of the logic in my suggestions. You definitely like the idea that success comes only if you take the time to let it grow. And you're the most patient of everybody here. You realize that speed is not the goal. It is quality that counts, right?

Fine. We agree on that.

Uhmm. Did you also see my comments in exactly nine places in the book that it doesn't make a difference how much you know or how much you're capable of doing if you don't actually do anything?

We've both heard the expression, "If you fail to plan, then you are planning to fail." But what does that mean? It means you need to go from thought to action. You don't need to talk with anybody, but you do need to act. Your time at the drawing board is over. You need to trust me on this. Now, off you go and act. If you do nothing besides rephrase and polish up your plans, then nothing will ever happen. And that would be a problem, right?

Since you, like the Red folks, are more interested in substantive issues than in relationship issues, there's a risk that you, too, will decide to do everything yourself. That would be most unfortunate. The idea that you're best at everything is incorrect. You aren't. Not even if you've taken the class. There is always someone better. Bring them into the process. Accept their help.

Your tendency to strive for perfection will prevent you from moving forward. Take this as a serious piece of advice from one perfectionist to another. Perfection is the ultimate threat to progress. Waiting for the perfect opportunity—just tweaking the plans a little more, looking for even better alternatives—that doesn't go anywhere. There is no perfect moment. The time has come to act.

The people you surround yourself with see your lovely plans and elegant presentations. What they're waiting for is something to happen. When they look at your documents, they also see goals that don't look too challenging. That's because you are a cautious general. Listen to others and see if you can challenge yourself a bit more.

Appoint somebody you really rely on to have a look at your plans and help you to evaluate everything you've laid out.

Your Method to Achieve Acceptable Quality

You need to start to trust other people. They know an awful lot of things that you don't have a clue about. You can start by trusting me when I say that the methods in this book really work.

You need to drop the idea that you don't really have any proof of that. Since you haven't followed somebody around for seven years, you don't have concrete evidence that this plan was what led to his success.

That's true. But look at your own method. Consider the place you are right now. You are there thanks to, or perhaps because of, your "homemade" method. If you're 100 percent satisfied with the result, then don't change anything. If you want more out of life, then you need to change things up.

If you want to experience the best quality life in terms of your health, your career, your financial position, your immediate family, and your long-term plans for the future, then it's time now to accept that all the answers don't exist.

Perhaps you're thinking that it doesn't feel right to invest five years of your life in something that might not work perfectly. I understand that, but I have one question for you: How long does it take to wait for five years and not do anything at all?

I know that you aren't afraid and that you don't feel hesitant because of low self-confidence. Rather you're waiting because you are wondering where you can get more concrete evidence. Okay, send me an email and I'll give you the details.

SUMMARY

Regardless of what your dominant colors are, or your primary driving forces, you have qualities that will definitely help you on your way forward. But, unfortunately, you also have qualities that could throw a wrench in the works. That's what I've tried to address here.

You could choose to ignore them. Or you could really understand them and do something about them. As usual, it's your choice and your responsibility.

I took note of the feedback that life gave me. It wasn't something that came completely naturally. I was an underachiever, performing far below my potential. Then, I got tired of feeling mediocre.

Over the years, I've changed my opinion of myself. Nowadays, for example, I control my red streak very well. It often made itself known in the presence of the wrong people when I opened my mouth and fired off some less-pleasant comments. I still don't have complete control over it. You only have to ask people in my inner circle. Or maybe don't do that.

The yellow column, which is also fairly high in my profile, was probably what people around me noticed most when I was younger. When I was young, I was a lot more sensitive about what people thought about me than I am today, so I made an effort to be popular. It's debatable whether that worked. My approach was to be the prankster who joked and kept people in a good mood and tried to be funny. I can still be funny, but that's more of a tool than a need these days.

I don't have any green to speak of. My apologies to all those I have forgotten to get in touch with.

And my blue factor, that's very high. I actually like it, because it gives me an annoyingly good memory for what people say to me, and I'm good at making plans. Now that I've learned to take those fancy plans and transform them into concrete action, I'm much better off.

29

Maintaining Your Success

Now you have the answers to 95 percent of all questions. If you follow the ideas I've presented, you'll come a long way no matter what your goal is. And I want to congratulate you on your desire to make new dreams for yourself. You won't regret it. Just remember one thing: it's easy to start new things, but not as easy to carry them out. Some laws of nature are hard to avoid. But there are solutions to that, too.

What does a rocket need in order to leave Earth? An awful lot of power and huge amounts of fuel. Breaking through the atmosphere and leaving Earth's orbit uses up almost all the fuel in the tanks.

But what's interesting is that this isn't a problem at all, even if the journey is going to be very long. Because once the rocket has left Earth's orbit, it needs hardly any power to maintain its speed.

The same principle applies when you're going to start a new direction in life. If you want to go from setback to success, you need to kick up the speed for a while. Work harder on your goal descriptions, your habits, keep a better check on your own ideas and the people around you.

But you also need to keep things in hand. Maintain your momentum.

Don't ease up until you have a head of steam and start seeing results. The risk is that you'll relax far too soon and start drifting off course.

If you've gone around with a few extra pounds for a few years and are now living a healthier lifestyle, you're going to see results after a while. You're going to notice that your pants are a bit looser around the waist and you'll have more energy.

Congratulations!

THIS IS A SERIOUSLY DANGEROUS PLACE

This is when you'll start thinking you've earned a reward.

The reward can be anything at all, from a tiny piece of chocolate to a fancy dinner out on a Saturday evening with your sweetheart. Or a month's vacation in some pleasant, sunny place.

It's not wrong to give yourself a reward for your progress, but this is where there's a risk that it will all go south. If you break your new good habits by celebrating with chocolate, you might sabotage the whole project. Because if you munched on chocolate all your life up until six months ago, it's going to take much longer than that to break the habit.

One little piece of chocolate leads to . . . what?

Exactly. Another piece of chocolate.

Who knows where it will end. The risk is that it ends in a stomachache and regret.

Reward yourself, by all means, but not with something that goes against your original goal. Buy yourself a sharp new shirt, or go for a day at the spa. Avoid rewarding yourself with something that caused your problem from the very beginning.

You need to stick to your new, healthy lifestyle—or whatever change you've made—until you've left Earth's gravity. And when you've reached your goal, then perhaps—and I repeat, perhaps—you can allow yourself a piece of chocolate. But you know what? The chances are that such a long time will have passed that you won't even want it. For real.

BUT HERE'S THE GOOD NEWS

Once you've gotten up to speed, it's going to be much simpler to keep your pace. Sticking to your plan will, after a while, feel like a quiet walk in a forest. You're going to wonder what you struggled with six months ago.

The same thing applies when you're saving money. If you've decided to set aside $100 every month until you have reached $5,000, then you can't stop at $2,000. That would be letting yourself down. You need to remind yourself why you need that $5,000. To start using some of the money to buy something meaningless would be stupid, really stupid. But it's very tempting.

Just like when you want to get into better physical shape, you need to hold on a little longer and make sure that you really do reach your goal of $5,000 in the bank. And you know what? Even though it might sound a bit sad: The more money you have in the bank, the more you'll want. When you have reached $5,000, you might very well want to aim for $10,000. This means you're going to be very careful about spending money when you're out shopping, and only buy things you actually need.

How do you reward yourself when it comes to saving money? Really, you shouldn't go shopping at all. But I can understand why you do. Perhaps you've written something down on your calendar for a year from now. If you've saved X amount, then you can go buy product Y. Or something like that. You need rewards, as I said. But remember—do the job first, then you get the reward.

If, before you've reached your goal, you fall for the sales trick—

"Save $50 if you buy this weekend"—then you're going to fall straight into the trap. Remember the simple math: If you pay $200 for something that really costs $250, you haven't saved $50. You've just consumed $200.

Stick to your tight budget until you've achieved momentum.

Once you've reached supersonic speed, it's easy to maintain that speed, but you need to accept that it might take some time to get there.

Don't let go too early.

Remember why you created your goal. Stick to the plan.

FORGET THE MIRACLE METHODS

Throughout this book, I've tried to impress upon you that you will have to have a degree of patience. You need to be content with the fact that there are no quick fixes. They don't exist.

There aren't any miracle methods. You can't get abs with the help of an electric thingamajig ten minutes every day in front of the TV. You can't count on becoming financially independent by investing in Bitcoins. Your relationship with your partner is not going to flourish after just one visit to a therapist.

It almost makes me feel sad every time I hear somebody exclaim, *If only it were simpler!*

Of course, I've also sighed in a similar way, but long ago I accepted the fact that the world doesn't work like that. In some cases, it's a hard and unjust society we live in. But when I sober up from my own self-pity, I realize that despite extremely difficult circumstances, an enormous number of people do succeed in what they take on. Why shouldn't I?

We're so impatient, so demanding, and we want such quick results that it's hard to achieve anything at all.

Bad habits are easy to build, but they can be very hard to live with.

Good habits take time and are hard to build, yes, that's true. But they're extremely easy to live with. So give them the time they need.

So stick to it. Once you're up to speed, you don't need to do much to maintain your pace. You're going to smile at your former self and wonder what you complained about.

Keep at it until you have some momentum. Then you're home free.

THE STRANGE AND UNTRUE IDEA OF LINEAR SUCCESS

Look at the figure on this page. It shows examples of things to focus on when you want to achieve success. It doesn't matter in what area. You do these things, work hard, and so on. Then you achieve success. You're at the top of your career, you have acquired honor and fame, you have money in the bank, or you have a body worthy of an Olympic athlete.

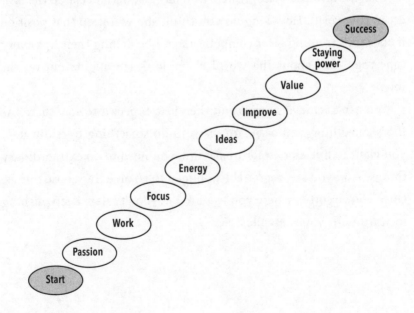

Great. Well done.

But what next?

The question about momentum still applies. Your effort and energy mean that you'll arrive where you want to be. But . . . what happens if you stop doing the right things? If you stop keeping track of your time, of your waistline, of what you put into your mouth, of how you talk to your partner? If you start getting up later in the morning and don't keep arriving early at work, the way you did when you were building your success? If you suddenly start wasting your new money instead of saving for retirement? What happens if you simply revert to your former, less-focused self? If you start to drift away . . . toward Laterville?

There are lots of examples of people who made their way to the top. But for one reason or another, they stopped focusing on growth or development. And soon they found they were no longer at the top. When you stop doing the things that took you there, then—first slowly, but soon much faster—you tend to return to a place that is often worse than where you started.

Imagine an athlete, a sprinter, who has just been declared the fastest in the world. How long do you think she will keep that position if she stops training? Her competitors will be licking their lips every time they read about the world champion's late nights out on the town.

You can't achieve success and then just expect it to stay there. As if it's something you own. You have to do something to retain it. If you want to live an extraordinary life, you need to do extraordinary things. And you are, regrettably, obliged to go on doing those things. Once you've gotten where you want to be—don't relax. Keep pushing forward with your new lifestyle.

WHAT SUCCESS *REALLY* LOOKS LIKE

Now look at this image. This is what success really looks like—when achieved in a nonlinear way. It's an ongoing cycle, not a straight line. Success demands that you keep your eye on the ball all the time.

If you want to achieve success, you must demand it of yourself through hard work and sharp focus—every day, for the rest of your life. In the world we live in, stopping is the same as starting to roll backward.

But the world doesn't care. It's up to you to decide what you want to do about this.

The world won't demand that you keep yourself in good shape and eat healthily so that you don't have a heart attack. You do, however, need to demand that of yourself if you want to live to be a hundred.

The world won't demand that you read books or develop yourself in some other way to increase your knowledge and make yourself more employable; you need to do that yourself if you want to build a career.

The world won't demand that you build up an immense emergency fund for your family, but if you want to do that, then you have to demand it of yourself. Otherwise you'll continue to go on living with just three months of rent in the bank.

You can choose to define success for yourself. That's what is so great about it. You, and only you, decide what is important for you. But you should be aware of the fact that success is something you are renting rather than something you own.

And that is one of the reasons why it's sometimes rather lonely at the top. Only a few people manage to get there—and stay there.

WRITING YOUR WAY TO MOMENTUM

Imagine an author like John Grisham. His first book was published more than thirty years ago. It took him five years to write while he was working as a lawyer in a little, unimportant firm in the South. Hardly anybody bought the book. Even fewer read it. Five thousand copies were sold, and he bought half of those himself and pressed them on people he knew. Do you know what that book is called? You would have to be a true Grisham fan to answer. The book is called *A Time to Kill*.

But while he knew how badly his first book was doing, he wrote *The Firm* as a gamble. That sold immediately, was made into a film starring Tom Cruise, and, in a flash, everyone knew who John Grisham was. His success was a fact. He wrote a book a year for ten years, and I think virtually every one ended up as a major movie. He must have earned buckets of money. He could leave his ordinary job and do what he wanted. John Grisham could have retired at the age of forty-five.

But he kept on publishing books. There's a new one almost every year, and has been for more than thirty years. Now, John Grisham certainly likes writing, but far fewer people would remember him if he'd stopped after ten books.

Besides, I happen to know (as an author, I'm curious about how the top writers do their work) that he has *not changed the writing process that took him to the top.* He still has other people do all the research so that the facts are correct. He still lets certain specific people read the first version. And he still pays attention to their feedback and makes changes as a result. And his books continue to sell. The reviews are fantastic. You don't need to love books by Grisham, you don't even need to like thrillers—but it's hard to ignore the fact that he's still doing it right, even though he, objectively, doesn't need to. Now he does it without any great effort. Because he's achieved momentum.

THE KEY INSIGHT

This is one of the most important lessons I myself have learned. You can't stop once you've started. Starting a journey toward the goal of your dreams—be it to see all the countries of the world before you die, or to be financially independent, or to have your own business and be able to work with your family, or to win an Olympic medal—is an active choice to live a different sort of life.

My task is not to judge somebody for how they've chosen to live their life. But for those of us who choose the path to success, it is an ongoing cycle.

I feel that I'm fairly successful, even though I, of course, can't compare with John Grisham. But I've been published in forty languages, and readers seem to like my books: they get in touch with me and tell me their stories. I lecture in many different places and meet fantastic people all year-round.

But the day I start being careless about my commitment, the day I can't be bothered to read other authors' books anymore, the day I convince myself that I already know everything, the day I stop pushing myself in my lectures and no longer test new things regardless of what my critics might say . . . that's the day I stop growing. And then it will all be downhill.

Like when you throw a ball up into the air. If you watch as it reaches its highest point, for a moment you might think it's hovering there. But it isn't. It turns in the air and then gravity pulls it down to earth again. Faster and faster.

YOU CAN'T CHANGE SOMEBODY ELSE, BUT YOU CAN CHANGE YOURSELF

When you think about that, it's fantastic news, isn't it? To have power over yourself and your own future. Now you just need to remind yourself that you have this power.

You can always decide what is most important for you and start there. You know how to break patterns, end old bad habits, start a new routine, begin new and better habits. A bright future awaits you.

And so my advice, once again: Start with something small that you'll succeed at. Gain a little self-confidence. Then try something bigger.

Make sure you keep working in the same direction until you've achieved momentum.

And then never let up.

POSTSCRIPT

In New York in 1934, the unemployed alcoholic William Griffith Wilson was admitted into a hospital to detox. In the hospital he had a spiritual awakening and started to convert other alcoholics. He worked hard but didn't succeed in converting many. When he complained to his wife that he didn't think that his method worked—nobody is sober!—she answered, "Oh, yes, *you* are sober."

Perhaps you've heard that story before. But it illustrates something I want you to take with you: By helping others to move ahead, you will also make yourself stronger. By trying to make others successful, showing them what you did, encouraging them, supporting them, saying that you believe in them, you yourself will benefit more than they do. There's no better way of building up yourself than by building up others. And besides, it feels good when you do something for others. So my request is this: if there is something in this book that works for you, tell others about it. Spread the word; show them what you did. By all means, give a copy of the book to everyone you meet. I've nothing against that, of course. But most of all, explain to those around you what you found useful.

So go back to the beginning of the book and read it again. This time have a pen and a sheet of paper next to you.

And one last thing. Let me know how it went. Because I collect success stories.

Further Reading

Brown, Brené. *Rising Strong*. Random House, 2015.

Burnett, Dean. *Idiot Brain: What Your Head Is Really Up To*. W. W. Norton, 2017.

Canfield, Jack. *Mastering the Art of Success*. Celebrity Press, 2017.

Carnegie, Dale. *How to Win Friends and Influence People*. Vermilion, 2009.

Cialdini, Robert B. *Yes! 50 Scientifically Proven Ways to Be Persuasive*. Free Press, 2008.

Covey, Stephen. *The 7 Habits of Highly Effective People*. Simon & Schuster, 1989.

———. *The 8th Habit: From Effectiveness to Greatness*. Simon & Schuster, 2006.

DeLuca, Fred. *Start Small, Finish Big: Fifteen Key Lessons to Start—and Run—Your Own Successful Business*. Mandevilla Press, 2012.

Duckworth, Angela. *Grit: The Power of Passion and Perseverance*. Scribner, 2016.

Duhigg, Charles. *The Power of Habit: Why We Do What We Do and How to Change*. Random House, 2014.

———. *Smarter, Faster, Better: The Secrets of Being Productive*. Random House, 2017.

Fabritius, Friederike, and Hans W. Hagemann. *The Leading Brain: Powerful Science-Based Strategies for Achieving Peak Performance*. TarcherPerigee, 2017.

Hill, Napoleon. *Success Habits*. Macmillan, 2019.

Jeffers, Susan. *Feel the Fear and Do It Anyway*. Ebury, 2017.

Jiang, Jia. *Rejection Proof: How I Beat Fear and Became Invincible Through 100 Days of Rejection*. Harmony Books, 2015.

Kenner, Soren, and Imran Rashid. *Offline: Free Your Mind from Smartphone and Social Media Stress*. Capstone, 2019.

Kishima, Ichiro, and Fumitake Koga. *The Courage to Be Disliked: How to Free Yourself, Change Your Life and Achieve Real Happiness*. Allen & Unwin, 2019.

Levinson, Steve, and Chris Cooper. *The Power to Get Things Done (Whether You Feel Like It or Not)*. TarcherPerigee, 2015.

Levitin, Daniel. *The Organized Mind: Thinking Straight in the Age of Information Overload*. Penguin Books, 2015.

Levy, Ariel. *The Rules Do Not Apply*. Little, Brown, 2018.

Robbins, Anthony. *Awaken the Giant Within: How to Take Immediate Control of Your Mental, Emotional, Physical and Financial Destiny!* Free Press, 2003.

Robinson, Ken, and Lou Aronica. *Finding Your Element: How to Discover Your Talents and Passions and Transform Your Life*. Penguin Books, 2014.

Schwartz, David J. *The Magic of Thinking Big*. Touchstone, 2015.

White, Jennifer. *Work Less, Make More: Stop Working So Hard and Create the Life You Really Want!* John Wiley & Sons, 1999.

Index